Strategic IT Portfolio Management

Governing Enterprise Transformation

Jeffrey D. Kaplan

Heartfelt thanks to:

Family and friends for support
Clients for challenges
PRTM colleagues for assistance
Daniel Penrice for editing

Contents

Reader Roadmap: Who Should Read This Book

| | Target Audience | |
Chapter / Section	Senior Executives	Business Unit and IT Managers
Introduction: Make IT Matter!	X	X
What Is IT Portfolio Management?	X	X
How We Got into This Mess—Learn from the Past	X	X
IT Portfolio Management: What It Can Do;		
How It Works	X	X
Design Principles	X	X
Governance Design	X	X
The Role of Senior Leadership (CxOs)	X	X
Portfolio Segmentation		X
Decision Rights		X
Special Types of IT Portfolios		X
Infrastructure Portfolios		X
Support (Service-Level) Portfolios		X
Application Preservation Portfolios		X
Workflow Design		X
Inventory and Calibration Work Stream		X
Strategic Analysis Work Stream	X	X
Decision-Making Work Stream	X	X
Chartering Work Stream		X
Interdependencies		X
Service Development Process		X
Resource Management		X
Enterprise Architecture and Standards	X	X
Financial Management	X	X
IT Governance Processes		X
Six Sigma		X
Enablers		X
Articulating—and Achieving—the Benefits of		
IT Portfolio Management	X	X
How to Drive Change		X
Epilogue: A Method for Strategic Transformation	X	X
Appendix: Business Case Analysis		X

This book outlines for senior executives the essential governance method to manage IT for value, including how to go about implementing a consistent, repeatable process. But before we get too far ahead of ourselves, it will be helpful to add some perspective. IT investment failures do not occur in a vacuum.

The *Introduction* provides a brief look at the topic of how organizations can *make IT matter,* a topic of great interest to shareholders and policymakers. A working definition is provided the chapter titled, *What Is IT Portfolio Management?*

No complex human problem can ever be comprehended, much less resolved, without reference to its history, and the IT dilemma of today is no different. The organizational behavior and financial management practices that the IT portfolio management method is designed to address arose in a specific historical context. Readers attempting to change their practices should understand the history of how organizations have managed their IT investments (IT management), and will find this briefly sketched out in the chapter titled, *How We Got into This Mess—Learn from the Past.*

Although the complex problems facing IT management today have been some 40 years in the making, they can be fixed by any organization that is willing to look hard at its existing portfolio practices, understand what is not working, and do the painstaking work of improving its portfolio management method. What the IT portfolio management method can do to address these problems and reverse past trends, and how it does so, are the subjects of *IT Portfolio Management: What It Can Do; How It Works.* Readers may wish to pay special attention to the reference model of the IT management system as a whole (and the place of portfolio management within it) presented in this chapter, as well as to the "design principles" of the IT portfolio management method laid out there.

We describe the value proposition of a highly efficient and effective IT portfolio management method in *Articulating—and Achieving—the Benefits of IT Portfolio Management,* and offer advice as to how to drive the kinds of organizational change that are necessary to realize these benefits. The value proposition is described in terms of both concrete impacts on the bottom line and qualitative improvements to organizational processes. This section is placed toward the end of the book because it is easier to appreciate the subtleties of the value proposition once the reader understands the challenges addressed by a robust portfolio management method.

The two chapters, *Governance Design* and *Workflow Design,* which are the longest in the book, take the reader into the guts of the IT portfolio management method. Designing the governance architecture includes the tasks of segmenting the portfolio, allocating decision rights, and addressing certain special types of IT portfolios (like infrastructure), all of which are covered in *Governance Design.* Designing the portfolio management workflow entails both the activities of the method itself and the interdependencies between the workflow and the rest of the IT management system, the two subjects that are discussed in the *Workflow Design* chapter.

Having designed the governance architecture and the workflow of the IT portfolio management method, organizations will want to design and incorporate various enablers that can be used to make the method more efficient and effective. These enablers include decision-support tools, metrics, best practices, and software applications. The use of each is the subject of *Enablers.*

Finally, in a brief epilogue, we consider the ultimate benefit of adopting and perfecting the IT portfolio management method: the achievement of a method that drives enterprise transformation. We believe this natural evolution of IT portfolio management is where best-in-class organizations are headed.

Introduction:
Make IT Matter!

*A problem is something you have hopes of changing. Anything else is a
fact of life.*

—C. R. Smith, Publishers Weekly

In both the private and public sectors, spending on information technology (IT) continues to increase. In the private sector, large corporations spend in excess of $500 million per year directly on IT products
and services. Direct IT spending (IT assets plus IT department personnel) now represents anywhere from 1% to 15% of corporate revenue
across all commercial sectors. A government agency may spend 10 times
more.[1] In addition, most organizations, whether businesses or government agencies, invest an incremental 20% to 60% in addition to what
they budget for IT. They spend this amount indirectly on non-IT staff
for oversight, requirements definition, testing, training, support, decision making, and so on, all in support of IT-related projects. The order
of magnitude of spending is consistent whether IT services are provided
by a third party (outsourced) or provided by in-house staff (in-sourced).

Organizations not only rely on information technology and IT
services to operate their businesses, IT is an integral enabler of growth
and value when combined with innovative business practices. The financial and telecommunication service industries, for example, would

---

[1] In fiscal year 2004, for example, the U.S. Department of Defense planned
to spend $27 billion. The civilian agencies spent in excess of $31 billion.
The Department of Health and Human Services spent over $4 billion. The
Department of Treasury, Department of Transportation, Department of
Justice, and National Aeronautics and Space Administration (NASA) each
had a total IT budget in excess of $2 billion.

come to a standstill if not for IT; they repeatedly look to innovative IT applications to differentiate their service offerings. Even the military and intelligence communities have turned to IT to provide an advantage on the battlefield and in the war on terrorism. IT has been an enabler of research and development (R&D) for decades, and organizations increasingly rely on IT to reduce R&D cost and cycle time.

So why do some continue to ask whether IT matters? The debate is a waste of time. IT matters. It is a fact of life. The issue at hand is what executives can *do* to make IT matter *more* . . . repeatedly, consistently, proactively, and predictably! Shareholders and policymakers seek a management mechanism to assure that growing IT investments drive commensurate *value*—an increase in net worth (economic, social, ethical, etc.). Even though IT spending as a percentage of total expenditures varies from one organization to the next,[2] little conclusive evidence indicates that organizations spending proportionately less on IT than their peers are any less successful or less well strategically positioned.[3] Some organizations just spend more on IT. Some organizations manage IT better than others do. So corporate shareholders and government policymakers continue to question whether the value returned from IT spending is sufficient. They ask for evidence, but they do not really want to see quantitative benchmarks that contrive value relative to what other organizations are doing. When asking for evidence, they are really asking for a better understanding of *what executives are doing to make IT matter.* If organizations are going to spend more and more on IT, then the incremental spending should make a difference. Senior leadership should be able to articulate how the incremental IT spending adds to the organization's net worth, as well as what is being done to reap increasing value from the existing installed base of IT assets.

Responding to the question is easy. Getting the organization to believe and *act* on the answer is the challenge. A surprising number of executives don't like to answer the question, for the most part, because

---

[2] Among firms of comparable size, the one with the largest IT budget may spend as much as 50% more than the company with the lowest IT budget.
[3] It does appear, however, that organizations that do not sustain competitive parity in terms of operational efficiency and effectiveness are disadvantaged. For example, companies that have not automated their workflow may be less productive than competitors, which can affect their competitive position.

they don't like the answer. They don't like to disclose that they lack the activity-based cost accounting practices to measure where IT spending is really going. They don't like to disclose that they're spending too much on marginal projects. They don't like to disclose that they're spending too much on minor enhancements to existing systems. They don't like to disclose that their predecessors allowed this spending year after year for decades. They don't like to disclose that changing this trend requires significant cultural change at all levels, including the most senior levels, in the IT department but more so in the business units. And they don't like to explain that reversing the trend requires investment if they want to do it without harming business performance. Shareholders, policymakers, and senior executives generally don't like to hear that they have to spend money to save money, especially when it is a result of suboptimal decisions made in the past. So, in many instances, an unspoken mutual agreement remains: executives won't ask and IT managers won't tell. This "agreement" lets everyone pretend that value from IT is optimized.

Why is the value from IT diminishing? Why do some organizations spend so much on IT and get so little return? The remainder of this chapter looks at some of the underlying reasons:

- Runaway demand from business units
- Obsessing about the urgent and leaving the important to chance
- Treating IT like a technology issue instead of managing it as a business issue
- Failure to evolve IT management as a discipline
- Failure of senior executives to hold themselves accountable
- Cutting costs, not budgets

Runaway Demand from Business Units

Every day, business unit managers make decisions that drive IT spending. Every time a manager makes a strategic business decision, that decision likely affects IT spending. Even mundane changes to product pricing, invoicing, and manufacturing often require reprogramming of legacy software applications. Decisions to open or close an office or relocate personnel within an office require IT services. In fact, a manager makes relatively few business improvement decisions without affecting IT spending or resources.

Because it is virtually impossible to transform the business significantly without affecting IT systems, it begs the question, *who really makes IT investment decisions?* Is it the IT department or the business units? One could claim that, in effect, the IT department doesn't make many IT investment decisions. They make many IT *execution* decisions, some of which affect *how much* is spent on IT, *how* it is spent, and *when*. But the IT department has relatively little authority when it comes to *whether* money is spent on IT and *where* investment funding is allocated. CIOs try to become involved early in strategic business initiatives requiring IT-enablement, but try as they may, business units routinely commit the organization to making big IT investments long before the IT department ever becomes involved.

We might not care about this blinding flash of the obvious except that the IT department—and not the business units—is typically tasked by senior officers to cut IT spending and align IT investments with business goals. The IT department is typically blamed when the senior officers do not see sufficient value returned from the level of IT spending. Yet, if the IT department does not actually drive IT investment decisions, how is it possible for them to be truly accountable for IT alignment and spending? If senior executives believe that IT investment does not align with business goals or significantly contribute to business performance, why do they repeatedly look to the IT department to solve this problem? *At the most basic level, the business units are ultimately accountable for optimizing IT investments, just as they are accountable for optimizing all their other investments and spending.* The problem in a large number of organizations is that business units have abdicated this accountability even though they continue to make decisions that affect IT spending. This disconnect between accountability and decision making is at the crux of the IT dilemma.

Obsessing About the Urgent and Leaving the Important to Chance

The broad role that business units require the IT department to play contributes to the IT dilemma. Many IT department managers spend huge amounts of time dealing with situations whose systemic cause is well beyond their span of control, and often beyond their ability even to influence. Because of the *urgency* behind these issues, the organization often neglects the *important* issues. Most IT departments are accountable for executing four different core missions. Although each of these missions shares the common thread of being technical in nature, each is a different discipline that requires diverse skills, behaviors, procedures, and performance metrics. The four missions are:

- **IT Service Provider:** Provide IT-enablement to the business in the form of software applications, computer systems, and telecommunications, and so on by providing IT development, delivery, operations, and administration.
- **Information Assurance Governor:** Seek to guarantee the availability, integrity, confidentiality, and nonrepudiation of the information and the assets that house it, to comply with regulatory requirements and provide for business continuity (a fiduciary role).
- **Business Architect:** Model the current and future business (operations as well as service offerings) to clarify how the organization must transform its people (accountabilities, responsibilities, organizational structure), processes (workflow, business rules, policies), and technology (data, applications, infrastructure) to achieve its core mission.
- **Transformation Agent:** Serve as a trusted advisor and change agent to the business and, in a complementary mission to the business architect, manage business transformation, helping identify and realize bottom-line improvements.

Some of these missions are more important than others, and some are more urgent. Some analysts argue that effectively managing just one of these missions is all that the average executive can handle, especially in a large organization that spends billions of dollars on IT initiatives. Moreover, the CIO role was originally conceived to lead the Transformation Agent and Business Architect missions. The remaining missions were intended to report to a vice president of IT. Yet today in many companies, the CIO is expected to manage all missions.[4]

---

[4] The missions were all consolidated under the CIO over time, primarily to save money and simplify the senior management team's span of control. Some wonder whether we traded away value from IT in exchange for the cost savings and simplification.

Chief executive officers (CEOs) and chief financial officers (CFOs) want to have "one belly button" that they can turn to when things go wrong with IT. They think that if they put everyone associated with these core missions in one department, put one person in charge of them, and hold that person accountable for everything having to do with IT, then this approach will improve the return on IT. This strategy is fundamentally flawed. It makes as much sense as holding the CFO accountable for every expense the corporation incurs. IT investment decisions, like financial investment decisions, cannot be contained in one organization and cannot be optimized by reorganizing boxes on the organization chart. Trying to consolidate all staff members responsible for IT into one department makes as much sense as trying to put all financial analysts in one department. It can be done, but does it make sense?

To understand better what we're dealing with, take a closer look at the IT service provider mission. The typical organization spends more time and mindshare fretting over IT service provision than it devotes to figuring out how to make IT matter.[5] Portions of this mission are arguably very tactical; the mission is considered by many managers and analysts to be a commodity, and yet it consumes the greatest amount of IT and business unit management attention. Although critical to the organization's survival, much of the service provider mission adds little value as compared to the other four missions. It is predominantly a supporting mission like accounting, facilities management, and procurement. To accomplish the mission, the IT service delivery model requires multiple disciplines such as customer management, research, development, service logistics, service supply chain, operations, and administration. In effect, best-in-class IT service providers operate a mini-business within the business. Hence the coining of the phrase, "run IT like a business."[6] The resources required to

---

[5]According to an IT Effectiveness Survey performed in 2002 by PRTM and *CIO Magazine,* CIOs and IT managers report that they spend an average 60% of their time on nonstrategic issues, such as managing routine IT services, and 40% on strategic issues, such as business transformation.
[6] Many practitioners over the years have misinterpreted this phrase to imply the IT department should become a profit center and offer their services to other companies. This misconception was fueled by corporate diversification

operate the IT service provider business consume more than 80% of the typical IT department's resources and management mindshare. Both IT managers and their business counterparts alike prefer that IT departments devote more time to performing more value-enhancing missions. Ideally, the organization would optimize service provision to the point where it ceases to distract the management team. However, too often the dynamic, complex nature of IT service provision combined with the broad role of the IT department prevents the IT department from ever fully optimizing service provision. The net result of runaway demand, combined with such a broad scope, is that service quality ultimately degrades. Most organizations cannot afford what the business units demand. With budgets constrained and demand growing, service level is the only lever that the IT department can adjust to balance the system. The IT department is forced to cut corners. Over time, the declining service level causes a breakdown in trust between the IT department and the business units, and collaboration degrades. This decline further affects service quality, which upsets the business units even more. This destructive cycle impairs the IT department's ability to fulfill its more strategic transformation and business architect roles.

This death spiral causes all sorts of dysfunctional organizational behavior that we can only begin to recount. For example, those IT managers who should be adding value and optimizing IT service processes instead spend an inordinate amount of time in meetings:

- Listening to how IT service quality does not meet the business's expectations—expectations that may have never been articulated to the CFO
- Trying to explain to business unit executives why service degradations are a direct result of IT budget cuts mandated by the CFO (oddly, the CFO is rarely present at these discussions)

---

trends and a very small number of large organizations that successfully spun off their IT departments to become commercial IT service providers. Although in-house IT service providers would do well to mirror their businesses after commercial IT service providers, the phrase "run IT like a business" has more to do with the business model for any effective and efficient IT service provider.

- Firefighting IT problems caused by inadequate IT service provision processes—a problem attributable to year-over-year budget cuts and repeated attempts to do more with fewer resources
- Trying to rebuild trust that was lost when past IT initiatives did not achieve the business objectives, mostly because the business didn't want to change its processes to accommodate the new IT system
- Debating why an obsession with "quick hits" (a common symptom of risk aversion caused by past failures) will not return as much value as one breakthrough system that transforms supply chain management

To someone outside the system, these scenarios seem ridiculous—even comical—yet they are the reality faced by most IT managers and are symptomatic of a fundamental breakdown in strategic priorities: *Issues of value play second fiddle to mundane IT service requests and will continue to do so as long as the root causes remain unaddressed.*

Treating IT Like a Technology Issue Instead of Managing It as a Business Issue

It is easy to lose sight of a simple truth: management behavior—*not* technology—is at the heart of the IT dilemma. People manage IT. People request IT. And people make IT investment decisions. Some of these people reside in the IT department, but most reside elsewhere. Many of these decision makers are unaware of the implications of their decisions. The people making the business decisions have, in many cases, little knowledge of the IT enablement they are asking for and what it can (and cannot) do for them. Some don't even realize they affect the technology. On a personal level, we forgive them for their ignorance, but at the top of the chain of command are senior officers, expected to understand all implications of their actions—and those of their delegates—when investing the organization's money in any asset, be it financial or technological. So even though ignorance may be their excuse, it isn't a reason to repeat past mistakes.

Changing this behavior requires organizations to better integrate their business planning processes with their IT planning process. Although plenty of energy allegedly goes into aligning business and IT investments, mere "alignment" just doesn't cut it anymore. The two planning processes need to become one. When budgeting, investment management, and decision-support processes do not fully account for IT, executives make business decisions with incomplete information—their situational awareness is impaired. To find evidence of this deficiency, map out the organization's budget process. The typical budget planning process requires the IT department to estimate the IT budget before the business units determine which initiatives they plan to pursue. How sensible is that approach? If business decisions should drive IT decisions—a fact we've known for decades—then why would a CFO ask the IT department to submit its budget without first understanding what the business plans to do and how IT plays into that strategy? Yet most organizations now follow this practice. Why is it done that way? Because it is how most organizations have always done it. Business strategy does *not* drive IT investment decisions. In more cases than not, the IT budget is decided before the business determines its strategy, and the two are aligned ex post by well-intentioned middle managers who, by the way, know the process is broken but are not empowered to fix it.

Failure to Evolve IT Management as a Discipline

The IT management discipline is one of the newest corporate disciplines, predated by management of the other functions (engineering, finance, human resources, logistics, manufacturing, marketing, sales, etc.). It has been around for only 40 years or so. Compared to the other disciplines, IT management practices have improved little over the past 20 years. Supply chain and customer management, for example, revolutionized the way that best-in-class organizations manage their supply-facing and customer-facing operations, reducing cost of goods sold, cash-to-cash cycle time, and order-fulfillment cycle time. Managers in high-technology organizations have cut research and development cycle time for new products by more than 50%. Financial management has vastly improved the fiscal awareness of most organizations. The fusion of these management capabilities has provided the senior leadership team with decision support and strategic management capabilities. How then has the management of information investments improved in the past 20 years? Not much, it seems. In 2003, MIT *Sloan Management Review* researched 130 *Fortune* 1,000 companies and found how immature their IT investment management practices are:[7]

- 41% of the companies surveyed did not have central oversight of IT spending.
- 46% did not document their applications and infrastructure well.
- 47% did not have central oversight of IT projects.
- 57% did not have project success criteria.
- 41% did not regularly calculate return on investment.

The organization could address these issues if it had efficient and effective processes, but too many IT management practices are disjoint, lacking consistent, repeatable, reliable processes to sustain them. The few industry standard IT processes that exist are immature and fragmented. Management has no reference model for end-to-end management of IT. In response, some organizations try to outsource the difficulties of IT service provision. Yet even if we outsource IT service provision we are still left with the other core missions. We are also still left with the IT governance activities, that is, the means the organization should be using to ensure accountability for IT spending. According to a 2004 study by *CIO Insight Magazine,* only one-third of CIOs and IT executives consider IT governance to be a strength in their organization.[8] At the end of the day, the organization retains accountability for IT spending decisions regardless of whether, or what, it outsources.

It is important to understand that the situation described here is not the fault of individual managers, practitioners, or vendors. If anything, it is the collective fault of all of these roles. We are where we are

---

[7] "Best Practices in IT Portfolio Management," *MIT Sloan Management Review,* Spring 2004.
[8] "The IT Organization: Why Is IT Morale So Bad?" *CIO Insight Magazine,* November 2004.

due to a systemic failure to manage and develop the IT management discipline. Industry has not taught IT management as an integrated business process. Instead, it has been taught as an amalgamation of best practices, checklists, models, software, and templates. IT investment is viewed as a "bolt-on" to corporate planning processes. Most executive training programs rotate up-and-coming managers through every key department *except* the IT department. As a result, many IT managers spend their entire career in the IT department and have no other perspective. In fact, in many organizations, the IT department is viewed by business unit managers as the least desirable place to work. Why? If one of the biggest line items in the general ledger is IT expense, why don't we rotate our best business unit managers through the IT department, and why don't we routinely rotate our best IT managers through the business units? The reason is that we still treat IT management as an art in spite of the fact that we know it is a proven discipline. Most managers blame IT practitioners for the IT condition, but it is due only to the heroic efforts of these passionate and dedicated practitioners that technology has transformed the corporate and government landscape as much as it has in the relatively brief time that IT has existed. Imagine what the technology could do if applied and managed in a more disciplined way and success did not depend on a small number of superheroes!

For some reason, senior leaders treat the IT department differently from every other department and then complain when it does not perform like the others. We have to stop treating IT and the IT discipline as if it were a different animal. It is not. Information technology is just like every other technology. The IT department is just like every other department (except that we have neglected its management practices). As you read this book, you will see that IT investment management has many parallels in other management disciplines. IT service development activities parallel those of commercial R&D organizations. IT service delivery and operations activities parallel those of corporate manufacturing and customer service departments. IT governance activities parallel corporate governance activities. IT is dynamic, but so are other disciplines, such as finance and logistics. IT is complex and uncertain, but no more complex or uncertain than engineering and demand forecasting. Get over IT! In concept, the fundamental management principles of all the disciplines are identical. We just need to do a little translation.

Failure of Senior Executives to Hold Themselves Accountable

In spite of past attempts to "fix" the IT department, the fundamental issues remain:

- Business transformation is fragmented.
- Projects fall short of expectations.
- Resource supply is misaligned with strategic intent.
- Project cycle times are too long and unpredictable.
- IT investments provide decreasing advantage.
- No multiyear IT financial forecast exists.
- IT operations expense increases year-over-year.

Tasking the IT department won't solve the IT dilemma. Reorganizing the IT department won't solve the dilemma. Decentralizing and centralizing the IT department won't solve the dilemma. Optimizing the IT department won't solve the dilemma. Outsourcing the IT department won't solve the dilemma. These solutions are fundamentally flawed because the problem is not the IT department.

The IT dilemma requires a systemic solution that alters the organization's decision-making behavior, something only the senior leadership team can accomplish. It requires involvement and cooperation among the entire senior leadership team. Delegating this transformation to middle managers is risky. Senior leaders can delegate day-to-day responsibility for execution but when they delegate accountability, overall performance suffers. The problem compounds over time. Over the past decades, most organizations dug a hole they are finding difficult and expensive to get out of.

Senior business leaders must retain accountability for ensuring proper IT investment decisions. Most middle managers lack the complete situational awareness required to make informed investment decisions and are biased by pressure to improve their departmental performance. It is not their fault. Middle managers are motivated to optimize their part, even at the expense of the whole. Senior business leaders are accountable for net worth, so they need to retain control and accountability for major investment decisions, including IT investment decisions. Senior leaders need to become more informed about the consequences of these decisions and more involved with assessing the nuances of the alternatives.

Cutting Costs, Not Budgets

Technology, including information technology, must be managed as a capital asset, and having too many assets is just as harmful as having too few. As we said, IT does not guarantee competitive advantage. Organizations need to use technology more precisely to improve organizational performance and, in so doing, gain competitive advantage in particular processes, achieve differentiated product or service offerings, or improve bottom-line performance. Cutting IT spending across the board—the all-too-frequent approach to soaring IT expenditures—is as likely to smother performance as it is to permanently reduce spending. Most attempts to cut the IT budget detract from investments that enable top-line growth, value, and competitive advantage. More often than not, budget reductions end up cutting new investments—integration budgets. Yet, these projects are what add value to the organization.

To avoid cutting off their nose to spite their face, organizational leaders need to cut *waste* and *low-value projects*, not budgets. They

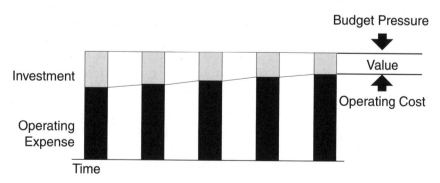

Effect of Budget Pressure and Growing Fixed Operating Cost

need to follow the flow of money to understand the true costs of providing IT services to the business units. They need to know how every IT project adds to the organization's ability to execute its mission or achieve its goals. Even though leaders may lack perfect understanding of each project's total impact, the organization should be able to trace the logic from a top-level business mission through to business improvement targets, to business improvement initiatives, to IT application investments, and all the way down to IT infrastructure investments. Said differently, every IT expense should be traceable to an IT service that business units require to meet their business mission. It should be clear how each project would affect the organization's operating performance. It should also be clear how each project would affect IT spending in years to come.[9] Yet instead of proceeding from such a clear rationale for proposed IT expenditures, organizations more typically require IT managers spend months each year debating with the finance department, the human resources department, and the leadership team about IT budgets and headcount. In the absence of such a rationale, IT managers are constantly doing too much with too little, but are not provided the means to prove it. Politics, pet pro-

---

[9] Furthermore, the place to cut IT expenditures is operations and maintenance (O&M) expenses. On average, 70% of IT spending goes toward sustaining the status quo. (And for some companies during the recent recession, this number grew to 100%.) But O&M is mostly a fixed cost in the short term. Another point to consider here is that for many organizations, the 10 most expensive IT systems comprise less than 50% of the budget, while the rest of the money is spent on tens or hundreds of systems, each with relatively low annual costs. This variety of systems makes it difficult to cut operating costs, because senior management can't simply slash the budget with broad policy decisions. Each system must be analyzed individually to determine whether it provides sufficient value, whether it should be decommissioned, and/or whether it can be consolidated or replaced by a more effective system. It is a time-consuming, exacting, and often costly process. It is why organizations under pressure to cut short-term costs are more likely to cut investment expenses rather than operating expenses, which makes legacy systems a concern today. However, the best way to address operating cost is to prevent it before new systems are installed, just as design-for-manufacturing dramatically reduces manufacturing expense ex ante.

jects, and squeaky wheels influence decisions rather than the effective balancing of organizational resources with organizational objectives.

To better understand how decisions to simply cut IT budgets can stifle organizational effectiveness and decrease the IT value equation—and, conversely, how proactive IT governance drives down cost and drives up value—consider this simplified diagram illustrating how the way in which different attempts at IT cost reductions can lead to either value erosion or value creation. Governance decisions to reduce the budget through cost cutting can stifle organizational effectiveness and decrease the IT value equation. In other words, such budget reductions can result in a lower overall return on IT investment. In contrast, carefully managing down the *demand* for IT services, or improving the *unit cost*[10] of service provision, perpetuates and improves competitive advantage from IT investments, thereby improving their value.

IT Cost Reduction Decision Implications

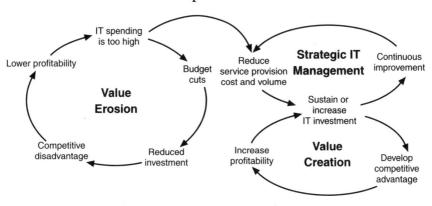

---

[10] The *unit cost* of a service is the cost for providing an incremental unit of service (hours, connections, devices, etc.). Unit cost uses cost accounting methods to calculate the cost pool for the service and the total number of units. The unit cost is a function of the cost pool, total units, and the incremental cost of providing one more unit of service. Holding the IT department accountable for unit cost allows the IT department to focus on their controllable (supply) costs as opposed to focusing on the aggregate cost, which is as much a factor of business demand for IT services.

Some will be skeptical of this claim because of the track record of organizations that have tried to get themselves out of the vicious circle depicted on the left side of the diagram and into the kind of virtuous cycle shown on the right side. Several analysts, in fact, reported that fewer than one-third of business transformation and cost reduction projects in the early 2000s were delivered on time, within budget, and with expected results. Many practitioners would have us believe that time and budget overruns are the "nature of the beast"—that IT is difficult to manage and that such high failure rates as these are necessary for innovation. People used to say the same things about marketing and new product development back in the 1980s, too. That premise proved to be invalid, and it is invalid for IT projects as well. In the 1980s, R&D managers thought that all they had to do was throw money at R&D to fuel innovation and expedite time-to-market for new products. Eventually chief technology officers (CTOs) learned that such tactics were a waste. R&D, it turns out, yields greater results when governed by a robust portfolio management method that ensures technology is driven by customer needs. Today, IT portfolio management is used by best-in-class organizations to reduce wasted IT spending and uncover hidden costs, freeing up resources to pursue projects that address true business needs.

Key Themes

- Spending on IT trends upward regardless of whether organizations outsource IT services or provide them in-house.
- IT has become an essential enabler of growth and value, used throughout the value chain to deliver products and services to customers.
- The issue at hand is what executives can do to make IT matter more . . . repeatedly, consistently, and predictably.
- Shareholders and policymakers seek a management mechanism to assure that growing IT investments drive commensurate value—an increase in net worth (economic, social, ethical, etc.).
- Value from IT diminishes for a number of reasons:
  - *Runaway demand from business units:* Business unit demand for IT drives IT spending. In effect, the business really makes IT investment decisions. Hence, business leaders should be accountable for IT spending, not merely the CIO.
  - *Obsessing about the urgent and leaving the important to chance:* IT managers are too often consumed by mundane IT service provision issues to devote time to the strategic issues (information assurance, transformation, and business architecture).
  - *Treating IT like a technology issues instead of managing it as a business issue:* Management behavior—not technology—is at the heart of the IT dilemma. Changing behavior requires organizations to better integrate their business planning and IT planning processes. Mere alignment is not enough. The two must become one.
  - *Failure to evolve IT management as a discipline:* The IT management discipline is one of the newest corporate disciplines and needs to be improved. The root cause of the IT dilemma is not bad people but rather bad processes.
  - *Failure of senior executives to hold themselves accountable:* The solution requires that we alter the organization's behavior. Leaders must regain and retain accountability for IT investment decisions.

- *Cutting costs, not budgets:* Technology must be managed as a capital asset. Leaders need to focus on cutting low-value projects, not cutting budgets. Cutting projects implies cutting all aspects, in the business units as well as the IT department. Focus on systemic cost and investment improvements, not budget reductions means that organizations will at times need to spend money to save money in the long run.

What Is IT Portfolio Management?

Good writers define reality; bad ones merely restate it.

—Edward Albee

If we've learned anything from IT value erosion, it is that neither the IT department nor the business department alone is capable of fully addressing the IT dilemma. They have to work together. Managing IT investments requires cross-organizational collaboration and decision making at the most senior levels. It requires systemic thinking—addressing and countering the root causes of unproductive IT expenditures instead of simply bandaging the symptoms.

To better manage IT and increase return on investment, organizations have to improve IT management processes as they improved management processes in every other discipline (product development, supply chain, sales, service, etc.). Although a clear formula can be followed, educators have not traditionally taught it as a process, and too many senior executives are either unwilling or unsure how to take advantage of it. In short, the only way we are going to get this right is if the organization's leadership team works together to make IT investment decisions, just as they do to make most every other major investment decision regarding products, sales, manufacturing, and facilities. Leadership needs to manage IT investments as a portfolio, the same as it manages other investments. Management of IT requires a process that systemically addresses the cost drivers and improves the IT management system holistically to keep the bubble from surfacing somewhere else.

This book provides managers with a process-based method, called IT portfolio management, that enables senior leadership to govern IT investments (projects and services). IT portfolio management contains the fundamental constructs required for efficient and effective governance. At times, some of these constructs may appear obvious. Each individual concept is relatively simple, and some readers may believe they're doing it already. But most of those talking about portfolio management aren't doing half of what they need to. The prerequisite for efficient and effective IT portfolio management is applying all constructs in tandem, which is more complex and requires a level of discipline and determination that most organizations lack. "Give a person a fish and they eat for a day, teach a person to fish and they can eat for a lifetime." This book instructs managers how to fish. This book contains no fish. If the reader is too hungry to learn, then they can hire someone to fish for them. We won't tell the reader what to fish for. Because organizational mission and capabilities should drive IT investment decisions, any generic advice from us or anybody else on what the reader should fish for would be worthless.

This book incorporates and applies decades of experience in portfolio management methods to govern technology, research, and process reengineering projects. Fundamentally, little difference exists between *technology* portfolio management, *information technology* portfolio management, *project* portfolio management, and *service* portfolio management. Only the implementation details differ. Project portfolio management originated as a means for high-technology companies to govern large, complex new product development projects. Many of our high-technology clients sought our assistance in applying the portfolio management methodology because they were struggling with constrained budgets and conflicting priorities as well as R&D projects that repeatedly fell behind schedule, overran budgets, and fell short of customer expectations. Sound familiar? Chief technology officers (CTOs) adopted portfolio management as a way to ensure that research and new product development aligned with market and product strategy. Portfolio management became the preferred method to:

- Weed out weak product concepts early so engineering resources could concentrate on the highest-value projects.
- Hold project teams accountable while executing complex projects, with multiple work streams and multiple departments.
- Align and govern the processes for product development, resource management, service development, and project financial management.

Many service providers later adopted portfolio management as a best-in-class method for governing *service development* and *service investment management*. In the 1990s, the concept began to permeate the IT industry as a best-in-class method for governing IT projects and services. Later in the 1990s, the concept was applied to business process reengineering, transformation, restructuring, merger, and acquisition initiatives.

IT Portfolio Management as a Method for Driving Value

To begin with the briefest possible definition, IT portfolio management is a *method for governing IT investments across the organization, and managing them for value.* Further defining the scope of the IT portfolio management method requires a few working definitions. One of the most fundamental problems in IT management is that it has no taxonomy, no common language. IT engineers have defined the technology's terminology reasonably well, but we lack a precise *IT management* nomenclature. We can't tell you how many times we sat in management meetings and listened to a group of executives talk past each other. They think they are communicating, but they're not. They disagree because each executive thinks they are hearing and saying the right thing, but each interprets the conversation differently. Similarly, the term *portfolio management* means a dozen different things to a dozen different people. Media hype and practitioner myopia have contributed to the sketchy picture of IT portfolio management. Some have marginalized it to a list of projects. Others think it is a committee structure. Still others think it is a project management office. Each paints the picture from his or her limited perspective. We will try not to get too pedantic, but we ask that you hang in there for a few pages while we establish a common understanding of what we're going to discuss in this book.

What is a *portfolio*? In mathematical terms, a *portfolio* is a set of investments. In plain English, it is a grouping of investments that share similar characteristics. Investments can be grouped according to where they reside in an organization's value chain (R&D, supply chain, customer management, etc.), by discipline (engineering, manufacturing, sales, service, IT, HR, finance, etc.), by relative size (cost, resources, etc.), by strategic value (benefits). Some progressive organizations group investments by strategic objective (mission), such as all investments that attempt to improve product margins by 5%. Most IT investments are projects. These projects are grouped in a manner called *portfolio segmentation,* which is discussed in more depth in the *Governance Design* chapter. Because portfolio segments are logical groupings (based on a project's characteristics), a single project may be a member of multiple segments. This approach to grouping provides the flexibility of having the same project, such as a big operating system upgrade, visible in multiple segments. Although it can be confusing, this method provides a way to manage the fact that the same infrastructure project likely has a different priority in each division. What is important to remember at the onset is that portfolios and segments are sets of projects with related objectives. Because the segments are not physical, they can evolve over time, adopting as the organization learns and evolves. Portfolio management is receptive to continuous improvement and adaptive to organizational change.

What is a *project?* "Who cares?" you ask. You will. The definition of a project is at the same time both important and irrelevant. It is important because the organization needs to define what a project is in order to design its portfolio management method. The organization needs to establish a set of guidelines that mandates which "projects" flow through the process and what activities will be allowed to circumvent portfolio management. Believe it or not, many portfolio management implementations go awry at this first step. Many IT departments get hung up trying to precisely define a project. Honestly, organizations spend hundreds of hours on this topic. For example, is a business initiative a project? Is an IT service a project? Is upgrading the storage on a computer in the data center a project? Is reconfiguring the network a project? If a customer calls the IT help desk and needs a computer repaired, is that a project? Are the only real projects those that involve application development resources? A lot of media and academia must think so, because they reference these situations in the hundreds of papers and articles published on portfolio management. Our definition is broader, more encompassing. The good news is that your initial definition does not need to be precise. Most people want to change it not long after they define it, evolving it over time as the process matures and the organization acclimates to using the process methodically.

Rather than trying to define a project per se, focus on defining *criteria* that determine which activities (a.k.a. projects) fall under the purview of portfolio management. For example, an organization might define criteria for level of project expense, capital, resources, duration, impact, risk, and so on. Avoid letting debates on this subject become a delay tactic. Take a cue from Nike and "Just Do It." Pick a set of criteria and move on, knowing that the organization can—and likely will—fine-tune the criteria later. Some organizations choose to rollout the portfolio management method to the big projects first. But *design it to handle all the projects*. Simple projects might require a "fast path" through the portfolio management workflow, but they still need to follow a method—preferably the same method.

One prerequisite for a project—and perhaps our only one—is that a project must have some *explicit desired outcome* (objective). If the organization cannot state the objective of a project, then it is not a project. Can a service be a project? Yes. The objective of a service is to fulfill a request. Can routine maintenance be a project? Yes. The objective of maintenance is to repair or prevent the failure of a component. Can running a data center be a project? Yes, if the performance criteria are crystal clear. Some ask whether it makes sense to think of these activities as projects because some can be small, and we may not want to manage thousands of activities the same way we manage big projects. We agree completely, but don't get ahead of us. We haven't discussed how we want to manage thousands of tiny projects, and we won't for a few chapters so try to be patient. We're simply trying to establish a working definition.

Our explicit desired outcome only need be observable (measurable) in a qualitative way. We prefer the outcome be measured in quantitative terms, because it allows more precision in our valuation. However, it does not need to be quantitative. The sole objective of some projects is to define the objectives for a bigger follow-on project, which is a reasonable desired outcome. In fact, this approach is a best practice when dealing with a highly ambiguous new project concept. As long as someone can evaluate the project result against a desired outcome, and make a value judgment about that desired outcome, then the basic tenets of portfolio management are preserved. Without an observable objective, however, it makes it difficult to value the project.

What do we mean by *management*? Now here's a vague term that can mean everything from making the decisions and owning the results (accountable), to doing the work (responsible), to contributing to the effort (consulted), to receiving project status (informed). Which are included in management? All of them. A holistic portfolio management method addresses the entire management spectrum, including all activities required to hold an organization accountable, govern the resources with responsibility to do the work, ensure all who need to provide input are consulted, and inform all key stakeholders. Nothing less will suffice for our purposes.

A team of senior managers, called the *portfolio management team* (*PMT*), generally carries out portfolio management. This team need not be newly formed. Many organizations use an established senior management team for this purpose. Others prefer to use a subset or create a new team. Often the determining criteria for whether to use a new or an existing team is that *the PMT is first and foremost a decision team*. Decision teams are not analytical teams, they are not research teams, and they are not discussion teams. Decision teams don't make recommendations. Decision teams make decisions! The implication is that the PMT must include senior managers with the authority to make portfolio decisions. In fact, the PMT includes *only* senior managers with the authority to *make* portfolio decisions for projects in that portfolio. Analytical teams or facilitators may support the PMT, but the PMT makes the decisions. Surprisingly few organizations have the discipline to follow through on this design principle. As a result, the PMT is relegated to a disempowered overhead activity that answers to the real decision makers. We will expand later upon how this limitation impedes the portfolio management method.

What do we mean by a *process-based method*? Most equate process with workflow, the repeatable tasks required to achieve a desired result consistently. However, that characteristic is only one element. We use the broadest possible definition that includes all elements. A *process-based method* includes all information (data), information technology (applications), performance measures (metrics), policies (rules, regulations), roles (expectations), tools (templates and applications), teams (organizational structure), and workflow (activities) that are typically documented as *guidelines*. It also includes all interfaces and interdependencies (commonly referred to as inputs and outputs) with other processes and practices. Success comes only when the organization implements all elements. We will simplify our terminology going forward, referring to this compilation of elements as a *process* or *method*.

Some clients ask, what is the difference between IT portfolio management, IT project management, and IT service development? They appear similar but they are *not* the same. All three are required for successful project execution. Portfolio management, as we have defined it, is an investment management method. Portfolio management intersects the other two processes throughout the project's life cycle. Project management and development are *execution* management best practices that ensure successful implementation. Early in the project's life cycle, the project's value proposition—the business case—is reviewed by the PMT. If approved, the PMT ensures the project has the resources, including the appropriate execution methodology and best practices, it requires to be successful. The PMT ensures that the project plans to follow the proper project management and IT service development processes. Once the project is chartered and the project governance structure is established, it only reengages with the portfolio management process when it provides status updates as to whether the project is operating within the initial parameters (scope, objectives, funding, resources, and results) established by the PMT. By managing on an exception basis for ongoing projects, the PMT does not need to reengage with the project except when it needs to redirect the initial parameters.

Project management is a methodology for administering projects. It originated as a set of best practices for intraproject work breakdown structure (tasks and plans), task interdependency management (critical path), resource and skill needs analysis (loading), and risk analysis and mitigation (mission assurance). In the IT discipline, project management must be carried out in conjunction with a service development process. Some organizations merge project management and service development into a single, integrated process. Others manage the project management discipline as a general discipline throughout the organization.

Service development ensures that all essential work streams are completed before a new IT service is launched. Service development is a process that every new IT service (application, messaging, infrastructure services, etc.) should follow once the PMT charters the project. The service development process typically integrates all work streams including application development, integration, infrastructure enablement, life cycle support, business process reengineering, organizational responsibilities reengineering, business rules reengineering, training, and communications. The service development process addresses people, process, and technology. Whereas a third-party IT service provider may not need to be concerned with business impact, the organization's IT service development process needs to look at the new IT services holistically as *information* services not *technology* services. Some organizations believe that the service development process is synonymous with their IT software development process, also referred to as an application development or systems integration process. Although true in some organizations, the service development process is all-inclusive whereas the software development process may only focus on the software work stream. Many organizations overlook the subtle difference, and hence run into trouble when rolling out new IT-enabled services to their business units and find that the organization is not prepared to use the new system. In more cases than not, the service development process is incomplete and the management team is unaware that their service development process is ad hoc.

Put these elements all together and we have our definition of IT portfolio management. The holistic scope allows us to map out all aspects of an organization's current method and see clearly what may need to change in order to increase portfolio value. The construct is scalable to any size project or portfolio. The scope includes all elements required to be successful and provide infinite scalability and flexibility to adapt to most any organization. Adapting the generic portfolio management method to different organizations merely requires us to reconfigure the elements to meet the idiosyncratic needs of particular ones.

The IT portfolio management method is needed and is effective in every type of organization: commercial, private, public, not-for-profit, government, and military. In all cases, the organization needs to make IT investment decisions so the organization needs a portfolio management method. We have yet to find an organization where this method does not work. It adds value to every organization, big or small. Portfolio management is highly effective where IT service provision is outsourced, because it ensures the business has control over investments made by third parties. Portfolio management works where IT service provision is retained in-house (in-sourced), because it facilitates collaborative decision making between the business managers and IT managers. Portfolio management complements Six Sigma, by providing organizations with a mechanism to review and fund improvement projects. Similarly, portfolio management complements every other quality management method. Portfolio management structures the fuzzy front-end of every IT systems development and reengineering methodology, by ensuring the business is actively engaged at the onset of the project where their participation is most critical. It doesn't matter whether an IT organization is CMM Level 1 or Level 4. All organizations make IT investment decisions. All organizations need IT portfolio management.

How We Got into This Mess—Learn from the Past

You learn from a conglomeration of the incredible past—whatever experience gotten in any way whatsoever.

—Bob Dylan, "Subterranean Homesick Blues & the Blond Waltz"

Unless you are playing dice or roulette, it is irrational to do the same thing over and over again and expect a different outcome each time. Yet it is what many organizations' efforts to reverse the downward spiral of IT overspending and value erosion have amounted to in recent years. Although few executives want to take the time to understand the root causes of their firms' seemingly intractable problems with IT, it is difficult to effect change in organizational behavior without understanding how particular behaviors came to be. It is not necessary to read the unabridged history of the evolution of IT and its impact on corporations and public agencies, but the short version offers some valuable lessons. It is helpful to consider IT management in context of its history lest we repeat the mistakes of the past.

IT is a product of its environment. A brief look at the past helps to reveal that today's IT troubles are not random or mysterious. Evolution of IT as a technology, a discipline, and a corporate function systemically created today's IT dilemma. This chapter synthesizes the changes that IT management underwent on its way to its present condition. The following generalizations might not apply to every organization, but most every organization has undergone at least some of these tribulations and most large corporations have undergone most of them.

The 40-year period from the mid-1960s until the present day saw the IT market emerge, mature, be disrupted and transformed, explode, peak, crash, and recover. The form factor of the technology began at the size of a garage, then progressively shrunk to the size of a file cabinet, a typewriter, a notebook, a postage stamp, and soon will be no

29

larger than a dust particle. The footprint of IT evolved from a single machine in one room in the basement to devices that sit on every desktop, to devices that sit in the palm of a hand. They may soon be woven into clothing. And while this transformation was happening, IT management was born and underwent its own often uneven and sometimes wrenching development. Its major crisis—from which the discipline has yet to recover—came as a result of the transition from the centralized mainframe to distributed computing. For the explosive growth of the personal computer (PC), as we shall see, drove not only a transformation of architecture but also of IT governance that, in turn, altered the way organizations procured, operated, and managed their IT.

The Mainframe Era

In the mainframe era, disciplined processes enabled IT staff members to provide systematic service to most every core business process. IT staff members optimized computing assets and protected them with strict governance procedures. Procedures were clearly defined and steadfast. IT was expensive, so to maximize return on investment (ROI), support staff members maximized mainframe asset utilization. IT practitioners designed their processes for this purpose, to keep the mainframe in use 24 hours per day, seven days per week, if possible.

IT management in the mainframe era also intentionally created a barrier between IT assets (and, therefore, the IT department) on the one hand, and their internal customers in the business departments (e.g., manufacturing, sales, and finance) on the other. Human and machine were disconnected by design, for their mutual well-being. IT originated, after all, as an obscure, expensive science conducted in a climate-controlled laboratory called a data center. The first computers were highly sensitive to heat, movement, and improper operation. To protect the computers, only computing specialists could enter the data center. Computer specialists created rigorous operating and maintenance processes and followed them religiously. IT processes were technocentric, designed to protect and optimize the computers. The rest of the organization came to worship at the doorstep of the data center when people needed computing support. The situation served most everyone's needs for a time. Few in the organization really wanted to understand the technology—or its keepers. Computer engineers designed the technology under the assumption that computer scientists would use it, not the novice. It took many years before engineers accepted that the novice might use the technology, and even then it required considerable schooling to learn the arcane programming languages. These characteristics made for a certain equilibrium between the IT department and the business departments.

Under these circumstances, most organizations also accepted that they needed to structure the way the organization worked to accommodate the computers and the IT staff. The organization saw the potential of computer technology and was willing to adapt to the technology in order to realize its benefits. Business staff designed their processes around mainframe computer schedules. Activities such as customer invoicing and sales reporting, for example, were scheduled in advance. Few business activities were processed real time.

IT staff members, meanwhile, became accustomed to business staff seeking them out with computing challenges. The definition of customer focus to the average IT staffer was responding accurately to business requests for information. IT staff response time was measured in weeks. The company valued technologically savvy IT staff. It was a technician's dream. No soft skills required. Warm, fuzzy people need not apply. If a programmer was a little eccentric, it was not a problem as long as the job got done. After all, programmers didn't interact with customers, and rarely interacted with mainstream business staff. They spent most of their time in the basement writing programs. Even as IT departments grew, the fundamentals did not change. IT costs were mostly comprised of assets. At the peak of the mainframe computer era, labor rarely exceeded a third of the IT budget. The mainframe computer industry emerged, peaked, and crashed in a couple of decades. It never died, but it is now a shadow of its former self.

From the Mainframe to the PC

The advent of distributed PCs disrupted the equilibrium in the computer marketplace as well as in the IT discipline. A few Silicon Valley engineers were dissatisfied with the mainframe operating model and found the mainframe too complex and costly for their computing needs. As a result, they created PCs and workstations. The birth of the

PC created a void in the marketplace, and thousands of companies rushed to fill it with new products. Industry growth was explosive. Technology proliferated and diversified. Catalyst after catalyst fueled the industry at a phenomenal growth rate. After the PC came, in rapid succession, the graphical user interface (e.g., Microsoft Windows and Apple Macintosh); thousands of single-user, business-specific applications; the network (intranet); thousands of multi-user, business-specific applications; the Internet; integrated enterprise-wide applications (ERP, CRM, etc.); Web-browser applications; and wireless technology.

The problem with the PC, from the standpoint of IT staff, was that it did not conform to the mainframe paradigm. It upset the equilibrium between the IT department and the rest of the organization. It broke the operating commandments. IT staff couldn't contain PCs in a lab. PCs needed to coexist within the organization in order to be effective. Engineers designed the PC for the layperson to use. Computer specialists gave it little notice because it was not, at first, a powerful device. Mainframe computers outperformed the PC 10:1 in all aspects. To the computer specialists, PCs were primitive in every sense. A relatively small subset of nonspecialists, referred to as *power users*, pushed the PC into the mainstream computing marketplace. Power users were frustrated with the mainframe governance model; they wanted to control the technology and its services. The mainframe service model impaired power users' creativity by requiring them to work through computer specialists. Some power users learned the cryptic mainframe programming languages, but they were limited in what they could do. They saw the potential for a device with which they could build complex models and store information themselves, accessible and changeable on a real-time basis. Power users didn't see the PC as limiting; they saw it as liberation from the strict rules and regulations of data center managers. Whereas the mainframe computers were cryptic, PCs were increasingly intuitive. Whereas one mainframe cost millions, one PC cost only thousands. Whereas most central IT organizations leased mainframe computers, most power users purchased PCs with money from departmental budgets. PCs established a new paradigm by changing operating procedures, service procedures, and financial management procedures. The explosive growth of the new technology drove a transformation of the IT architecture and governance structure, which in turn altered the way organizations procured, operated, and managed their IT. All the while, most organizations were oblivious to the impact these changes would have on the underlying IT cost structure.

The initial impression—that the PC would lower the IT cost structure—was a misconception caused by grossly misunderstanding the ripple effects of this new technology. Decision makers failed to predict the explosive industry innovation or its impact on the adoption rate for IT. Most underestimated what it would take to make the technology effective. Few understood the impact on the financial ledger. Although each individual PC was relatively cheap, organizations evolved to the point where, today, most have more computers than employees. Large corporations have tens of thousands of computers. Hundreds of routers and switches, which are in essence specialized computers, and miles of cabling interconnect this distributed *network* of computers. Each computer requires its own software (license). Because laypeople use PCs, the software interface had to be easy to use. The more vendors made business applications easier to use, the more business staff used the computers, and so the more business staff demanded from the applications. The more demanded of the software, the more expensive it became in the aggregate, to the point where it was actually more costly to maintain than the old centralized mainframe environment. Organizations also now required more IT support in more places, and it was increasingly impossible to rely on a few specialists housed in centralized offices to support the enterprise. Every major campus demanded its own support staff. Business staff members became accustomed to having their own on-site support staff to provide high-touch IT support services on demand. All these elements cost money, too.

At the same time that IT costs were increasing in this way, responsibility for IT was decentralized to the four corners of the organization. The distributed nature of IT was the catalyst for today's IT dilemma, but it didn't *cause* the dilemma. *The dilemma was caused by a breakdown in IT governance, resulting in a subtle but fundamental change in procurement and asset management.* Whereas previously a central IT department controlled IT decision making and influenced vendor decisions, now this decision making was decentralized to site leadership teams, department heads, and other organizational groups. Whereas a disciplined method had once controlled IT expenditures and executives who were experienced in IT management controlled IT investments, organizations now decentralized responsibility for IT decisions to most every departmental middle manager. The new decision makers had neither the situational awareness nor the experience, in some cases, to make these decisions effectively. Previously managers involved in IT decision making had typically reported up the chain of command to one person responsible for IT, including the entire IT budget. The final decision-making authority was manifest in one "belly button." Responsibility for IT assets was now dispersed. Each department manager made IT investment decisions, implicitly or explicitly. Business leaders influenced the IT budget and allocation decisions whenever they decided to pursue a new business initiative that required IT enablement. Soon a typical organization did little without affecting IT assets or services.

Even in organizations where the CIO approved all IT expenditures, it only appeared that they made the decisions. The IT department may have decided what product to buy or may have allocated IT department resources to a business initiative, but it was more often the business decision to pursue a business initiative in the first place that set the IT agenda. More typical were organizations that decentralized the IT budget to dozens, if not hundreds, of departments. There was no central control, except perhaps from the CEO, who had no time for it. Everyone was responsible and nobody was accountable. Every manager made his or her own decisions, and from their individual perspectives those decisions were appropriate. Organizations as a whole spent money on IT like adolescents who had just been given their first credit card.

The Cost Crisis

Left unchecked in this way, the cost of computing now grew out of control. Costs grew out of control not because of the IT department but in spite of the IT department. Most IT managers were fully aware of what was happening; but in addition to being powerless to stop it, they were also afraid of becoming outcasts by speaking out against the changes. The trend was indiscernible at first, different for each company and industry. Most managers knew the paradigm was changing, but it was not readily apparent how, and how fast. It took approximately five years for the PC to mature to the point that the masses wanted to use it. It took another decade before it hit the radar screen of most senior executives. The growth was not sudden and disruptive. Had it been so, the effects would have been immediately apparent and organizations could have adjusted. Instead, growth was surreptitious. It was like slowly turning up the heat on a frog in a pot of water. (The frog can't tell when to jump out of the pot.) Senior officers (CxOs) didn't notice IT expenditures creeping up until it was too late. Few senior executives looked critically at IT spending from an enterprise perspective until about the year 2000, when aggregate financial effects began to erode the bottom line.

Three events converged to create a spike in IT spending at about this time. Year 2000 (Y2K) was the first event. Prior to Y2K, dates were stored as two digits.[1] Software developers failed to anticipate what would happen when the year changed from "99" to "00." Organizations went into a tizzy because they had not planned for the change. In some instances, the IT staff members who had built many of the applications had long since left the organization. Many other organizations had been using applications purchased from vendors that were no longer in business. Still other applications were woefully out of date because the organization hadn't upgraded them for years. All these organizations had no idea what would happen to their applications on January 1, 2000. It was a mess. Yet most organizations, unwilling or unable to assess their risk objectively, succumbed to the Y2K frenzy. The more organizations that succumbed, the more others jumped into the fray to try to take advantage of the situation. Some IT managers used Y2K as an excuse to increase their staff and budgets, or get rid of old software applications. Many other IT managers were fully aware of what was happening but were powerless to act. Their business and IT management peers chastised them if they raised any alarms. Because organizations had decentralized decision rights, it was relatively easy

---

[1] The year 1999, for example, was stored as 99. The software incremented the date by adding 1 to the number. The challenge was that most software applications would stop working when they attempted to store the number 100 in a two-digit storage area. Software applications were not programmed to reset the number to 00. Much of the software was written decades previously when the programmers never anticipated the situation.

for departmental managers to take advantage of the situation. Many organizations wrote off more hardware and software against a Y2K expense than they really needed. In this way they funded the IT spending frenzy of the late 1990s.

The next major event saw enterprise resource planning (ERP), integrated financial systems, customer relationship management (CRM), and e-business become the silver bullets for fixing the Y2K problem and simultaneously reducing operating expense. Chief operating officers (COOs) thought these applications were going to transform everything from order management to manufacturing to receivables to sales. ERP was going to drastically reduce inventory expense, reduce cash-to-cash cycle time, and perhaps even eliminate world hunger if we were lucky. (At least that was the way some managers and vendors made it sound.) Middle managers sold senior executives on implementing ERP, CRM, and e-business in many cases based on fear that their organizations would be left behind. Perhaps business managers listened too much to the vendors. More than likely, they didn't listen enough. At least they didn't listen to the vendors' disclaimers about needing to change operational business processes and responsibilities, or to their warnings against customizing the software to retrofit existing workflows. In most cases, organizations customized the software applications to automate their existing inefficient and ineffective business processes. Performance improvements, as a result, were marginalized, while the increased amortization and operating expense of the customization often adversely affected the value proposition.

The vendors were not without fault, however. They didn't realize just how different every industry was. Vendors initially thought they could produce a generic application and have every industry follow a generic set of business processes. They quickly learned that their software needed to accommodate business process nuances unique to each industry. In time, the vendors evolved the applications to meet these unique industry needs. Yet organizations that had already made the purchase claimed that they couldn't wait for the software to catch up. Perhaps they really couldn't wait, or perhaps they didn't want to admit that they had made a mistake. Most were under the gun to get the software installed in time to take a Y2K write-off. Because the organization couldn't use generic applications, they customized the ones they had just bought. In the end, practically all projects overran their

Compounding Effect of Technology Events on IT Operating Expense

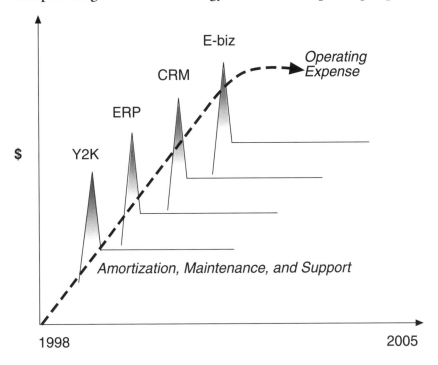

budgets and increased the net annual IT operating expense. With costs much higher than expected, the business case assumptions changed, but few middle managers revisited their decisions. Rather than write off the sunk cost, they went ahead with the deployment. At any other time, organizations might have forced middle managers to mitigate the expense, but they now wrote it off against the Y2K slush fund—a skeleton they'd prefer to hide away in the closet.

The third major event accounting for the IT spending spike of recent years occurred in the mid-1990s, when a number of corporations began amortizing the implementation cost of large applications. The effect did not become completely evident, however, until the Y2K and ERP spending began. Previously corporations had amortized large hardware and software purchases but not the entire implementation cost, which might be 2 to 10 times what they had paid for the hardware and software. Instead, they made the investment decision based on the implementation cost being a direct expense in the current year.

Now organizations could amortize the expense and spread it over three, five, or more years, depending on the expected life of the application. This tactic lowered the bar for new investments, which at first seemed like a good thing. Once IT depreciation and amortization expenses began to amass over two to three years, however, CFOs began to see the impact on the balance sheet. CFOs were driving by looking in the rearview mirror and didn't see the wreck in the middle of the road until they ran into it in the around the year 2000. They had neglected to adjust their financial planning and forecasting methods in light of the accounting change, despite all the money they had spent integrating their financial systems. It is a sad irony that what caused CFOs to overlook the buildup of IT expenses was a lack of good financial management applications. It was a bit like the chef starving to death in the kitchen.

Trying to Come to Terms with the Cost Crisis

From the late 1980s thru the late 1990s, business unit demand for IT assets and services had come to drive unprecedented levels of IT spending. Rapid business spending on IT over this period caused departmental IT budgets and asset ledgers to swell to the point where they eventually set off warning bells in the CFO's office. Over the next few years, corporate officers generally experienced a rude awakening as to the impact of distributed computing. Fixed IT assets were piling up. Fixed IT expenses compounded with every new application acquired. Labor costs associated with the implementation and maintenance of these new applications grew to the point where 60% of the IT budget consisted of labor. The number of IT employees was growing faster than the growth rates of organizations themselves, and many of these employees were among the highest-paid staff members. To CxOs, the growth seemed alarming. They had no visibility into the portfolio of IT investments, past or present. Without situational awareness, CxOs were unable to react effectively to the situation. With their decision processes impaired by this lack of transparency into who was spending what and why, most CxOs did what many managers do when a crisis occurs—they looked for someone to blame.

In an attempt to get their arms around the IT dilemma, most organizations reconsolidated responsibility for distributed IT assets and services under the IT department. IT departmental managers inherited a mess; a hodge-podge of assets, processes, and skill sets. Meanwhile, the ever-increasing demand for IT continued. The scapegoat became the IT department. IT departments came under fire from the CFO to cut spending, even though the problem was one of demand management more than supply management. It was easier for CxOs to constrain the supply of IT services than it was for them to stem spending in the business units, or so they thought. The only alternative would have been to blame the entire management team, but CxOs couldn't do that because CxOs *were* the management team.

With the IT cost structure now consisting mostly of fixed assets and fixed operating expense, not much surplus spending was available to cut. Most IT managers had already cut discretionary spending to the bone to fund increased business demand for IT services. Labor and expense for operating fixed assets were effectively set in the short term. The only way to reduce fixed costs was to improve operating process efficiency and effectiveness systemically, which took time and money. CxOs had neither. Organizations were under pressure from the financial community to deliver immediate results. The financial community wanted not only investment reform but also short-term bottom-line improvement. Unfortunately, CxOs couldn't erase the past just because the financial community suddenly woken up to what was happening. The assets were already on the books and most couldn't afford to retire them. They couldn't decommission the applications without affecting the business, and without decommissioning the applications they had few options for what they could do for free. So the senior leadership of most organizations became increasingly frustrated. The money had to come from somewhere, so as most CIOs cut the infrastructure budgets, CxOs cut the business units' budgets. In the end, the majority of the savings came from the very budgets that enabled organizational stability and growth. It was a price that had to be paid eventually, but it was hoped that with luck the organization could postpone these investments until the crisis had passed. With luck, competitors would be in the same situation and would not be able to take advantage of this temporary competitive weakness. Most organizations turned out to be lucky.

Meanwhile, as the IT function took the brunt of the blame for the crisis, trust in IT, IT vendors, and the IT department fell precipitously. Many of the highest-caliber IT staff members left the profession to

IT Stakeholder Frustrations

Senior Leadership	*Business Units*
What do you mean it doesn't work that way?	Can't it be done faster?
Why is it late? I need it now!	Can we make one small change?
It cost how much?!	I don't care what it costs, I need it!
But they said it was low risk!	Don't worry; we'll handle the people issues!

Suppliers	*IT Practitioners*
Sure, we can do that! Trust us!	Who makes the decisions?
Did we mention it might cost more?	What should I do? Which is more important?
You want what? That will cost extra. . . .	Why is everything a rush?
	I have no time for training!

pursue general business or consulting careers. They were sick of seeing businesses throw good money after bad. Seeing the problem clearly but not having the authority to solve it frustrated them. The majority remained in IT and waited for the ax to fall. Downsizing was long overdue. Outsourcing was also a possibility. Some hoped to get an early retirement package. Others simply felt that any change would be for the better. IT practitioners had long ago learned that their IT skills did not give them job security. The technology kept changing. Most practitioners were constantly concerned that they would become obsolete or have their work outsourced. The half-life of IT staff skill sets was two years. After that, IT staff members required retraining or they risked obsolescence, so they typically retooled their technical skills every four to seven years. At first, organizations rewarded IT practitioners for writing the best programs as fast as they could. IT practitioners did not need to understand the business in depth as long as they could make the technology hum. A few years later the organization wanted IT practitioners to become specialists in technology integration. A few years after that, it wanted IT practitioners to have an M.B.A. and become business reengineering experts and change agents. Later came demand for even more skills, such as enterprise resource planning (ERP), integrated financial systems, customer relationship management (CRM), e-business, and decision support. At the same time, the organization expected IT practitioners to learn how to perform comprehensive needs analysis, business case analysis, and total cost of ownership (TCO) financial modeling.

They were supposed to run a distributed computing enterprise and a worldwide support organization, drive cost out of the system, increase productivity, and retain employees, because the organization could not afford to cross-train or perform succession planning. To make matters worse, the organization repeatedly talked about outsourcing these IT practitioners along with everything they had created over the past decade, to save the company money. Or else, people thought that maybe the IT department should get an SEI CMM Level 4 certification, or implement ITIL service management, or implement Six Sigma, and so on and so forth.

To sum up, over the course of 40 years the IT discipline evolved from an obscure science, to a cost of doing business, to a strategic enabler, to one of the largest line items on the general ledger and the bane of senior executives. Myopic managers spent decades building up the IT budget. They spent millions replacing hundreds of homegrown mainframe applications with PC-based departmental applications. Then they found themselves with hundreds of point solutions on multiple platforms that didn't share information effectively. Organizations entered valuable information into applications that had inferior reporting and decision-support capabilities so they couldn't get the information out of the systems and, hence, didn't even realize the full value from these investments. Some organizations customized these applications in the hopes of getting them to work together more effectively, but that move added cost. Others tried to glue applications together but that approach required additional investment. Those who could afford it added expensive data warehouses to mine the information. Others spent millions replacing all the applications with new integrated applications that required considerable effort and investment, and posed considerable risk. Senior executives had little tolerance for replacing applications, considering the mess that most organizations already had on their asset ledger. No broad-stroke policy or mandate would change the situation.

Solving the problem required analysis on a case-by-case basis, but most organizations lacked the patience for this task. The problems were complex and required careful planning, but few managers plan well. The solutions required a high degree of collaboration between IT and the business departments, but organizational silos and the blame game became a barrier to collaboration. Implementing these solutions carried a degree of risk, but few organizations effectively mitigated risk. Some managers decided to wait to see what the future brought. Some are still waiting for the next silver bullet—as if the last silver bullets hadn't done enough damage.

In fact, most organizations poorly equipped managers to deal with the IT condition. Only recently have business schools begun to teach IT management. Most managers haven't known how to apply the principles of lean thinking to IT to reduce operating expense. They haven't known how to use Six Sigma principles to optimize IT cycle time and unit cost. They haven't known how to apply IT standard processes to improve service levels. What little they were taught in school about managing IT focused mostly on software development and project management. They hadn't learned to run IT like every other business unit. They hadn't learned how to balance IT service supply with business demand. They hadn't learned how to increase the value from IT enablement.

Due to neglect and repeated bad decisions, the IT condition became so complex and convoluted that few managers could effectively manage all the information technology, the IT discipline, and the IT staff. The head of the IT department and the IT management team were expected to wear multiple hats. They had to run an IT service organization, manage the technology and asset life cycles, fix the bad investment decisions made by their peers and predecessors, and be change agents for the senior leadership team. They had corporate fiduciary responsibilities (e.g., security), service delivery responsibilities (e.g., help desk, application development), and diplomatic responsibilities (e.g., transformation). Moreover, it was up to them to figure out which decisions were which. The organization expected IT managers to have exceptional management and leadership skills while most IT managers never received any formal IT management training. Why did senior leadership expect more from their IT managers than they expected from other managers, and where were the IT managers supposed to obtain these skills?

Facing this skill shortage in the IT management ranks, some organizations brought in managers from the finance department to try to solve the alleged IT problem. It seemed like a good idea. One of the biggest problems was budget overrun, which looked like a financial problem—so why not bring in financial managers? Unfortunately, financial managers knew nothing about managing technology, programmers, and technicians. They knew nothing about managing services. The financial managers knew how to account for spending, but not how to prevent IT operating expenses. They knew financial accounting but didn't realize that cost accounting was the answer. They were insufficiently educated for governing risk associated with technical decision making. They were inexperienced at managing large complex projects, and most of these managers failed.

Other organizations tried to solve the problem by bringing in managers from the large systems integration companies. This idea also sounded good. If these firms were smart enough to run large IT projects, why not hire these professionals? But these managers were essentially project managers, and the IT condition was not wholly addressable by project management. The IT condition was a product of decades of bad decisions, decentralized execution without enterprise coordination, corporate politics and bullies, ad hoc processes, average employees earning average compensation, complacency, and ignorance. Most of these new managers used best-in-class IT management processes, but they had never implemented them. In their old jobs, the focus had been on profit. In their new ones, the focus was on value with efficiency. The IT department was a cost center, which introduced a new set of economics. Systems integration firms didn't have to deal with out-of-control business unit demand and unreasonable requests, which was the purview of the corporate IT department. In their new jobs, these managers *were* the IT department. These new managers were acquainted with the basic economics of supply and demand, but were unskilled at managing a captive IT service provider within what was effectively a monopolistic economy. In the end, most of these managers were able to make some improvement. Organizations benefited from importing raw management talent into the IT ranks, but most organizations fared only marginally better than before. Things changed, but performance did not improve significantly.

Some senior leaders then lost patience and turned to outsourcing as a solution, only to find that *outsourcing results are ambiguous.* An August 2002, *CIO Magazine* survey[2] reported that 40% of survey respondents outsourced IT service delivery primarily with the intent of lowering IT expenses. Only half achieved a net reduction in expenses. Outsourcings reduced unit cost if the outsourcer provided services

---

[2] "By the Numbers: Upward and Onward with Outsourcing," *CIO Magazine,* August 1, 2002, p. 26.

more efficiently or obtained greater economies of scale. Many factors affected whether the outsourcers could provide this advantage, including the way the contract was written, the way the outsourcer was managed, and the limitations placed on the outsourcer regarding how to run IT service provision. Organizations with weak demand management for IT services further exacerbated the situation. Although the CFO and the IT management team had previously constrained IT spending by controlling the supply of IT resources, many organizations inadvertently eliminated this constraint when they outsourced IT service provision. These same organizations did not have strong governance processes to oversee project and service investments. In effect, they abdicated responsibility for investment management to the outsourcer. Some allowed any manager to submit requests to the outsourcer. The volume of IT services grew. The business units enjoyed a vast new pool of IT service provider capability, but it came at a bottom-line cost. Again, the CFO was caught unaware until it was too late, for the money was already spent by the time the CFO saw the bottom-line effect, and this time the organization had a contract with a third party to exacerbate the situation.

At this point senior leadership, as we have already noted, tried to cap IT budgets, but these constraints had unfortunate side effects. When senior leaders attempted to cap IT department head count, IT contractor expenses went through the roof because IT managers supplemented internal resources with outside ones, often paying two to four times as much to contractors than they would to their own staffs. When senior leaders tried to freeze contractor expenses, IT department throughput dropped, and the business units hired their own IT support staff to compensate for the shortage of in-house IT resources. IT resources once again began to be dispersed throughout the organization. The bubble kept getting pushed around but never went away, and even continued to grow and grow and grow.

Sweeping budget cuts didn't work well in dealing with runaway IT spending either. Senior leaders could stem spending in the current fiscal year, but this solution was not sustainable. A cap on spending affected new investments more so than life cycle costs. Once an organization deploys a new application, the application's operating costs are fixed for the life of the asset. Improving the efficiency of operations typically requires an investment in operations (processes or systems). No money was allocated to operating improvements. The nature of fixed operating costs thus isolated operating budgets from the effects of most budget cuts. The cost reduction inadvertently came from the investment budget. This cut reduced spending reserved for IT projects that supported new business endeavors and initiatives (i.e., higher-value activities). Organizations that cut the operating budget didn't improve efficiency; they merely reduced service volume or service levels, which reduced overall IT effectiveness. By capping IT spending, senior leaders bit off their noses to spite their faces. Budget constraints stifled organizational growth and value by preventing deployment of technology to automate business operations. In the meantime, fixed operating expense continued to amass. Some unfortunate organizations saw their IT operations costs grow to more than 90% of the IT budget, leaving only 10% to support business initiatives. Some of these organizations had to postpone needed-to-play investments, and as a result found themselves at a competitive disadvantage. Most every organization adopted the bad habits of cutting corners and insufficiently funding IT projects in an effort to do more with less. Rather than understand the situation and make the really hard decision of what not to investment in, most senior leaders just told everyone to tighten their belts. The alleged cost savings resulted in design and quality problems that ultimately drove up downstream operating cost . . . again.

Breaking the Death Spiral

All of this history brings us to where we are today. The mess that IT has become within so many organizations is not the nature of the beast. It is just a result of human nature. There is no beast, except for what organizations have created. Looking back on the history we have just sketched, we can see that it is our fault that the IT department doesn't have a clearly defined scope and set of responsibilities. It is our fault that the IT discipline lacks standard processes. Some may believe that ad hoc operating processes and dysfunctional behavior are a small price to pay for the tremendous innovation that the IT discipline brought about in such a relatively short time, but the shareholders don't see it that way. If the IT discipline is dysfunctional it is because we continue to send our IT personnel mixed messages. Organizations continue to ask IT managers and staff to fill a role and execute a set of responsibilities that are broader, more dynamic, and more political than most every other role in the corporation. If organizations want the IT department to improve, they need to stop expanding its scope of responsibilities while cutting the IT budget. They need to stop looking at IT as the productivity silver bullet (and blaming the IT department) and realize that organizations need business transformation, not technology. They need to start managing financing for IT the same as financing for engineering and manufacturing. As the first and most important step in this direction, they need to take IT investment decisions out of the hands of application integrators, accountants, analysts, and middle managers and put them into the hands of the leaders who are accountable for business results. All of which is to say simply that they need to design and implement a good IT portfolio management method.

Key Themes

- In the mainframe era, IT and the IT department were separated from the business departments of the organization, which subordinated their activities to the requirements of the technology.
- The advent of the PC, which had to coexist within the organization to be effective, drove a transformation of IT architecture and governance, altering the way organizations procured, operated, and managed their IT.
- By the end of the 1990s, IT spending was out of control. Three events at the end of the decade that particularly contributed to the problem were Y2K; the advent of ERP, integrated financial systems, CRM, and e-business; and a change in accounting practices to amortize the expense of implementing hardware and software.
- By the time CFOs woke up to the problem, fixed IT assets and expenses were piling up. Senior management responded by cutting IT infrastructure and business unit budgets, even though these funds were the ones that enabled organizational stability and growth.
- IT departments took the brunt of the blame, even though IT managers had never had the opportunity to acquire the know-how for managing IT investment more effectively.
- Bringing in outside managers and outsourcing IT failed to produce significant improvements in performance or any improvement at all.
- The way to break the death spiral that IT investment has entered is to design and implement a good IT portfolio management method.

IT Portfolio Management: What It Can Do; How It Works

No matter how long or how hard they strive, no matter how extensive their education as a species, no matter what they experience of the small heavens and larger hells they create for themselves, it seems that humans are destined to see their technological accomplishments always exceed their ability to understand themselves.

—Alan Dean Foster, *The Chronicles of Riddick*

One way to begin understanding what a good IT portfolio management method can do for an organization, and how it does it, is to consider some examples of organizations that needed to rationalize their IT portfolios. Perhaps you will recognize your organization in one of these scenarios:

- A government agency decentralized IT decision making. Each department made its own IT investment decisions. The large IT budget wasn't achieving the agency's goals. The agency's IT planning process did little more than staple each department's plan together. No rationalization of projects across departments took place. Each project was outsourced to a different service provider, so the service providers couldn't help. The service providers were accountable to the project managers but the project managers and leadership team were not held accountable for *results*. Instead, agency managers evaluated success based on successful execution of the project. If the project delivered its objectives, it was declared a success. The agency needed to facilitate departmental collaboration, ensure agency goals were properly enabled by IT, and hold each department accountable for results—not just for project execution.
- A financial service start-up went public with unprecedented success. Business growth exceeded everyone's expectations at 50% to 100% per year. Yet the IT infrastructure couldn't handle

the growth. Existing management methods were ineffective because the company had too many top priority projects and lacked the qualified staff to do them all. Management needed to balance the *urgent* projects necessary to keep the business running with the *important* projects necessary for growth. A business-led process was required to manage investment decision making and balance IT and business resources.

- An insurance company neglected its IT governance for so long that the IT department was completely out of alignment with the business units. IT service levels didn't meet business requirements. IT projects were falling short of business expectations. The relationship between the business and IT departments had deteriorated into finger-pointing, shouting matches, and threats. The only way to resolve this situation was to force the senior managers to work collaboratively. The first step was to establish a rudimentary process that held IT and business managers jointly accountable for decision making. They needed to be forced to work as a team, with everyone equally to blame if they did not achieve sufficient return on IT investments.

Even though the need for rationalizing an organization's IT portfolio may be more plainly visible in some cases than in others, it doesn't require any deep organizational soul-searching to see the need when it exists. Most senior executives intuitively know when they have an opportunity to improve IT investment management. CxOs know IT is not delivering sufficient value when IT investments do not improve bottom-line business performance. Supply chain managers, meanwhile, know IT is not delivering sufficient value when they do not have situational awareness of demand and supply after spending millions on new IT. Sales, marketing, and service managers know IT is not delivering sufficient value when they cannot get a 360-degree view of their customers' needs, orders, and concerns. Engineering managers know IT is not delivering sufficient value when they lack information required to better leverage platforms, reduce product cost, and improve time-to-market. In all cases, they know they are spending money on technology but their bottom line and value equation are not improved.

Here are some questions to help managers, at both the corporate and middle levels, to determine whether the organization needs to revisit its IT portfolio management methods:

- Do you have a 2- to 3-year forecast of IT spending?
- Can you identify which IT investments contribute to true competitive advantage?
- Can you confirm that IT spending priorities align with strategic priorities?
- Do projects end on schedule, within budget, delivering per expectations repeatedly and with consistent methods?
- Can you identify which IT projects are interdependent with people and process initiatives?
- Does IT operating expense increase commensurate with business growth?
- Do you know your business requirements for IT service level and do you manage your IT service provider against these targets?

A simple way of stating the benefits of effective IT portfolio management is that, when it has been successfully implemented, it enables organizations to answer "yes" to these questions.

Before we begin looking in detail at the IT portfolio management method, it is important to realize that every organization manages IT investments, even organizations that have outsourced their IT department. Everyone implicitly or explicitly decides how and where to spend the IT budget. Everyone implicitly or explicitly prioritizes projects. The question then is not whether to implement portfolio management. Like it or not, portfolio management is already implemented—even if only in an ad hoc, informal, uninstitutionalized way. The question is whether the organization performs portfolio management efficiently and effectively. If the portfolio management method is not well understood within the organization or people have not bought in to the design, then an opportunity exists to create a more *institutionalized* process, with the aim of increasing its efficiency and effectiveness. Ambiguity, delay, or excessive overhead in portfolio decision making presents an opportunity to create a more *efficient* portfolio management method. If the organization should be able to obtain greater value from IT investments, or more for each dollar invested, then the organization has an opportunity to create a more *effective* portfolio management method. Unfortunately, most companies suffer from some combination of poorly institutionalized, inefficient, and ineffective processes. This situation is what makes portfolio management improvements so complex.

Beyond these general considerations of institutionalization, efficiency, and effectiveness, two more particular reasons motivate a focus on optimizing IT portfolio management. First, governance of an IT investment is best applied early in a project or service's life cycle, and IT portfolio management provides a method for achieving it. Second, IT portfolio management is a major control point in the IT management system generally. Let's examine each of these statements in turn.

Governance of a new IT project is most effective when senior leaders involve themselves *before* a project or service is initiated. The old saying, "An ounce of prevention is worth a pound of cure" is really true in this case. Reactive governance is an oxymoron. An IT project's life cycle consists of six phases that we label *concept, plan/design, build/integrate/ test, certify, deploy,* and *retire.* (See the diagram that follows.) When senior leadership engages with a project early in its life cycle, it can ensure that the project concept is worth pursuing compared to other potential opportunities. Senior leaders can optimize the project's scope, objective, approach, planning, and resources. If they do not become engaged until later in the project life cycle, major design and investment decisions have already been made. At best, all that senior leaders can do at this point is keep the project on track. At worst, senior leaders revisit, reverse, or change design and investment decisions, which invariably creates wasted spending in the form of rework or unused work products.

An Ounce of Prevention Is Worth a Pound of Cure

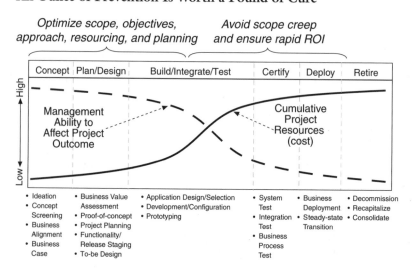

The IT Management System (Process Overview)

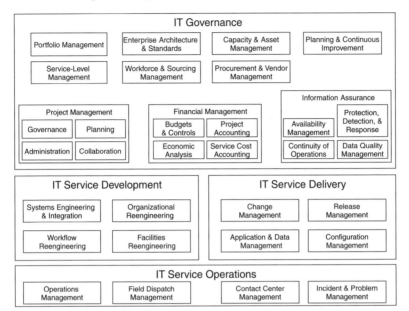

Besides being a way of ensuring that governance of IT investments is applied early in a project or service's life cycle, IT portfolio management is the control point for making IT investment decisions for the entire IT management system. The IT management system consists of four major elements: *governance, service development, service delivery,* and *service operations.* The place of IT portfolio management within this overall system is illustrated by the following figure.

The figure illustrates a notional reference model of the major activities (processes) required of most IT organizations.[1] It is important

---

[1] This IT management model is consistent with other IT industry frameworks. We grant permission to copy the diagram in whole or in part. The last thing the IT industry needs is another proprietary framework. The best thing that could happen would be if all the disparate IT associations (ITIL, SEI, COBIT, etc.), as well as academics who study and teach IT management, were to consolidate their frameworks into one definitive, comprehensive, public-domain reference model that would align industry terminology and create a single blueprint for IT managers. A common reference model would, among other things, help IT and business managers to govern the IT discipline. With standardized processes, the industry could implement end-to-end metrics that measure service effectiveness and efficiency, rather than continuing to rely on benchmarking with too heavy a focus on component cost.

to note that this is not an organizational model. The activities depicted here may or may not reside within the IT department, and some may not even reside within the organization if IT services are outsourced. As the figure shows, IT governance should bridge the other three elements of the IT management system. To do otherwise causes fragmented planning, dysfunction, and disharmony within and across the IT management system. When managers say that they succeed by hiring "good people," it is because the people they hire have an innate ability to manage within the IT management system. Some are even able to perceive the system itself.

To manage a process effectively and efficiently one needs to manage the *control points*, where key decisions are made. IT portfolio management is where the *real* financial management decisions are made. Proper governance of IT portfolio management is crucial to the governance of other IT management processes such as financial management. Senior leadership may formulate the financial forecast and plan, but the month-to-month decisions that drive spending behavior are what determine the long-term cost structure and value equation (benefit). The resulting spending profile is the de facto expression of strategic intent.

Take, for example, one large enterprise management project that we know of that was initiated without complete buy-in from the organization. The project had a run rate of close to $1 million a month. It stalled early in its life cycle due to disagreements among the various departments regarding its scope and objectives. The project then spun its wheels for several months, producing various ad hoc deliverables for the organization to help it make up its collective mind. The project team planned, re-planned, and planned again. It prepared for review after review and ran workshop after workshop in an attempt to drive the organization to consensus. The reviews and workshops required the highest-caliber, most expensive resources on the team. In the end, the organization terminated the project because the leadership couldn't come to consensus.

Does this scenario sound unrealistic? Would you say that it couldn't happen in your organization? Yet the odds are 80% that it does, albeit on a smaller scale. Maybe not as much money is wasted. As you become open to, and practiced in, the systemic thinking that IT portfolio management entails, you begin to uncover a vast number of problems that stem from ineffective, inefficient, or incomplete decision making. When you add up the hours, the numbers can give you a rude awakening.

Another way of describing IT portfolio management's function as a control point for the entire IT management system is to say that IT portfolio management governs an internal market economy built around supply and demand for information technology and related services. In absence of a trade economy where senior leaders buy and IT managers sell IT goods and services, portfolio management becomes the clearinghouse for IT investments. The portfolio management process makes "buy decisions" by approving investments. The portfolio management process makes "sell decisions" by approving resource allocations and service levels. When portfolio management is lacking or weak (i.e., undisciplined or merely tacit), supply and demand go unchecked and the internal market economy invariably becomes imbalanced. Buy decisions are made without full understanding of the implications (cost). Sell decisions are made without full understanding of the impact (value).

Portfolio management decisions to invest in a new application service affect an organization's cost structure for years to come. Portfolio management decisions to invest in a new transformation initiative, such as supply chain improvements, affect not only the IT budget but also the supply chain cost structure for the foreseeable future. Portfolio management is one of the most influential processes in the IT management system. It is the rudder that steers the ship. Turn the portfolio management rudder and funds flow in a different direction—from one budget into another. The wake generated by the ship and rudder represents the total cost of ownership (TCO) for IT investments, and it extends far out. TCO not only contains the three-to-five-year depreciation cycle but also includes every expenditure associated with the IT services and IT assets for their entire life cycle, which could last 10 to 20 years. Every penny spent on operating, maintaining, and upgrading the IT adds to its TCO. Sometimes it is necessary to minimize the wake. At other times it is more important to turn the ship quickly. Automation cannot replace knowledge and judgment, so steering the ship remains a manual process supported by various tools and controls. This book zeroes in on the rudder—portfolio management— but we also address the interdependencies with other IT management processes. It is important for managers to understand not only how to work the rudder, but also the effect that using it will have on the rest of the ship.

With portfolio management, managers can decide how much control they want to build into their processes. Some managers value the organizational willpower provided by a highly disciplined process. Others fear that implementing a process will stifle innovation. Generally, a well-defined and disciplined portfolio management process actually channels constructive innovation.

Portfolio management defines the decision-making process crisply so that innovation is focused on results, and so that the decision-making process does not have to be reinvented with each decision— something that costs organizations thousands of hours and millions of dollars each year. Every organization has some type of decision-making process. For some organizations, this process is ad hoc. They manage informally via the chain of command. Even when they implicitly or explicitly choose not to decide, they still make a decision. The more concealed the decision-making process, the more hours the organization wastes revisiting how to make decisions. The organization wastes time and resources trying to figure out who can make the decisions. It wastes time and resources trying to schedule and coordinate decision makers. It wastes time and resources reinventing what deliverables are required as input to decision making. It wastes time and resources trying to make decisions with incomplete information; debating subjective deliverables; miscommunicating due to lack of clear definitions and templates; trying to drive to consensus among miscommunication and all this process confusion; and repeatedly revisiting discussions because of decisions made incorrectly.

Efficient portfolio management should minimize such waste by ensuring that projects do not receive funding or resources until the business case is sound, and is reviewed relative to the other projects in the portfolio. The portfolio management team (PMT) does not have time to review every project in detail; however, it cannot delegate *accountability* for portfolio results. If it delegates *responsibility,* then it needs a method to ensure that those to whom it delegates effectively execute that responsibility. Roughly 10% to 20% of most total project

Typical Pipeline of Programs

PHASE 0	PHASE 1	PHASE 2	PHASE 3	PHASE 4
Concept	Plan/Design	Build/Integrate/Test	Certify	Deploy

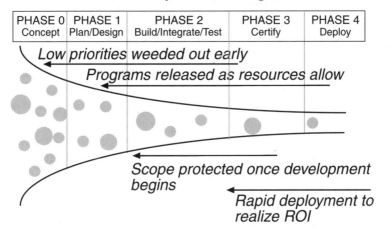

Changes to Scope

Emergency Requests

Overload

Overlooked Opportunities

Rework

Bottleneck

Best-in-Class Pipeline of Programs

PHASE 0	PHASE 1	PHASE 2	PHASE 3	PHASE 4
Concept	Plan/Design	Build/Integrate/Test	Certify	Deploy

Low priorities weeded out early

Programs released as resources allow

Scope protected once development begins

Rapid deployment to realize ROI

budgets is spent developing and achieving buy-in to the business case (needs, requirements, objectives, scope, approach, and plans). The PMT must ensure that each business case is created and maintained using a consistent approach, with the proper checks and balances governing the final project results. It is the only way to assure quality. PMTs are successfully managing IT portfolios when a controlled investment review process effectively governs funding and resources and an ongoing project governance structure is in place.

Good portfolio management ensures accountability by building it into the process. The process holds the project sponsor accountable for achieving results. The sponsor may delegate responsibility for execution to a service development process that manages the tactical implementation of each individual project. Nevertheless, the sponsor who chartered the project and established the project team structure retains accountability for overall results. If the project does not generate results, the buck stops with the sponsor. The PMT must hold the sponsor accountable, not the project manager. We are constantly amazed at the number of senior executives earning well over $250,000 per year who think that a project manager earning less than $100,000 is accountable for ensuring the success of the organization's $5 million strategic project. Although it is true that some of these executives are just looking for a scapegoat and others are abdicating their responsibilities, many loyal and dedicated executives genuinely think that one individual contributor can transform the workflow, responsibilities, and applications for hundreds of employees without proactive involvement of senior leadership. They just don't understand what it takes to navigate the personal agendas (politics), behavioral norms (culture), and middle management hierarchy (bureaucracy) to get the organization to change. They really do think that the definition of "involvement" is to sit in their armchairs and quarterback the game. When the project fails, they blame the project manager. Their definition of accountability consists of destroying project managers' careers when they fail. (And management wonders why there is a shortage of project managers!) A good portfolio management method builds accountability into the process and, in so doing, increases the overall value of the portfolio (i.e., return on investment).

Accountability is difficult to measure objectively but easy to observe. When accountability exists, multimillion-dollar strategic IT implementations rarely go awry. With accountability, large supply chain projects do not overrun by 30%. With accountability, a $15 million salesforce automation application isn't underutilized because the sales staff members don't want to use it. The fact that these incidents exist is evidence of a lack of accountability. Mistakes happen, but when mistakes are so large, they transcend normal risk thresholds and point to a fundamental breakdown in governance.

Effective and efficient portfolio management also manages project interdependencies as well as interdepartmental workflow. In most organizations, no central team is accountable for managing these interactions. Project steering committees are accountable for specific projects, but who is accountable for managing across projects? The answer is that the project portfolio management process needs to manage *all interactions,* both cross-project and cross-departmental. Suppose that a company planned to implement not a single CRM application but three discrete applications: contact management, incident management, and campaign management. Suppose that all of these applications are dependent on a "customer master database," all three will be used by the contact center, and all three need to be tightly integrated to provide maximum value. Even though expert project managers might think to manage outside their project scope, most do not have the time to do it effectively. In some cases, the solution might be as simple as the PMT directing the project managers to work together or tasking a project management office to coordinate. In most cases, some rescoping or timeline adjustments need to be made— changes that the project managers might not be able to make. It is often politically incorrect, and can be career-debilitating, to suggest to a project sponsor that a project's scope be changed to accommodate some other project. Someone needs to watch to make sure that the sequencing and timing of project deliverables meet the greater organization's needs. Without portfolio management coordination, these activities occur only through the heroic efforts of individuals. Without effective portfolio management, project teams need to broaden their perspectives, manage outside their comfort zone, and be willing to go above and beyond the call of duty. But average managers do *not* manage this way. They manage within their box on the organizational chart and don't think about managing the white space between boxes, which is what makes them average. Organizations rarely have enough heroes to put the heroes in charge of every project, hence the need for a robust portfolio management process.

Design Principles

Portfolio management is not an end; it is a means to an end. It is easy to become so caught up in the details of implementing IT portfolio management (which we will examine in the next few chapters) that one loses sight of the objectives. Keep in mind the following themes during a portfolio management implementation. Consider them design principles. You won't remember every practice and word of advice in this book, but try to remember these fundamental tenets.

Design Principle #1: Implementing Portfolio Management Is a Transformation Project, Not a Technology Project

Truly implementing project portfolio management processes requires transformation. That concept may be a blinding flash of the obvious to many, but we would be remiss if we didn't warn the reader that a leading cause of failure in these implementations is overlooking how portfolio management will change the organization. Many organizations set off to improve portfolio management, but do not really want to change the way they make decisions. In the end, they may implement some portfolio management tools or analytics, but they have no meaningful impact on the bottom line or the value returned. Often in these situations, the tools are grossly underutilized and have a negative return on investment. Many organizations would have been better off had they not bothered with portfolio management at all and expended the resources on something more productive.

We counsel senior managers to articulate their goals clearly, when they set out to implement portfolio management. Consider the example of one of the largest pharmaceutical companies in the world. It tasked its IT managers with implementing IT project portfolio management, and to their credit, the IT managers collaborated with the business managers. They inventoried their projects, developed all sorts of taxonomies to characterize them, went through a time-consuming and painful process of force ranking the projects, and then declared victory. They didn't reallocate resources. They didn't change the scope of projects. They didn't cancel projects. They added only a few projects. When we asked them what the point of the exercise had been, they replied, "To implement portfolio management." "But if you weren't going to change the decision-making process, why implement portfolio management?" we asked. "Because it is a best practice," they answered, "and we want to be a world-class IT organization." Alas! They missed the point. Implementing portfolio management is not a best practice. *Managing your portfolio* is a best practice! Surprisingly, this type of mishap occurs quite frequently. Senior management improperly or ambiguously defines the goals of implementing project portfolio management and doesn't sufficiently engage to ensure accountability for results. They may not really understand what it means to implement a portfolio management process. In this example, the executive team mandated the effort but middle managers had no intention of relinquishing control over portfolio decision making.

We say more toward the end of the book about the importance of a robust change management process as part of any implementation of IT portfolio management. For now, it is important to recall that, as we noted in the introduction, IT management generally is more about *people* and *processes* than it is about technology. Moreover, when we say that IT portfolio management is a change project, we need to keep in mind that what we are trying to change, above all, is the way the organization makes *decisions* about IT investment.

Design Principle #2: Focus on Transparency

Portfolio management should increase the transparency of the portfolio of projects, rush requests, skunk works, and back-channel requests. Really good portfolio management processes ensure that all projects are visible to all decision makers. Portfolio management can provide immediate return on investment and a short payback period simply by educating senior leadership about what projects are in queue, thereby enabling senior leadership to make more informed investment decisions. When we implemented portfolio management at a large computer equipment company, they saved $2 million in the first few months simply by bringing to light what was in the portfolio. When he saw the inventory for the first time, the division senior vice president was elated. He had never previously seen how the money was being spent. He then proceeded to redline $2 million worth of projects that he deemed unworthy of investment. Within the first few hours of the pilot, the division redeployed part of the $2 million to more strategic projects and let the remainder flow to the bottom line as an expense reduction. The change effort more than paid for itself on the first day. We do not necessarily endorse this unilateral approach to decision making, but it helps illustrate the point that sometimes portfolio management achieves tremendous value simply by providing management with optics. It may be easy for IT managers to overlook this benefit, given that they have the visibility on a day-to-day basis. However, senior leadership typically does not enjoy such visibility into what is being spent, where, and why. Senior leaders lack the transparency that IT managers benefit from.

Portfolio management should also improve communication within the IT management system, leading to more transparency in the organizational relationships involved. Providing a common nomenclature, definitions, and classifications is another way that portfolio management adds tremendous value from the outset. It helps senior managers communicate on the same wavelength. As we have already noted, senior managers often have their own languages that their peers do not necessarily speak. Managers might walk away from a meeting in agreement, but each has a different understanding of the discussion. Consider one case where we were facilitating an organization's senior leadership team through a project operational-readiness review. The project team was making the case that it was ready to deploy the new application to the business unit. The project manager said that the new application would "not significantly impact the availability" of the order management process. The sales director walked away interpreting that statement as zero downtime. The IT manager meant that order management applications would be down for only a few hours, which would not significantly impact the availability statistics. But what is the definition of *significant*? What is the definition of *impact*? *Downtime*? *Disruption*? All are vague and misused terms. This simple example shows how expectations can be mismanaged. Now consider that the average project has several IT team members working with several business team members. The odds of miscommunication grow exponentially.

The issue of assessing project risk offers a great example of how implementing a better taxonomy can improve communication in ways that lead to more transparent decision making. Take, for instance, two projects with the same level of risk. Jeff, the project manager of project A, is risk-averse. Jeff doesn't like taking risks and will be more pessimistic about the expected outcome. Scott, the project manager of project B, is risk-neutral. Scott is more comfortable with taking risk so his assessment of the situation is more objective. Left to their own devices, Scott will rate Project B's risk as "medium" while Jeff will rate Project A's risk as "high." These ratings don't even factor in how politics impact risk assessment. Political pressure can easily sway a project manager to change a risk rating when it might have career ramifications. Instead, suppose we break down risk into its various component factors. We know that risk comprises some factors that are within an organization's span of control and others that are outside of it. At a minimum, we can categorize risk as "controllable" or "uncontrollable." Then we can depict the major drivers of risk in each category. For example, we could break controllable risk into resource constraints, organizational impact, and project interdependencies. We could similarly break down uncontrollable risk into technology uncertainty, vendor viability, and the uniqueness of the project within the organization. Now we have a classification of risks and a scorecard. Instead of rating risk per se as high, medium, or low, we can have the project managers rate each risk factor. We might even go as far as establishing an index so that we can compare risk ratings across projects more objectively. This comparison would help us understand why Jeff thinks the risk is high. By providing transparency into the drivers of risk, we empower the senior leadership team to have a meaningful discussion about the risk rating on Jeff's project. Perhaps the leadership team will agree with Jeff and will raise the risk rating on Scott's project. Or perhaps Jeff's risk rating is high because it is dependent on Scott's project, so that the right way to manage this risk is to ensure that Scott's project is completed on time. Instead of having an abstract discussion of risk, the leadership team can engage in a meaningful dialogue with concrete implications for mitigating and managing it.

Some might argue that creating these taxonomies is the purview of project management, not portfolio management. Yet the issue of purview is irrelevant: the taxonomy is required regardless of which process owner creates it. How can the PMT compare and evaluate many projects without a universal nomenclature? Risk is only one factor that benefits from this type of analysis. Qualitative benefits is another. Many types of projects, from research projects to administrative ones, cannot be evaluated purely against financial measures. Sometimes a new application is just a cost of doing business, like painting the walls or repairing a fence. Dissecting qualitative benefits into comparable factors and drivers that can be compared across dissimilar projects enables senior leadership to better understand, compare, and contrast project benefits in the hope of selecting the highest-value projects. A few examples of other factors include the following:

- *Organizational impact:* How will the project disrupt day-to-day business operations? (Number of users, hours of downtime, lost revenue, etc.)
- *Customer satisfaction impact:* How will the project directly improve customer satisfaction? (Increase in customer satisfaction rating, cycle time improvement, additional customer functionality, etc.)
- *Employee satisfaction impact:* How will the project directly improve employee satisfaction? (Increase in employee satisfaction rating, enhancement of employee career management, quality of life improvement, etc.)
- *Resource skill/level requirements:* How will this project affect the skills required to run day-to-day business operations? (Number of unique skills, depth of knowledge, breadth of knowledge, etc.)

Finally, besides providing insight into return on IT investment and improving communication within the organization, the increased transparency that IT portfolio management infuses into the IT management system rationalizes decision making in ways that both improve the quality of decisions and gain legitimacy for them within the organization. The more you can take subjectivity out of project management information, the more you enable projects to succeed based on their own merits. By instilling better optics, you reduce the politics in portfolio decision making, and thereby level the playing field.

Design Principle #3: Integration Is Paramount to Sustained Success

The principle of transparency is closely bound up with the design principle of integration. In the IT portfolio management process, integration must take place at two different levels: between the business units and the IT department (as we have seen), and within the IT management system itself.

First and foremost, organizations that wish to implement better IT portfolio management need to integrate their planning and decision-making processes across the enterprise. New practices must compel business and IT managers to jointly plan and make decisions. Even if IT department planning was optimized and we had proper decision-support tools, the output would be ineffective unless the business managers were forced to collaborate. More often than not, the business managers will abdicate their responsibility for IT planning, because either they don't have the time or don't know what is required. Some abdicate because planning requires business managers to consider the possibility that business initiatives are more complex or more costly than they'd like. Yet, IT department planning becomes a waste of resources when performed in isolation from business planning. IT managers must collaborate with their "customers" just as commercial service providers must do. Commercial service providers who spend insufficient time collaborating with their customers eventually lose business to the competition. In-house service providers who spend insufficient time collaborating with *their* customers eventually lose customer insight . . . or their jobs. The secret to most IT executives' success is that they spend quality time with their customers. They collaborate to plan, develop, and deliver IT services. Sometimes they even collaborate to source IT services. When done effectively, repeatedly, and consistently, collaboration provides holistic (business and IT) governance over IT investments, IT assets, and IT services.

In presenting the design principle of "Focus on Transparency," we discussed how senior management, in particular, can benefit from greater transparency in the IT portfolio. Providing transparency, in turn, typically requires integration with other management processes and data. Portfolio management endeavors fail when they add overhead, such as tasking the organization with a lot of redundant data entry. Let's face facts. Most organizations are already trying to do too much with too little. Most everyone is stressed and can't absorb more work without something falling off their plates. When extra work can be avoided, it is not only irresponsible but also downright inconsiderate not to do whatever you can to avoid creating redundancies. Adding administrative resources to run around and collect these data is a waste of time and money, and is considered poor quality management.

It may do more harm than good to implement a portfolio method that creates a lot of overhead, duplicate data entry, and overlapping decision teams. These redundancies are what happen when organizations don't appreciate that portfolio management is part of a broader IT management system. They parse out the processes in an attempt to divide and conquer process design. They give one manager responsibility for service development improvement, another manager responsibility for portfolio management improvement, a third manager responsibility for resource management improvement, and so on. Although this tactic may spread the work, it is no way to design a management system. The resulting system is a hodgepodge of policies, procedures, templates, and guidelines. Together, the whole becomes *less* than the sum of the parts because of the inefficiencies. The resulting IT management system is a *kludge,* and may even cause an organization to backslide, performing worse after changing the process than it had before the effort began. Project managers have to submit data multiple times to multiple decision makers. They revisit decisions because senior leadership doesn't have all the information it needs when it needs it. They second-guess or actually reverse decisions because multiple teams work under overlapping authorities. Gaps and overlaps in delegations of authority erode accountability, and responsibility becomes unclear. No matter how well-coordinated, synchronized, and integrated the IT management improvement initiatives may be, if they are not designed as a complete, integrated process they will not serve the long-term needs of the organization.

The most effective portfolio management processes tightly integrate with adjacent processes. They have clear accountability and clear responsibility. Information is entered only once. Decisions are made only once. For example, the information entered into a service request feeds the project charter documentation. Project charter documentation feeds the business case. The business case feeds portfolio analysis and technology planning. Portfolio analysis feeds and is fed by resource management. Technology, portfolio, and resource management feed budgeting. Budgeting feeds IT financial management project and service accounting. Accounting feeds the project phase reviews and status reviews. Even though this format all sounds very logical, it takes time to accomplish. It requires a shared vision and careful process design before distributed implementation can actually be achieved.

Lack of a well-integrated IT management process architecture can end up emasculating portfolio management. Left to their own devices, people involved in IT management processes will second-guess IT portfolio decisions. For example, service development decisions obviously affect project scope. Even though it does not typically make cross-project decisions, a good service development process addresses project scope and objectives. Hence, the service development and portfolio management processes need to be tightly integrated to avoid indecision and unnecessary redirects. The delegation of authority and responsibility needs to be explicit. Typically, the project team makes a recommendation and some leadership team approves the scope. If the project decision team is not synchronized with the portfolio decision team, then decisions are made in disconnected fashion and need to be reconciled. Having to reconcile the two perspectives not only creates overhead but also appears to the organization as evidence of indecisiveness or conflict, thereby undermining confidence in either process's effectiveness.

When tightly integrated, project and portfolio management are mutually reinforcing. You will find that most portfolio management information is already being—or should already have been—collected by the project managers. Unfortunately, because project administration and accounting are rarely well-structured, the requisite information is typically stored in e-mails, spreadsheets, documents, and presentations. It is often in free-formatted text. To integrate the information, the organization needs a repository. To aggregate the information, the organization needs common taxonomies. What typically happens when you initiate portfolio management is that either project teams are reluctant to tell executives what they need to know, or they spew reams of documentation at the executives. Each executive reviews several projects, so executives are inundated with documents. Of course they do not have time to read everything put in front of them—and it doesn't help that every document is formatted differently with its own unique terminology—so they cherry-pick what to read. They wade through slide shows and text documents to draw their own conclusions regarding the project. Their situational awareness is incomplete and inaccurate, so they are incapable of making optimal decisions. By using common taxonomies to help integrate processes in the IT management system, organizations can give decision makers the tools they actually need.

Rather than looking at portfolio management as a data *collection and reporting* exercise, look at it as a data *integration and analysis* exercise. The data are out there but we need to integrate them, which requires us to move them to another repository or change the format. Storing the data in discrete Microsoft project files, spreadsheets, and presentations just doesn't cut it anymore. Implementing portfolio management requires changing the way we make decisions *across* a portfolio of projects. This process, in turn, requires decision-support capabilities (analysis and charts).

Implementing portfolio management provides an opportunity to obliterate reams of ad hoc project documents and store the information in them consistently and concisely in one repository. It provides an opportunity to streamline project reviews by imposing a consistent format for all projects to follow when reporting to senior leadership. Ideally, project status reports should not include any slides. Projects should report status via automated queries and dashboards, and free up face-to-face meeting time to resolve issues and make decisions. By

Portfolio Management Data Integration

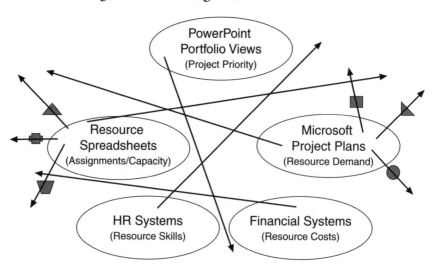

overlooking the opportunity to consolidate and integrate project information, you fail to take advantage of the fundamental catalysts for change in your organization. We discuss software tools later in the book. For now, suffice it to say that they are an integral part of any transformation effort. The tools should never become the primary focus of your change effort, but they enable integration of information and decision support. When implemented properly, they become a facilitator of information transparency, integration, and change.

Design Principle #4: Plan to Plan Well

The very need for improved portfolio management is evidence of a need for strategic integration across departments: finance, IT, and business planning. Regrettably, recent transformations in financial management have not fused with IT management processes. Everyone agrees that financial planning and portfolio management must be seamless, yet most managers are reluctant to integrate because budgeting is a "financial" process and portfolio management is an "IT" process. The same holds for "IT" planning and "business" planning, which in today's technology-enabled world are really two sides of the same coin. This compartmentalized view of IT management creates inefficiencies that cost corporations thousands of management hours each year. As in the pharmaceutical company example, prioritizing projects is pointless, as is adjusting priorities, if the business planning and budgeting process is going to overturn those decisions when it comes time to develop the annual plan. Best-in-class companies alter their annual planning calendar to embed portfolio management strategy, analysis, and decision making into the financial and business planning cycle.

Most organizations, in fact, need to revisit their fundamental planning and decision-making methods. Because most organizations have become so dynamic, changing business plans quarterly, organizations must integrate IT planning into their *quarterly* planning activities as well as the annual budgeting and long-range planning activities. IT planning has become an ongoing activity, not something one can effectively carry out once a year, a month or two before the budget is due. Planning is one of the most important and most neglected IT management processes. Engineers, technologists, and programmers generally like to design, tinker, and study. As a whole, they don't like to plan. Most IT managers are engineers and technologists, promoted into jobs that they are not empowered to do effectively, in part because they have never been taught what, or how, to plan. They also lack fundamental management systems to provide them with requisite planning information, and are not disposed to go out of their way to champion new systems to provide it, mostly because they are already under so much pressure from the organization to reduce IT costs. Furthermore, they know that they will only have to administer these same systems and enter the planning data—creating more work that they will invariably have to do with the same amount of resources because budgets have been cut to the bone.

Instead of expending a lot of energy on implementing a fancy project prioritization system, why not use the opportunity to implement portfolio management as a means of addressing some of these systemic breakdowns in the IT management system? Why not repair the fundamental disconnect in workflow that causes misalignment, rather than merely bandaging the symptom? Why not fundamentally change the sequence and method for IT decision making so that IT plans are synchronized with business plans? Portfolio management is a *decision-making process* rather than a transaction or operational one. The purpose of portfolio management is to structure the thought process of senior leadership to help them make better decisions, based on logical and organizational knowledge. Because available information is typically incomplete, many portfolio decisions are imperfect decisions. Imperfect decisions are difficult to make because they require a manager to fill information gaps with personal judgment. In the case of projects that deploy or enable entirely new capabilities, managers might need to take a leap of faith that the new capability will achieve the desired business result. Imperfect decisions are inherently more risky than decisions made with complete information. Mitigating the risk requires that we prevent managers from treating the decisions too subjectively. To accomplish this task, we use a process-based approach that structures the workflow and guides managers through the analytics first, postponing the application of intuition and judgment to near the end of the decision-making process. This process-based approach allows managers to depend on other enabling processes and practices, which provide valuable information to portfolio decision makers while also assuring senior leaders that projects are doing everything they can to ensure the desired results are achieved.

Because decision-making processes are different from operational and transactional ones, we recommend following a slightly different sequence when designing the IT portfolio management method than one would use designing other processes. Typically, an organization would begin its process design exercise by mapping out the workflow. For the reasons discussed previously, it is better to first determine the portfolio governance architecture *before* designing the workflow. The workflow is more easily designed with increased awareness of the governance architecture, which revolves primarily around portfolio segmentation and decision rights. Also, the governance architecture will be where much of management's resistance to change occurs. With that out of the way, it is easier to work on the basic blocking of how the work gets done. Workflow design will need to address not only portfolio management activities but also interdependencies with adjacent IT management processes (process inputs and outputs). Lastly, the organization will want to design and incorporate various enablers that make the process more efficient and effective. Enablers include decision-support tools, metrics, best practices, and software applications.

Begin with the value proposition for change—that is, the business case, including both the financial rationale for implementing IT portfolio management and an explanation of what's in it for all those managers whose authority may be affected and whose behavior will have to change. Without this value proposition, it will be near to impossible to rally the organization to the cause. Next, define the governance architecture so people are clear from the outset about who will be making which decisions. Then design the workflow, including the portfolio management activities as well as the inputs from, and outputs to, other processes. (The workflow should be relatively straightforward if all the supporting processes are in place, but can be a complex task if these supporting processes are ad hoc.) Lastly, focus on the portfolio process enablers, including decision-support, performance metrics, best practices, and software tools. In most instances, the organization will be able to pilot the process with relatively few enablers, improving continuously over time as the process matures and is embraced.

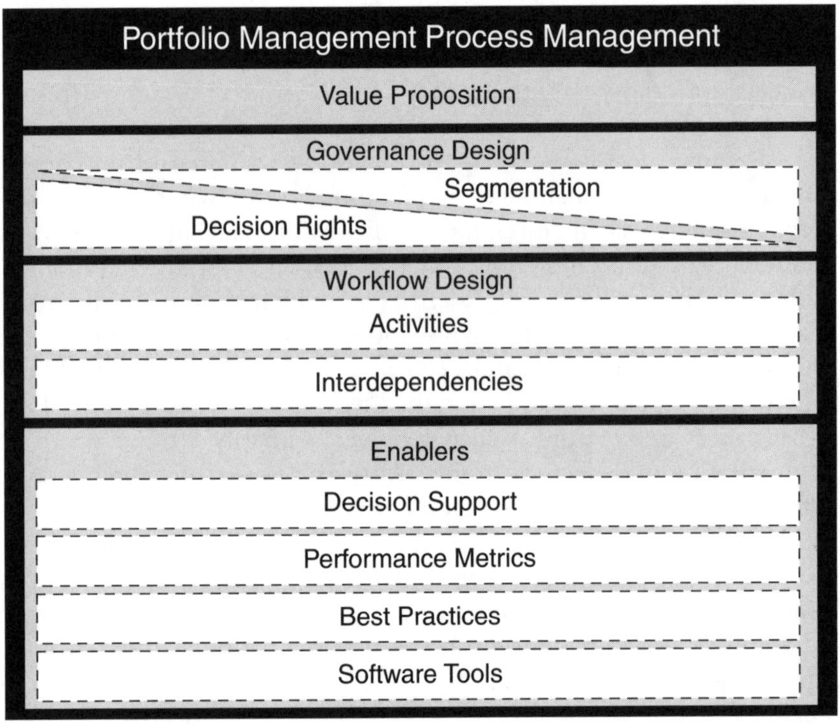

Portfolio Management Process Management

Value Proposition

Governance Design

Segmentation

Decision Rights

Workflow Design

Activities

Interdependencies

Enablers

Decision Support

Performance Metrics

Best Practices

Software Tools

Key Themes

- Most managers intuitively know when their organization's IT investments are not delivering sufficient value.
- Every organization manages IT investments, even if only in an ad hoc way.
- Most companies suffer from some combination of poorly institutionalized, inefficient, and ineffective processes.
- Governance of IT investments is best applied early in a project's life cycle, which is one reason for implementing IT portfolio management.
- IT portfolio management is a major control point in the IT management system generally, which consists of governance, service development, service delivery, and service operations.
- Portfolio management defines the decision-making process so that innovation is focused on results.
- Efficient portfolio management minimizes waste by ensuring projects do not receive funding or resources until the business case is sound.
- Good portfolio management ensures accountability by building it into the process.
- Effective and efficient portfolio management manages interdependencies with the rest of the IT management system as well as interdepartmental workflow.
- Implementing portfolio management is a transformation project, not a technology project (Design Principle #1).
- Portfolio management focuses on transparency (Design Principle #2).
- Integration (between the IT department and the business units, and within the IT department itself) is paramount to sustained success (Design Principle #3).
- Portfolio management is a rare opportunity to revisit enterprise planning and decision-making methods (Design Principle #4).
- The process of designing and implementing the IT portfolio management method follows a sequence of these activities: formulating the value proposition for change; defining governance architecture (portfolio segmentation and decision rights); designing the workflow (activities and the management of interdependencies); and utilizing portfolio process enablers (decision-support, performance metrics, best practices, and software tools).

Governance Design

If all responsibility is imposed on you, then you may want to exploit the moment and want to be overwhelmed by the responsibility; yet if you try, you will notice that nothing was imposed on you, but that you are yourself this responsibility.

—Franz Kafka (1883–1924), *The Fourth Notebook*

The Role of Senior Leadership (CxOs)

Economy does not lie in sparing money, but in spending it wisely.

—Thomas Henry Huxley

Accountability is a term thrown around a lot in management circles. But what does it mean when it comes to IT portfolio management? A central feature of the IT portfolio management method is that it demands accountability—complete with both the authority necessary to meet objectives and real consequences for failure to do so—for IT investment decisions. As we have already noted, it demands accountability from the senior management team in particular. And, finally, it builds accountability into the portfolio management process itself. Few people willingly embrace the idea of being held truly accountable for the consequences of their decisions and actions, and so if the IT portfolio management process is designed for those with the highest scruples and levels of intestinal fortitude, it will fail more often than not. Better to recognize that even heroes stray from the path of righteousness now and then, and thus to design the process for the average manager.

Beyond these general principles, we can identify five particular areas in which executive accountability needs to be exercised in IT portfolio management:

1. Portfolio strategy
2. Project strategy
3. Resource management
4. Fiscal management
5. Service quality

Let's look at each of these areas in turn.

Executive Accountability 1: Portfolio Strategy

Senior managers have the perspective to determine whether "strategic" projects truly provide competitive advantage. Only senior managers can ratify the business value of IT investments, regardless of whether the value is measured in financial terms (NPV, ROI, etc.) or operational terms (speed, cost, precision, etc.). Senior managers cannot delegate these accountabilities because others in the organization typically do not have comparable perspective and knowledge. They also cannot delegate these accountabilities because at the end of the year, the senior managers are the ones who have to answer to the board of directors.

The role of the CxO is to manage the internal market economy for IT services. A micro-economy for IT services exists within every organization. The microeconomy for IT services defines how business and IT decision makers will behave. Projects will only succeed if equilibrium exists in the economy. To achieve equilibrium, the supply of IT services must balance the demand for IT services. If supply is constrained, the internal market will react by seeking substitutes. Substitutes for IT services are typically contractors who do not have accountability for their actions and who are managed by employees with insufficient IT management experience. Again, the best way to lower IT investment levels is to govern business unit demand for IT services, including demand for new systems, enhancements to existing systems, and higher service-level requirements for existing system operations. Constraining demand for IT services from the business units is not easy for senior leaders to accomplish but is vital to sound IT investment management.

Senior executives are accountable for optimizing spending allocations to maximize value. CxOs manage the demand side of the equation of the internal market economy by understanding how and when IT investments impact the bottom line. CxOs make sure the organization does *the right projects right at the right time.* The amount of nonobligatory (discretionary) spending that a company can use on strategic projects is relatively small, less than 10% of IT spending for some companies. Delegating or abdicating CxO accountability invariably results in suboptimal decisions favoring pet projects or departmental efforts over strategic endeavors. A cross-organizational senior management team that has a broad perspective on project implications and retains accountability for achieving results can best manage alignment between the IT portfolio as a whole and overall strategic objectives.

Executive Accountability 2: Project Strategy

Senior executives are also accountable for aligning project scope and objectives with organizational strategy. A robust IT management process has clearly defined and synchronized phase-gates that involve executives in clarifying goals and ensuring that project objectives enable improved business performance. Later in the project life cycle, executives make certain that the project stays on target, ensuring that they do not lose sight of its objectives in the frenzy of executing the project plan. Improving the governance and execution of strategic projects can reduce project expenses by as much as 40%. In other words, your $20 million CRM project might have been executed for $12 million. Furthermore, the payback on many of these projects can be increased by up to 25% by fine-tuning the plan to accelerate business results. The numbers are staggering, and many who have been accountable for projects in the past will refute these statistics, despite the fact that most industry analysts and trade surveys support them. The most successful business transformation projects of the past two decades have succeeded on the strength of clear accountability for results.

Executive Accountability 3: Resource Management

Senior executives are accountable for optimizing throughput and organizational effectiveness. Resource constraints are a leading cause of failed projects. Resources often are stretched too thin because people—financial investors, managers, and staff—are too impatient. It is natural to fall prey to the urge to start every project as soon as possible, but executives must resist this temptation. Most business managers assume that starting an IT project sooner will cause it to end sooner. Payback, however, is a function of *time-to-results*, not time-to-start. Overloaded resources compromise time-to-results. Overhead in the form of task switching, scheduling, and the like increases with every project added to an individual's workload. Despite that fact, companies continue to stuff as many projects as possible into the project pipeline, thus overloading demand on resources and creating unnecessary overhead and waste. Then they blame the IT department for slow throughput and poor results.

Executive Accountability 4: Fiscal Management

Senior management must ensure that IT spending is commensurate with need and the fiscal environment. Only senior managers have the perspective and authority to ration the level of spending on "nice to have" projects, deferring them until funding becomes available. Portfolio management provides senior managers with the ability to align the ebb and flow of IT spending with economic conditions. Senior managers have an appreciation for fixed costs and their affect on the organization in the long run.

Senior executives are accountable for forearming themselves with knowledge of future investments and ensuring that those investments are sound and that forecasts are comprehensive. Without this knowledge, organizations cannot manage the long-term financial forecast. CFOs are often more frustrated by an inability to forecast IT investments than they are by actual levels of investment. Some claim that technology spending cannot be forecasted. They are wrong. Perhaps it cannot be predicted with certainty, but it can be forecasted. If organizations can forecast sales, they can forecast technology spending. If organizations can forecast R&D budgets, they can forecast IT budgets. Technology decisions are based on a strong understanding of organizational need, removing technology bias and personal agendas from the equation. Many of the best CTOs are people who have the broadest and deepest understanding of the business as well as of what it takes to succeed in the current market. Best-in-class CTOs sort out the technology building blocks that most effectively enable the organization's strategy. These CTOs draw up technology roadmaps that outline the timing and sequencing of investments over a 24–36 month timeline. Even though these roadmaps are not perfect, they do provide line-of-sight to potential rough-order-of-magnitude investments. They improve financial forecasts and better equip senior managers to make investment decisions. With enough advance notice, managers adjust investment timing to better accommodate business and economic cycles.

As part of IT portfolio fiscal management, senior executives are also accountable for procuring efficient IT services. IT service efficiency is measured in terms of unit cost, the cost or price for providing one unit of service. Examples include the average cost for one hour of software application programming; the average cost to answer one help desk inquiry; the average cost to supply intranet connectivity to one desktop computer; and the average cost to supply and maintain one desktop computer.

Executive Accountability 5: Service Quality

Unit cost comparisons are complicated by the need to adjust for varying service levels. For example, providing a help desk service 24 hours a day, seven days a week, is more expensive than providing that service only on weekdays. A promise to repair a desktop computer in four hours is more expensive than an eight-hour response time. Senior executives are accountable for ensuring the IT department or third-party service provider supplies a cost-competitive service at a level commensurate with business needs (which may differ from user desires).

Whether IT service is outsourced or in-sourced, CxOs are accountable for defining IT service quality requirements and aligning these requirements with business needs. The IT service provider is accountable for delivering service quality and managing service cost. Senior executives need to choose between a culture of personal initiative and self-sufficiency, or high-touch services and amenities. Introducing new IT service requirements is as much a cultural change as it is a technology change, and it needs to be driven from the top if it is going to have any reasonable impact on bottom-line performance.

To see the relationship between service requirements and performance in the clearest possible terms, consider that most organizations spend millions to manage PCs. A large portion of this cost is for "desktop support" services where small armies of people staff help desks and run around fixing PC software and helping end-users. Most organizations could reduce the average cost of managing PCs by as much as 50% by controlling the PC software configuration (i.e., remotely managing the software) and requiring provision of online help and training. But most employees install whatever software they want, whenever they want—usually because they want to, rarely because they need to. Every incremental software application and hardware device, in turn, adds to the support cost, even if only a small amount. Many of these applications do not have online help. Some organizations do not even distribute instruction manuals for applications they purchase, so the people who use these applications call a help desk when they have a question. These phone calls add up when one considers that in most organizations thousands of people are using thousands of computers. One large telecommunications company reported that its average telephone help desk call cost $20, while the cost of providing the same help online is 50¢. These numbers are typical of most mid-sized to large organizations. Now imagine spending less on support services and more on proactively improving application quality and online help to avoid all these telephone calls. A one-time expense of $100,000 up front to improve online help and testing could reduce annual operating expenses by $100,000 per year or more.

Portfolio Segmentation

You see, I divide men into three categories: those who have a lot of money, those who have none at all, and those who have a little. The first want to keep what they have: their interest is to maintain order; the second want to take what they do not have: their interest is to destroy the existing order and to establish one which is profitable to them. They each are realists, people with whom one can agree. The third group want to overthrow the social order to take what they do not have, while still preserving it so that no one takes away what they have. Thus, they preserve in fact what they destroy in theory, or they destroy in fact what they seem to preserve. Those are the idealists.

—Jean-Paul Sartre (1905–1980), *The Devil and the Good Lord*

Most organizations delegate decision making to each departmental manager with an IT budget. It is an understandable practice, but not an efficient or an effective one. Organizations don't delegate facility-building decisions to each manager, so why IT decisions? It is because managers are still making decisions with the assumption that applications serve only one department. Managers are evaluated based on departmental performance, so many do not focus on enterprise-wide *process* improvement. Each manager makes decisions about his or her own piece of the IT budget. This practice reinforces organizational silos. Managers become myopic, designing functional processes instead of cross-functional ones. Hence, dividing up the IT portfolio by department may not be the right approach. More often than not, it reinforces the same behavior we are trying to change by implementing portfolio management.

The answer to this problem is to divide the portfolio in a more rational way, through a method that we call portfolio segmentation. We recommend that organizations start portfolio segmentation using a "clean sheet of paper." In other words, do not start with preconceived notions of how IT investment decisions should be delegated. Start by assuming that nobody has any right to make any IT decision. Then segment the portfolio in a way that reinforces the right behaviors. Portfolio *segmentation* is the act of dividing the projects in a portfolio into different "buckets" (a.k.a. portfolios, subportfolios, segments, etc.). Segmentation influences the effectiveness and efficiency of the portfolio management method by changing the way the organization makes trade-off decisions and aligns project scope with the organization's mission. Eventually, for each portfolio segment, a manager or team of managers will be delegated the authority to make decisions, but try not to let that authority designation bias your thinking. Don't come at it from an organizational perspective, or even an application perspective. Think about the portfolio from a business process perspective. Consider which core business processes add value to the organization, and consider grouping applications in keeping with business process areas.

When segmenting the portfolio, first think about your goals. Think about what is *not* working today. Ask some basic questions:

- Do people in different departments work together effectively for the common good?
  - Do departmental silos limit or impair projects?
  - Is there sufficient process-wide collaboration?
  - Do people make cross-process decisions effectively?

- Do managers select urgent projects in lieu of other, actually more important ones?
  - Do they start strategic projects too late?
  - Do they neglect infrastructure decisions?

- Do managers lack perspective (situational awareness)?
  - Do they make decisions from too low a level?
  - Do they make decisions from too high a level?
  - Do they understand the issues?
  - Do they micromanage?

- Do managers think holistically?
  - Do they try to manage lots of small interdependent projects, many of which might be managed as fewer, bigger projects?
  - Do they think in terms of complete, end-to-end solutions (people, process, and technology)?

One popular segmentation scheme is to create one big segment of all "IT projects." If you are going to compare every project against every other project, then you might skip the discussion on segmentation. Yet for many organizations, the set of all "IT projects" is a large set indeed. Take, for example, a large corporation. If they were to look at their entire IT portfolio as one big segment, it would contain thousands of projects. Making trade-off and scoping decisions on every project in that portfolio would be a daunting task.

In fact, we have yet to work with an organization mature enough to manage all projects in one portfolio, with one set of decision makers. Some organizations approach us with the intent of treating all IT projects equally, prioritizing based on each project's individual merits. However well-intentioned they might be, more often than not this approach is too big of a step for them to take. Most organizations are fortunate to be able to master portfolio management for a particular department or discipline, let alone trying to master it for the entire portfolio all at the same time. For most senior leaders, looking at all projects is too much to handle at first, especially when they often have little to no visibility into any projects to start with. Having a grand vision is a good thing, but don't try to get there in one big step. Be realistic about how much change your organization can absorb. Factor in how much motivation there really is to change. Pace yourself. Segmentation allows you to implement portfolio management piece-by-piece or division-by-division.

If you are not really going to perform a trade-off analysis between two specific projects, and the two projects are not highly interdependent, then don't create unnecessary overhead and strife by putting them into the same portfolio segment. By dividing and conquering, you can segment the portfolio to more easily evaluate each project against criteria that are meaningful for particular segments. If you really want to implement portfolio management across the entire organization, you might begin by implementing portfolio management for each core business process. Then compare and contrast portfolio criteria across the various segments. If you still want to manage IT as one big segment, making trade-off decisions across process areas, it will be easier to consolidate decision-making authority once each area is following a consistent process with a greater degree of discipline.

Some clients also approach us asking if they can manage IT projects in the same portfolio as non-IT projects such as capital improvements, product development, and organizational transformation. The answer is yes, but the prior discussion is even more relevant. The valuation criteria for product development projects may be different from the IT project criteria. Start by implementing a basic portfolio management method in each department, and then consolidate decision-making authority after you get a handle on what is in the portfolio and how decisions should be made. In other words, *normalize* the processes before you try to consolidate pieces of it. Most change management experts would agree that it is much easier to consolidate well-managed, controlled processes than divergent, ad hoc, or misunderstood ones. So use a standard process architecture, but when implementing major portfolio improvements, segment the "mega" portfolio when you first implement the changes.

All the projects in a particular portfolio segment should share common valuation criteria, called *value driver*. A value driver is some measure of valuation, and may be quantitative or qualitative. Most portfolio segments have more than one value driver. Some managers prefer to have a balanced scorecard of value drivers while others want to look at only one. The number depends on the complexity of your organization's mission. If you can sum up the mission using one value driver and you are comfortable that this value driver is objectively calculated, then one will suffice. Life is rarely that simple, so most managers consider several value drivers when making portfolio decisions. The most common value drivers are financial such as revenue, cost, return on investment (ROI), and net present value (NPV). Many CFOs want to boil everything down to NPV. However, many IT projects are a cost of doing business. They don't return a positive NPV (i.e., the present value of Cost+Benefits≤0). For organizations that do not measure their bottom line financially, such as military and civil agencies, cost is a factor but not the only one, and may not be the primary one when considering value returned from IT projects. Hence, most managers in such organizations consider other value drivers that provide insight into the value of their IT projects. Other value drivers might include customer satisfaction, employee satisfaction, service-level improvement, defect reduction, cycle time improvement, and mission assurance. Typically, portfolio value drivers have targets or objectives associated with them. For example, a corporation might establish a target of achieving a 2% reduction in cost of goods sold (COGS) from its portfolio of supply chain improvements. All value drivers need to measure relative value returned from each project in the portfolio.

In segmenting your IT project portfolio, think of it in the same way that you might think of a diversified personal financial portfolio.

For example, a financial portfolio may contain three segments of financial assets: cash, stocks, and bonds. Each can be further segmented. For example stocks break down into domestic, international, value, growth, large cap, small cap, and so on. We typically have a target to achieve a specific return on stocks. We can attempt to achieve this target by buying the services of mutual funds or build our own portfolio of individual stocks. As a rule, however, we do not like to compare the return on stocks with the return on bonds or cash savings. Each serves a different purpose and their targets are different. We invest in cash for liquidity. We might invest in bonds for stability during economic downturns. We might invest in stocks for growth. Comparing a stock with a bond is somewhat pointless. We know the bond will have a lower long-term return. We invest in it for a different reason. Sometimes long-term assured value is more important than short-term growth. Those who made investment decisions solely on the basis of near-term return probably lost a lot of money in the stock market crash. When you buy a one-legged stool, you expect it to fall over eventually. These same principles apply to IT. Sometimes we cannot or should not compare individual IT projects against each other. For the same reasons we don't want to compare the return on a particular stock with the return on a particular bond, we may not want to compare an infrastructure project against a supply chain project. We probably want to allocate a percentage of our investment to each of these two segments and then evaluate separately the investments within each segment.

Segmentation needs to be aligned with the internal economics of the organization. Having cash investments not only gives one a degree of security but also serves a need for liquidity. Everyone needs to keep cash at hand to cover periodic expenses. These expenses are fixed and short-term costs of doing business. We may not want to pay them, but most of them are a result of long-term commitments. (It is like taking out a car loan. We don't want to pay the loan but we have to or we lose the car.) Comparing investments across industries, and sometimes within industries, can be insightful or can be a complete waste of time. It is like comparing the investments of a lower-income family against those of a family earning in the top 5%. The exercise is futile. Each family has different priorities and, hence, different investment options.

The same principle holds for organizations wishing to compare projects across companies or business units with varied economics. It may not be appropriate to compare one business unit's IT projects against another's. Business units with higher margins, for example, are going to be able to invest differently than business units with low margins. Diversified business units may each have vastly different economics and valuation criteria than more concentrated ones, rendering such comparisons irrelevant. Countercyclical business units may need to stagger investments on different timelines to correspond with different business cycles. In these situations, trying to make trade-off or consolidation decisions across business units could do more harm than good. Most managers don't see this point when they try to rationalize and consolidate applications across business units. Just because two business units have a supply chain application, it may not necessarily hold true that they should share the same one. Consider the business unit's market and economics when you segment.

Portfolio segmentation is not rocket science, but it does require some forethought. Portfolio segmentation is going to become the nucleus around which the portfolio management process is designed. Segmentation will drive design of team structures, process timing, and prioritization criteria. You can change segmentation after you implement the portfolio management process, but changing it right after you've rolled it out may cause a loss of credibility and create unnecessary strife. Try to get segmentation at least close to right (80% right, say) the first time.

Here are a few case studies to consider:

A services company was struggling because it wanted to launch a new service line, but the demands of the established, highly profitable service lines always took precedence. Every time management reviewed and prioritized projects, it allocated funds to the established service lines because of their greater revenue and ROI. The company was not accounting for potential future revenue streams, even though existing services would become obsolete in a few years. Establishing the new service line was paramount to ensuring a competitive advantage in future years. When implementing portfolio management, the company intentionally separated the new service line projects from the established ones. They also consolidated all the established service offerings into one portfolio, whereas previously they had been distinct. Now the first funding decision made during a review of

(continued)

the portfolios is how much to invest in future versus present service lines. Projects in the new service portfolio no longer need to compete against projects in the established service portfolio. And projects in the established service portfolio have to compete against all other similar projects.

A manufacturing company had previously allocated funds to IT projects on a functional basis, using a snowplow budget-allocation methodology (last year's budget plus or minus some percentage determined by the CFO). This method presented a challenge. Over time, the budgets evolved to correlate with the size of each department. Sales, for example, had a large IT budget because it was a large department. There was limited consideration of portfolio value. If the marketing department had a killer IT project concept, it was politically difficult to take IT funding from the sales department to give to marketing; whereas the marketing department needed to plead with the executive team to get funding for projects, the sales organization did not need to justify projects of similar size and lesser value. When the company implemented portfolio management, it put all the IT projects into one big portfolio. It then divided the IT portfolio into investments, enhancements, and infrastructure. Now allocation of IT funds is not done by default, and each department must justify every project based on its individual merit. The senior leadership team determines which project concepts will be funded and when.

The R&D business unit of a pharmaceutical company didn't formally manage any of its portfolios—business process or information technology. With plenty of money to go around, the business unit didn't bother to prioritize. In the early 2000s, growing market pressures to cut costs motivated the firm to cut

(continued)

project spending. This, in turn, led it to implement portfolio management for its business improvement projects, ranging from process redesign to applications implementation. Previously each department (clinical supply, clinical development, regulatory, clinical submissions, etc.) had made its own portfolio decisions. This silo-based decision making led to inefficiencies, caused by suboptimal decisions and a lack of integration (of workflow and data) across departments. When the business unit revisited its IT portfolio management process, it decided to pool its IT funds to force cross-departmental dialogue and decision making. Now the portfolio management process is a catalyst for increased cross-departmental collaboration and cooperation. The company prioritizes and funds all projects based on fit with business strategy. This approach allows it to leverage R&D's entire IT budget when addressing top strategic issues.

In these examples, the organizations used portfolio segmentation to change the way they considered and selected new projects. In each case, the process provided short-term benefits in the form of improved decision making. In all the cases, senior leadership benefited from the process within the first few months of implementation. The segmentation and valuation criteria provided the organization with a new thought process that was more strategic and objective, and a decision-making process that was both repeatable and consistent.

Following are the most common IT project segments and brief suggestions about how to evaluate each type:

Financial Improvement Investments: This category is the easiest to evaluate. These projects have a direct impact on the bottom-line financial performance of the company, typically in the form of cash flow, revenue enhancement, or cost reduction. Managers should evaluate these projects based on their NPV, which takes into account the dollar benefit returned and the timing of the benefits (time-value of money). Unfortunately, only a small number of IT projects fall cleanly into this category. Most overlap with one or more of the following categories.

Mission-Critical Investments: Some projects are *needed to play;* they are a cost of doing business. Without question, the organization can't live without them and must invest in them. Examples of such projects include launch of a new business unit, manufacturing capacity expansion, cyber security, or tactical applications for the military. The trick in managing these project portfolios is clarifying accountability for decision making. The investment decisions focus on *how much* to invest. Many organizations over-invest in mission-critical investments. Once management decides to invest, it abdicates accountability for deciding how much to invest. As a result, it spends too much. There are many ways to achieve a mission, just like there are many ways to travel from one place to another. We can take a car, train, or airplane. If we take a car we can drive a Ferrari, Toyota, or Hyundai. We can lease or buy. All these options may all get us where we want to go, but they have different cost implications and each offers a different set of advantages. Mission-critical portfolio decisions need to delve into value drivers that help determine how much is enough. Too often, engineers will try to come up with the perfect solution. The perfect solution usually costs too much. How much mission assurance is enough? Define what is at stake. Come up with solution options. Define the threat. Define the vulnerability. Assess the risk of each option.

Enabling Investments (a.k.a. Subprojects): Some IT projects are really part of a larger initiative or project. The IT implementation is just one thread of work that needs to be executed concurrently with other activities such as process redesign, organizational change, and facilities construction. In these instances, the IT implementation may not be a separate business case because it is an integral part of a larger initiative. The larger initiative cannot move forward without it. In these situations, the larger initiative—including the IT project—should be approved and managed as a single endeavor rather than parsed into its individual subprojects. It is too easy for the larger initiative to blame the subprojects for failure, and vice versa. Fund the overarching initiative. Hold one manager accountable for results and let that manager decide how best to manage IT investments. If you were building a new factory, would you assign accountability for the electrical work to a completely separate organization? Probably not. You would have the same architect and general contractor manage all aspects of the build-out. So why treat IT differently? If a change effort wants an IT implementation, hold those who say they need it accountable.

For example, an employee portal that provides convenient access to employee-benefit and career-planning tools might be highly valued by a company that values investment in its human resource development. We can't easily calculate the financial benefit of the project, but we might consider employee satisfaction to be an organizational objective. So we might allocate some amount of investment to the HR manager in exchange for a measurable improvement in employee satisfaction ratings. There may not be a separate business case for the IT implementation. We would hold the HR manager accountable for a measurable improvement in employee satisfaction and let him or her decide whether the IT implementation is the best investment toward that end. The problem this may cause is that it will not motivate collaboration between departments. What if, in this same example, we had multiple HR managers in multiple divisions, or wanted to integrate the HR applications with the financial applications? Managers typically want to control their own destinies, so they may be more inclined to install their own applications rather than collaborate with others. This situation is a management problem. One way to mitigate it is to limit funds, so that managers must pool resources to be successful. This game is difficult to play and often requires a lot of senior management facilitation to be successful. Another way to mitigate this problem is to put all applications under the same IT manager, in the hope that the IT department can facilitate better leverage. At some point, however, the IT managers will get in over their heads and won't be able to facilitate effectively. (They are IT managers, not professional negotiators.) In truly critical situations, such as those pertaining to the life and death of a person or a business, recognize that duplication may be unavoidable, which may not be a bad thing as long as it results in sustained competitive advantage.

When Is Consolidation a Bad Idea?

The IT department of a large multibillion dollar company decided it would be good to consolidate ERP applications across its four business units. Presently, four applications were running on two different platforms, and all had extensive customization. The consolidation would save millions in O&M expenses. However, it would add considerable amortization expense. The amortization expense would decrease business profitability, but the financial community would never stand for lower profitability. If they executed the project, the business units would have to shore up net profits. In the end, the business leaders decided the consolidation offered little competitive advantage. They decided on other, less risky ways to save money. The project was shelved. Was the decision right or wrong? The decision not to pursue this particular course of action was sound. However, alternate approaches existed that offered less risk and greater financial stability. Shelving the solution was the right decision. Deciding to shelve the entire project concept was imprudent.

Foundational Investments: Foundational projects are prerequisites for other projects. For example before building a new store, a retail chain might first perform market research to determine where it has too many or too few stores. Similarly, in order to implement a new application, the organization might first need to install or expand a computer network. Installation of a network requires many decisions that originate not only from that one application's requirements but also from longer-term needs of the organization. The network is expensive. Installing too little or too much capacity will affect the bottom line or preclude other, more valuable investments. Yet the network needs to support not only the new application but also all future applications implemented over the next five years. These types of foundational projects should be evaluated based on how instrumental they are for achieving long-term goals. Such an evaluation can be a challenge, because foundational project drivers are qualitative. If senior executives do not have, or do not agree on, a five-year plan, then their opinions will differ greatly when it comes time to decide how much to spend on these foundational projects. If future capacity requirements are not well thought out, then the "how much" question becomes not only qualitative but also subjective. Even with alignment on the plan, much debate often occurs around foundational projects. Everyone might agree that a new network is required, for example, but may not agree on the significance of the network. Some may want state-of-the-art technology, while others might want to deploy proven, mature technology.

Foundational project decisions become even further complicated when foundational projects are funded by allocating the cost to multiple departments or business units. The funding decisions affect the financial performance of each business unit. Also, because executive compensation is often dependent on business unit financial performance, the issues impact managers on a personal level. Such situations are not unique to commercial firms. When military applications are affected, senior leadership may be faced with life-or-death situations. When civil applications are affected, public officials have to answer to government leaders, the media, or the public. Different decision makers may have different agendas, which makes it difficult to drive to consensus. The answer to such dilemmas is to ground foundational investment decisions in long-term strategies. Absence of a long-term strategy should trigger management action to develop that strategy, not to make foundational investment decisions without it. The strategy should drive the foundational investments. You wouldn't let the horse out of the barn without a harness, so don't let foundational projects launch without a strategic plan. Foundational decisions require value drivers that define the extent to which foundational projects support the strategic plan, and the cost-effectiveness of these projects. Determine whether the functional project is aligned with specific requirements called out in the strategic plan. Determine whether the project is providing the right capability at a commensurate cost. (We discuss foundational projects again later, in the context of infrastructure portfolios in the section of this chapter on *Special Types of IT Portfolios*.)

A subset of foundational projects that managers need to scrutinize are innovative applications and research projects. Typically, these projects include those that are new to the world, or at least new to the organization. Merriam-Webster defines *innovation* as "a new idea, method, or device." The challenge of evaluating a new idea is that we can only estimate its value, and often only qualitatively. Sometimes it is not possible to estimate its expected value with sufficient accuracy. So senior managers must monitor innovation investments using the same techniques used for applied research and start-up ventures. It is like using an "options" approach to technology implementation, because managers can "opt" to terminate the project at any point they feel the value is insufficient to justify the risk and future cost stream (development plus operations).

Fortunately, little is new under the sun. Most innovative projects are new to the organization but not new to the world. For those that are new to the world, heuristics and outside experts can assist in the assessment, provided the project team is not too arrogant to seek outside help or too poor to pay for it. Senior managers need to ensure that adequate and appropriate outside help is sought for innovative projects. IT engineers, by nature, like to tinker. Left to their own devices, they are more likely to reinvent the wheel than to buy one. These types of decisions directly impact the bottom line and are the purview of the senior management team, not of some engineer who won't have to explain to the CEO why the project is 50% over budget and behind schedule.

Decision Rights

Rights that do not flow from duty well performed are not worth having.
—Mohandas K. Gandhi, *Non-Violence in Peace and War*

Portfolio segmentation and decision making go hand in hand. As we have seen, the purpose of portfolio segmentation is to simplify the portfolio management process. Portfolio segmentation enables delegation of decision making for a particular segment of IT projects to a subset of managers. Portfolio decision rights concern the "who" and "how" of portfolio decision making. *Portfolio governance architecture* defines who has the responsibility to make which decisions about the portfolio and its various segments. It should address all decision making, from cross-project decisions all the way up to and including cross-portfolio (inter-segment) decisions. If you attempt to define only a piece of the decision-making authority without understanding the entire architecture, you risk creating overlapping or redundant delegations of authority, or leaving gaps in decision making.

A leading cause of IT project failure is ineffective decision making, which can mean either making the wrong decisions or making decisions that the organization rejects. Many managers think that by making all the decisions themselves, they increase their personal power base. However true it may be, by making decisions unilaterally managers are probably also making them from a narrow perspective. In so doing, they assume greater risk of failure. Cross-discipline decision making reduces this risk. It enables managers to look at problems from multiple perspectives. In addition, a well-defined, efficient cross-functional decision-making process can improve organizational buy-in with a relatively minor impact on decision-making cycle time.

Contrary to popular belief, IT managers do not make most IT investment decisions. In fact, most IT managers have relatively little decision authority when it comes to determining how and how much to spend. Business requirements determine need. Budgets determine spending. Non-IT managers determine end-user involvement. IT project managers are really more facilitators than they are decision makers per se. Hence, portfolio management must be executed cross-functionally by IT and business (non-IT) managers working collaboratively. This process begins at the top of the organization and trickles down. Some CEOs would prefer that the CIO be accountable for the overall IT portfolio. But the CIO is no more accountable for the overall IT portfolio than the CFO is accountable for the entire organization's budget. The CIO does not make all the IT investment decisions, so the CIO cannot be accountable for the overall IT portfolio. The CIO has many IT management responsibilities and should be accountable for certain IT spending decisions, yet the senior leadership team is accountable for the overall IT portfolio. It is accountable for the level of spending as well as the value returned from that spending.

Can a management team can be accountable? A team can be accountable, but it must be accountable *as a team*. If team members are allowed to blame each other for the consequences of the team's actions, then accountability breaks down. If the CFO abdicates accountability to the CIO, then the CFO is at fault. If the COO blames the CIO yet refuses to personally play an active role in IT management, then the COO is at fault. If the CIO is expected to manage the IT organization, but the business managers are allowed to dictate how the IT organization operates and organizes, then the leadership team is at fault. Teams lack accountability when the team members abdicate decision rights to their peers. Teams can be accountable as long as nobody else is blamed when things go wrong.

The Role of the Portfolio Management Team (PMT)

The portfolio management team (PMT) is ultimately accountable for ensuring optimum return on a portfolio of IT investments. The PMT is a senior leadership team consisting of organizational leaders who have been delegated the authority to make portfolio decisions. (According to a 2003 *CIO Magazine* survey,[1] approximately 50% of companies utilize an executive-level PMT.) One thing that the team structure enables is the sharing of risk management. If any one manager really was accountable for the large endeavors that an IT portfolio represents, we might never undertake them for fear of failure. A PMT, with its cross-functional perspective and decision-making power, can manage the risk. From this perspective, the purpose of a team is to do together what we might not have the capability, courage, or conviction to do as individuals.

A cross-functional PMT also has the authority to hold all associated managers accountable. Each organization has skin in the game. The organization succeeds or fails as a team. Social pressure to do the right thing is usually all the PMT members need to hold one another accountable. No one organization can point fingers at another when a project goes awry, because each member is accountable for ensuring the project stays on track. If a major implementation goes awry, it typically fails because of breakdowns in both the IT and the business organizations. The PMT members know it, and PMT members work together to fix it.[2]

---

[1] "Best Practices of Resourceful CIOs," CIO Magazine, August 4, 2003.
[2] Some organizations like to add an impartial chairperson or facilitator to the team. Sometimes this person is the chief executive for the division, but we've also seen the CFO fill this roll. The purpose of a chairperson is to mediate, arbitrate, and retain organizational objectivity. Occasionally, a PMT can fall prey to groupthink and become overly committed to a project. The chairperson needs to lead the team by ensuring portfolio analysis is objective and insightful.

Basic portfolio management requires that each portfolio segment have one subteam accountable for all of that segment's decisions—a subject to which we will return. However, the PMT assumes fiduciary responsibility for the portfolio *as a whole* to make sure that the right investments are made at the right time. It accomplishes this task by ensuring that the portfolio of IT projects and services meets the strategic needs of the business, and that high-caliber teams execute these projects as efficiently and effectively as possible. The PMT's responsibilities require that membership be composed of senior managers who have the authority to make all portfolio decisions. Decision rights have to do primarily with financial allocation and project scope. The PMT members must be able to authorize the portfolio's spending and resource allocation. If the PMT is not the executive leadership team, then responsibility for the occasional exceptionally large project might have to be escalated to the executive leadership team for capital spending approval, but the PMT should be able to handle most portfolio decisions. If the PMT does not have the appropriate delegation of authority, then the need to consult other people causes inefficiencies. Decisions could be revisited, second-guessed, or reversed. It is pointless to have someone on the PMT who can't make the requisite decisions, who is not really responsible or accountable for decisions but merely consulted.

For typical organizations, the responsibilities of a PMT include the following:

- Provide transorganizational leadership:
  - Rapidly resolve cross-organizational strategic conflicts (vision, mission, strategic intent).
  - Rapidly resolve cross-project conflicts (cross-project interdependencies, gaps, overlaps).
- Optimize the portfolio of IT projects:
  - Optimize value proposition for all projects.
  - Ensure project governance (oversight, team structure, etc.).
  - Balance demand for funding and resources with supply.
- Ensure IT fiscal management:
  - Ensure service levels are aligned with business need.
  - Ensure service provider costs (prices) are commensurate with value delivered.
  - Hold central service providers accountable for fulfilling contracts.

- Approve acquisition of fixed assets (capital purchases).
- Approve resource plan (employees vs. contractor vs. outsourcing).
- Ensure the IT portfolio management process is effective and efficient.

Although we have spoken here of the "typical" organization, exactly how PMTs are structured and how they carry out the responsibilities described will, of course, vary from one organizational context and situation to the next. To take the simplest example, in smaller organizations the PMT might consist of the CEO, COO, and the various department heads. In a large, multidivision company, an executive PMT consisting of senior corporate leadership might oversee the various divisional PMTs. At either end of this spectrum or at points in between, organizations can segment their portfolios—and hence their PMTs—based on the financial statement, the business process, or the business unit organization, as depicted in the following series of figures.

Despite this range of possible structures for portfolio governance, it is possible to offer a few more general observations about how the

Departmental PMT Structure

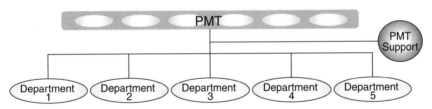

General Ledger PMT Structure

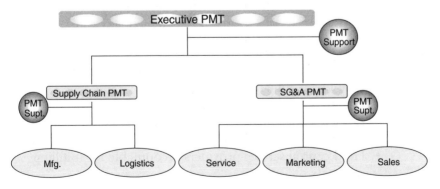

Core Business Process PMT Structure

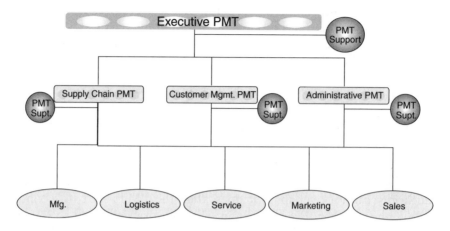

Business Unit PMT Structure

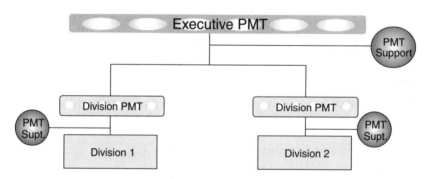

portfolio management process functions in this regard. For example, it is common for PMTs with senior leadership to delegate responsibility for certain portfolio management activities and decisions to subteams. (In terms of the four portfolio management work streams outlined in the *Workflow Design* chapter,[3] it is common for the PMT to delegate responsibility for the inventory and calibration and chartering work streams to others, as well as the legwork—although not the accountability—for strategic analysis and decision making, which con-

---

[3] Inventory and calibration, strategic analysis, decision making, and chartering.

stitute the heart of the portfolio management process.) Indeed, as noted previously, each segment of the portfolio could have its own sub-team, a more junior-level PMT to which accountability is delegated. A corporate PMT comprised of division heads might create a sales and marketing PMT, for instance, to handle all projects that impact only sales and marketing business processes. Other frequently seen examples of executive-level teams delegating responsibility for IT portfolio management activities include the delegation of individual project responsibility to a steering committee and project team, or the delegation of authority by the senior-level PMT for small projects (such as enhancements and maintenance) to a life cycle management PMT.

When an organization has multiple PMTs, their decision-making authority cannot overlap. If it does, then the PMTs start to second-guess one another. Even if certain decisions are delegated to lower-level teams, it is essential that the buck stop with the senior-level PMT. The senior-level PMT is ultimately accountable for ensuring that all IT investment decisions are made in the best interests of the organization. If decision making is delegated, then the PMT is accountable for eliminating ambiguity in roles and responsibilities. Many organizations delegate the portfolio analysis while the PMT retains decision-making responsibility. Some companies have senior PMTs review decisions made by junior-level teams, but this process is not efficient and is really just an excuse for not dealing with the decision rights issues outright. The junior-level teams are led to believe that they have authority to make decisions, but this tactic is deceptive and often ends in frustration and organizational inefficiency.

IT Governance Architecture in the Large Organization

Let's look at what the portfolio management governance structure might look like in a large organization with multiple, semiautonomous divisions, each having multiple disciplines (functional organizations). The top level of decision making is

(continued)

the executive PMT, responsible for establishing budgets and performance targets for each division. The executive PMT manages bottom-line performance of each division, rather than micromanaging. The executive PMT delegates most IT management responsibility to the divisional PMTs with the exception of cross-divisional projects and those that are either large or critical to the enterprise. The executive PMT functions as the top-level PMT for these critical few projects, with the understanding that responsibility for 95% of PMT decisions is delegated. The divisional PMTs are accountable for the remaining 95% of project decisions. However, many of those decisions are application life cycle decisions that affect only one department. Hence, the divisional PMTs establish departmental PMTs for sales, marketing, services, and engineering. The departmental PMTs manage the enabling-project portfolios.

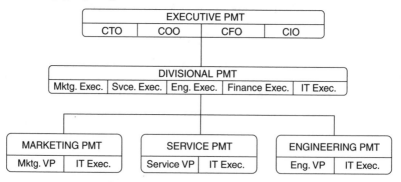

The executive PMT is concerned with the amount of money spent on IT projects. An organization we are familiar with had once used a "blank check" approach to IT spending. As a result, the spending level grew steadily over the course of a decade. To reverse this trend, the executive PMT placed increasing pressure on divisional PMT members to reduce IT spending. The divisional PMT was concerned that it was not getting an optimal return on IT-enabled projects. So it placed a cap on total IT spending to introduce some creative tension into the decision process. Projects now needed to be evaluated and approved based on merit. However, each division represents a $5 to

(*continued*)

$10 billion business, so even the divisional PMTs do not want to micromanage their portfolios. They want to manage the funding and the results strategically. Thus departmental PMTs were created to handle management and operational decisions. The divisional executive vice president (EVP) chairs the divisional PMT, which includes the senior VPs from each major function (sales, engineering, operations, HR, legal, etc.). The divisional PMT retains accountability for all capital projects and any large noncapital projects that require cross-functional decision making (e.g., organizational restructuring, major software upgrades, outsourcing). All divisional projects in the portfolio segment roll up to the divisional PMT. Each departmental PMT reviews each project proposal based on merit, and ensures that the divisional management team is committed to making the project successful. At the time of project approval, each PMT appoints a steering committee, or project governance team, responsible for the project. The project governance team manages all aspects of the project execution until a major change occurs in the project's charter (scope, structure, and objectives) or budget, in which case the PMT reengages.

The allocation of decision-making authority between the PMT and other actors such as project management teams, functional teams, and so forth—and also among multiple PMTs in organizations that have more than one—is what the issue of IT portfolio "decision rights" is ultimately all about. A helpful way of framing the various questions about decision rights, as you design your PMT segmentation and structure, is to think of IT portfolio decision making as two-dimensional. Horizontal (cross-organizational) decisions are made across functions, disciplines, and processes. Vertical decisions are made within a single organization. Let's consider each of these dimensions in turn.

The Importance of the Cross-Organizational Dimension

The most effective portfolio management teams are those that are cross-disciplinary, where leaders from affected disciplines come together as a single decision team to analyze projects and make decisions.

The IT management process by nature cuts across organizational boundaries. IT must therefore be governed cross-divisionally. Remember that our definition of *management* requires accountability for decisions, which are increasingly cross-discipline and cross-organizational, no matter what the focal point of a decision might be. Our definition of *process* is holistic and includes all activities required to make those decisions, regardless of whether the work is performed by IT practitioners or business practitioners. Typically, large IT projects, in particular, require collaboration among IT practitioners, business practitioners, and finance practitioners in order to implement a new business solution comprehensively. If not all these disciplines are represented on the portfolio decision team, decisions tend to be made sequentially or iteratively, which can consume hundreds of hours. Worse yet, the project can get too far out in front of the decision-making process, increasing the risk of the project getting off track, generating more waste, and losing organizational buy-in and support.

Portfolio management is an effective catalyst for bringing decision makers together to collaboratively make meaningful decisions, thereby breaking down organizational silos. Most executives are well intentioned and will try to do what they think is right. Yet each one makes decisions based on available information and his or her perspective in the organization. Those who lack a broad perspective may make a suboptimal decision. Cross-functional portfolio management processes help remedy this dilemma by injecting a broader perspective into the decision-making process. Through the involvement of all the relevant disciplines and key stakeholders, analysis becomes more comprehensive.

Now many of you are no doubt thinking that even though cross-functional decision making might be more effective, it is not necessarily as efficient. A single executive can usually make a decision faster than a team of executives. We can't argue with that generalization. It is true that keeping the scope of the portfolio within one organization makes decision making simple and fast—as long as decisions affect only that one organization. However, as soon as decisions affect multiple organizations, this decision-making structure becomes both less effective and less efficient. Now consider the nature of most IT and business transformation projects. How many of them really only impact one organization? At a minimum, IT projects typically affect two organizations: the IT service provider and business function. Today, fewer and fewer business solutions of any kind affect only one department. R&D projects affect at least engineering, manufacturing, and marketing. CRM projects affect marketing, sales, and customer support. Supply chain projects affect procurement, manufacturing, logistics, reverse logistics (returns), and service. In light of these interrelationships, can decisions affecting them made in unilateral fashion possibly stick? Will the decision pass muster when other disciplines become involved? Or will peers or leaders in the other disciplines second-guess and reverse the decision down the road? Decision-making cycle time is not the only metric to consider. Too many managers try to control decision making rather than facilitate it. Still, is a decision that does not stick really a decision?

With regard to the question of cycle time, standing up a cross-organizational portfolio governance structure may at first appear inefficient. Yet when you add up the time it takes for each individual project to achieve cross-organizational buy-in, it becomes clear that it takes much more time, and presents a much greater risk, without a cross-organizational portfolio management process. The average organization suffers from meeting overload, and adding a portfolio meeting to the mix may meet with resistance. Consider, then, how many of those existing meetings are spent on project coordination and governance. How many of those meetings could be avoided if decisions were made crisply and decisively? How many meetings could be avoided if you could lock all the stakeholders into one room and not let them out until they made a decision? In our experience, many of these meetings could be eliminated with an effective, efficient, integrated project and portfolio management process. Organizational productivity can increase as much as 20% by streamlining project and portfolio management processes. Even though this productivity increase may not translate directly into a 20% cost savings, what executive wouldn't highly value the increase in productivity?

Research and practical experience reveals that big (step-function) breakthroughs in performance come from integrating processes across organizations. Reducing organizational hand-offs, eliminating redundant paperwork and data entry, and improving collaboration and communication often provide greater benefits than optimizing workflows within one functional organization. The same is true for decision making. Aligning multiple organizations with a common goal and ensuring real, lasting cross-organizational buy-in takes time, diplomacy, and skill. However, the benefits in terms of both the quality of the decisions and the energy and commitment with which the organization implements them can be enormous.

The Dangers of Silo-Based Decision Making

Why is cross-organizational decision making so important? For one manufacturing company, the answer did not become clear until it was too late. The company had sales, order management, and support departments that were mostly autonomous. Each department began its efficiency engagement by defining core business workflows and then proceeded to add automation (IT) to optimize the processes. The sales department implemented a best-in-class Siebel contact management application. The order management department implemented Oracle's application, because it seamlessly integrated with the department's Oracle financials applications. The support department implemented a Clarify incident management application because it provided the best balance between price and performance. As these improvement efforts were initiated in the various departmental silos, nobody considered the need to integrate applications across departments.

The decisions to implement these three applications were made independently by three well-intentioned and well-trained managers, each earnestly trying to optimize the company's performance. Each investment decision was cost-justified, with appropriate ROI calculations that cleared the corporate financial hurdles. When reviewed individually, each decision was financially sound. However, none of these decisions was the optimal one for the corporation. No attempt was made to manage between and across departments. Huge inefficiencies in cross-departmental workflow now remain. Thousands of hours are wasted managing the integration of these three best-in-class applications. Where software integration is not affordable, hours are wasted retyping information. More time is wasted handling customer inquiries in the contact center. The contact center agents need to load all three applications to handle customer calls: agents track calls in Clarify to ensure an audit trail of customer needs; agents need to load Oracle to retrieve and modify order information; and if customers have presales questions, agents need to retrieve product pricing information from Siebel. Yet it often happens that sales orders are not entered into the order management application before customers start calling, so

(continued)

on top of using three applications, contact center agents and sales agents must play phone tag trying to address customer concerns. Customers cannot understand why it is so difficult for them. Sales managers are frustrated because salesforce productivity is impaired by "customer service issues" that the contact center manager should be handling. Contact center management is frustrated because it is on the hook to reduce call-handling time and cost. Contact center agents are stressed from constantly taking the heat from customers, the salesforce, and management for delays, even though the root cause is a broken process with fragmented applications.

Although the company optimized each of the three separate applications, it failed to greatly improve customers' experience. Recognizing this deficiency, the firm decided to establish a cross-functional project team to integrate workflow. On the front end, it wants to provide sales staff the ability to quote a promise date for new orders. This capability, in turn, requires a considerable amount of real-time integration with the order management applications. On the back end, the company wants to provide customer support with visibility into sales history, invoices, and other customer information. This level of service also requires real-time integration with the order management applications, while building an integrated customer database will necessitate some degree of automation with the sales applications as well. The integration project is costing as much as, or more than, any one of the previous three application implementations and is adding considerable incremental maintenance costs due to the custom interfaces. At first it had seemed logical to the company for each department to manage its own decisions. Once the departmental productivity issues were addressed, it became clear that the real opportunities for improvement involved *inter*departmental issues. It would have been better if the company had used an integrated PMT for managing the entire portfolio. Perhaps then it would have taken a more customer-facing quality management approach, beginning with an understanding of interdepartmental business architecture. Perhaps then it would have seen that by suboptimizing the parts it was sacrificing overall corporate performance. Perhaps then it would have selected a different application architecture that optimized the cross-functional flow of information.

Intraorganizational Decision Rights: How Far Up or How Far Down?

In determining decision rights in cases that do not require cross-organizational decision making, the key question is simple: To delegate or not to delegate? Delegation is a double-edged sword. Effectively delegating decisions down into an organization can ensure that they are made by managers with situational awareness. Decisions are made closer to where the action occurs, and senior leaders are spared the need to spend time immersed in project details. A downside comes with delegating decisions downward, however. Field managers may lack a broad perspective. Functional or departmental managers often develop a narrow perspective and bias. Regardless of how much breadth of vision managers below the senior levels of the organization may or may not have, delegating decision making may suboptimize ROI and impair visibility into performance. As visibility into performance is impaired, so too is accountability for performance. Managers tell their bosses what they think the bosses want to hear. Bad news is filtered out as it bubbles up the chain of command. Good news is exaggerated. The more links in the chain, the more diluted the message. Few executives in large organizations truly hear what is going on in the field. They piece the picture together with snippets of information, often heard from their peers and their customers rather than their staff. This tendency explains why senior leaders are so often unaware of major project breakdowns until it is too late.

Let's use a typical customer relationship management (CRM) initiative to illustrate this dilemma. Do we want senior leaders to evaluate the initiative based on net benefits? We can calculate those numbers well enough: perhaps the initiative costs $10 million, promises a 40% ROI, and has a three-year project life cycle. Are these figures all management needs to know? Do executives have sufficient situational awareness to make the "go/no-go" decision? Or do they also need to know that the CRM initiative is comprised of ten $1 million subprojects, each taking 9 to 18 months? Do they need to know that the ROI on these projects ranges from 0% to 70%? Sequencing of these projects affects the payback period. Another critical consideration is that a couple of these projects are high-risk, because they involve significant changes to process and decision rights. The remaining projects are so low-risk as to be no-brainers. Getting the higher ROI, however, hinges on the riskier projects. So how much situational awareness do decision makers need to have? Should senior leaders be allowed line-item veto of subprojects, or should they look at the initiative as one big project? These fundamental issues come into play when defining portfolio governance architecture. Delegation puts these decisions into the hands of middle managers, who may understand the details but lack organizational perspective (or accountability) to make the right decisions. Providing greater situational awareness might increase the ability of middle managers to make the right decisions, but once you begin delegating portfolio decisions, how do you ensure the right people make the right ones?

The bigger and more interdependent the organization, the more important it is to carefully consider delegation and decision rights. Small organizations may have the luxury of retaining decision making among a small group of people who have full situational awareness. The executive team members in small organizations perform many roles and are often hands-on. When an organization has only a few layers, people share a common situational awareness. As organizations grow, however, situational awareness becomes attenuated. Large organizations struggle with this issue. Either situational awareness needs to be brought up the chain of command—often a difficult task—or decisions need to be delegated to leaders in the field who are closer to the action. Fortunately, the advent of portfolio and program management processes—and the enabling software applications—allows senior leadership both to make the important decisions on projects *and* to delegate implementation responsibility, while retaining visibility into performance. Effective governance determines not only who is allowed to make decisions but also promotes common situational awareness among all decision makers.

As executives delegate, their level of involvement declines. The PMT, then, needs to maintain a careful balancing act between delegation and involvement. If we want senior executive accountability for portfolio value, the PMT needs to stay involved. The term *involvement* is a vague and overused one in the IT industry. Dozens of surveys cite lack of leadership involvement as *a major contributor to project failure.* Few of those reports define what it really means to be involved. If I read the e-mail messages, status reports, and presentations that you send me, am I involved? If I sit in your meetings, am I involved? Perhaps not—maybe all that overhead is a waste of time. In our experience, involvement requires two-way, constructive communication. A manager must both hear and comprehend the message. Not only the words but also their meaning. This same manager must provide constructive feedback, sharing the wisdom of his or her perspective and experience. So when we discuss managers' level of involvement, we do so in the context of what messages they internalize and how they use this information to influence decisions.

We want to emphasize that project governance is distinct from portfolio governance, on the one hand, and project management, on the other. The PMT is accountable for making sure that projects receive the governance they require to be successful. The PMT must assemble a project governance team that has the decision-making authority, and the accountability, to make a project successful. We do not favor the term *steering committee* because it brings to mind someone out on the ocean whose job it is merely to turn the boat. The project governance team needs to provide much more than a vector check. It is more like the captain of a ship than like the navigator. The project governance team is like the captain in being accountable for the project end-to-end. It is accountable for navigation, engine control, scheduling, route, morale, and delivery of the cargo to its destination. Like a ship's captain, the project governance team need not do all the work itself—it has a crew of project team members. But at the end of the voyage, the project governance team must be held accountable by the PMT for the project's results. If the project sinks, then the project governance team should go down with the ship. One way to hold the project governance team accountable is to make it answer for the financial or operational results of the project, regardless of whether it succeeds or fails. For example, a COO might hold a project governance team responsible for a 15% reduction in operating expense regardless of whether an ERP project is successful or not. If the project governance team is on the hook for the 15% reduction, it is more likely to make sound business decisions.

Staying on Track

Although certain principles, which we have just considered, guide the PMT through the process of structuring and allocating decision rights for the IT portfolio, no single right approach dictates which decisions are made by the PMT versus the project governance team versus the project management team versus some other group. To avoid the many wrong answers that are out there, the trick is to take advantage of the PMT's senior perspective and authority, while not burdening it with micromanaging projects. You can use the following heuristics to help determine your decision rights.

- *Heuristic #1:* Cross-discipline and cross-departmental strategic decisions are always the purview of the PMT. These decisions are best made early in a project's life cycle to avoid a lot of wasted expense. Examples of these types of strategic decisions include transferring responsibilities between organizations and optimizing cross-organizational workflows. Get the big operating assumptions out of the way at the outset of the project, and then delegate execution to a cross-organizational governance and project team.

- *Heuristic #2:* Authorization for major new investments and large investments in an existing technology platform is the purview of the PMT. These decisions have long-term impact on the operating cost structure, introducing additional fixed costs to operate, maintain, and support the new asset. The organization should be committed to optimizing platform utilization. Return on software assets comes from using the features to automate and eliminate work, both within and across functions. Hundreds of organizations have used ERP and CRM software merely to automate inherently inefficient processes that need to be fundamentally reconfigured, because the organization was not committed to changing its way of doing business. The PMT needs to ensure that the organization is committed to change *before* it invests in a new software asset! The PMT also needs to avoid overinvestment in technology. The degree of automation determines organizational efficiency, not the amount of technology deployed.

Beyond these rules of thumb, it is important to warn against some of the distractions that can lead the PMT off track as it tries to maintain the balance between delegation and involvement. By the time they design and implement the portfolio management process, many organizations forget that the purpose of the PMT is not merely to prioritize projects. In fact, too many organizations spend too much time prioritizing. Some spend so much time prioritizing that they find their priorities are obsolete before they finish the exercise. Prioritization is a noble effort, but it is not the end game. By definition, a higher-priority project should take precedence over lower-priority ones. In theory, this principle means that the higher-priority project should be able to "steal" resources from a lower-priority one if necessary. However, in the real world priorities change constantly, and middle managers don't like to put one customer on hold to serve another. We can't afford to prioritize on a quarterly or monthly basis in our Internet-enabled, high-speed, dynamic world. We prioritize daily. That's what most managers do. They manage day-to-day issues. When the production application fails, we reprioritize to pull experts in to fix the problem. When clients have questions or issues, we reprioritize to meet with them. Important activities are superseded by urgent ones. It is naïve to believe that because we label a project as *important* our resources will not address *urgent* requests as they arise.

If we had to summarize its role, we'd say that the PMT assures that the portfolio of projects meets business expectations for value and cost, and assures that projects meet those expectations. To say that the PMT simply prioritizes the portfolio is a gross understatement. When a project deviates from plan, the PMT needs to understand how it affects the rest of the portfolio. When a project varies from its plan, it affects budgets and resources of interdependent, parallel, successor, and future projects. For that reason, project planning relates closely to portfolio management. By designing a portfolio management process that simply prioritizes projects, we mislead the PMT and set it up to fail. Prioritization is only one decision that the PMT makes. The PMT charters projects. It defines project scope, objectives, and governance structure. It oversees project variance-to-plan and holds project governance teams accountable for project-specific results. It presides over interim reviews when project scope changes significantly. It resolves project interdependency and cross-functional issues that cannot be resolved during the normal course of executing the project. And it assigns resources (people, funding, and assets). All of these aspects happen dynamically.

The PMT is accountable to senior leadership for portfolio results. It is accountable for the value produced by the portfolio. The "M" in PMT stands for management, and we expect the PMT to manage the portfolio, using the portfolio management process. If an organization is not satisfied with the value returned from its investments, then PMT members shouldn't complain to some project manager who probably earns less than any of them do. The buck stops with the PMT. By making decisions about chartering and resources, the PMT is accountable for the projects that do the work. Projects are responsible for planning and delivering to plan. Are projects accountable for results? Not for bottom-line results. The PMT is accountable for bottom-line results, because the PMT decided on the scope, resources, and funding of the project. Responsibility rolls downhill, but accountability defies gravity. As the king of the hill, the PMT is accountable for ensuring projects do the right things and do them right. The PMT ensures that projects consult the right subject-matter experts and involve the right stakeholders to make the project successful. The PMT has the prerogative to delegate execution responsibility to a project governance team if it wants to, but it cannot delegate accountability for results.

The PMT structure affects organizational behavior broadly and deeply. As a result, it can be a change management challenge. Many organizations bring in high-caliber, experienced consultants just for this piece of the portfolio management implementation. Failing to implement the right PMT can render worthless one's entire portfolio management process. Given that most organizations expect portfolio management to increase accountability, it would be unfortunate if one went to all the trouble of setting up a portfolio management process and didn't appreciably affect accountabilities and responsibilities. If the PMT does not assert the proper authority over the portfolio, accountability suffers. If the PMT does not enable timely decisions, organizational performance suffers. If the PMT tries to micromanage projects, the process becomes bureaucratic and efficiency suffers. If the PMT and individual project approval teams are not integrated and rationalized, they will create overhead and conflict in decision making.

Documenting Rules and Policies

Once we account for all portfolio decisions at every level of the organization, we need to clearly document the business rules and policies so that everyone in the organization understands who is accountable and responsible for executing the process. This documentation needs to be integrated with the portfolio management process workflow, which we discuss later in the book. A good framework to use when documenting management roles is *RACI*, which allows you to clearly articulate who is:

- *Responsible (R):* The people who do the work
- *Accountable (A):* The people with ultimate decision authority who are answerable for results
- *Consulted (C):* The people who have an important perspective or subject-matter expertise
- *Informed (I):* The people who need to know what is happening

We're much better off ensuring that we have at least executive-level buy-in to the governance structure before we pilot the process. Performing the RACI analysis often uncovers gaps in roles and responsibilities, and it is a great management tool for achieving buy-in—or at least identifying areas of dissent—among all stakeholders. If decision rights are ambiguous, we risk a number of dysfunctional behaviors including second-guessing decisions, too many people on the PMT to manage effectively, and teams with insufficient empowerment to make decisions. It is much more difficult to resolve these issues once we start to use the process than it is to mitigate these factors in advance. Once we include people on a team, it can be difficult to remove them. And once we establish a PMT, we don't want to tell the organization that the executive team doesn't support its decisions. Organizations can be skeptical and may lose confidence in the process if management teams appear uncooperative or unsupportive.

Organizations need to provide resources to facilitate the analysis and documentation of the rules and policies associated with the portfolio management process. Senior managers have little discretionary time and portfolio management requires a significant amount of data collection, validation, and analysis. Thus we need to figure out who is going to do all the work between meetings. Even if we implement applications at the outset to automate these tasks, we still need to facilitate the process for the first 6 to 12 months, until the organization is accustomed to using the new system. The tasks and decisions will become apparent as the process flow is designed. (Some are described in the next chapter.)

Sample RACI Chart

	PMT	PMO	Eng	Ops	
Define Customer Requirements	A		R	C	A = Accountable
Research Technology Trends	I		A/R	C	R = Responsible
Determine Strategic Project Priorities	A	R	C	C	C = Consulted
Develop Technology Architecture	I		A/R	C	I = Informed
Develop Architecture Migration Plan	A		R	R	
Propose Changes to Architecture		A	R	C	
Approve Changes to Architecture	A	R	C	C	
Determine Tactical Project Priorities	A	R	C	C	

To use the RACI model, first make a list of all tasks and decisions. The sequence of the list is not important, but you will find it helpful to sort the list somewhat chronologically. Next to the list, create a column for every role (decision team, project team, project manager, discipline manager, etc.). Some people prefer to create columns for organizations, but if we are designing a cross-departmental portfolio process that can become confusing. It is often easier to focus on roles rather than named resources or organizations. Then we can map the organizations to roles. This approach also creates a degree of organizational independence: in the event of reorganization, we can simply reassign roles and team membership rather than changing the process.

Special Types of IT Portfolios

We greatly underestimate the serious implications to our own future. . . .
Things move with such terrific speed these days, that it is really essential
to us to think in broader terms.

                              —Franklin D. Roosevelt, *The Roosevelt Letters*

When designing a portfolio management process, many organizations
focus solely on new development and integration projects. However,
most organizations spend less than 30% of their IT budgets on new development and integration projects. The remaining 70% is spent
sustaining the status quo—operating, maintaining, changing, and
supporting the installed base of IT that is distributed throughout the
enterprise (desktop, work area, network, and data center). The PMT
also manages this sustaining spending. Although we might want to
pilot a new portfolio process on the new development and integration
projects, the PMT should not abdicate responsibility for the sustaining segments.

New development and integration are so highly integrated with
sustaining the installed base that it is rarely possible to implement a
new system without affecting the installed base of applications and infrastructure. Installing a new application will affect existing IT operations. Increasingly, new applications need to be integrated with
existing applications, which may require enhancements to the old applications, which in turn affects application availability. Often these
new applications affect infrastructure, by requiring upgrades in capacity or geographical expansion. (For example, many projects have failed
because they neglected to forecast the impact of an application on network traffic.) The average new development and integration project
has enhancement tasks, infrastructure tasks, data center tasks, training
tasks, and support (help desk) tasks. Some organizations treat each
such task as a separate project ("lots of small projects"), while others
treat them as one big initiative. Regardless of how management organizes the projects for success, all the tasks related to the new application are interdependent and need to be coordinated.[4] Each task affects

---

[4] Each method presents its particular pros and cons. Perhaps the most important consideration is whether the assigned project manager can effectively manage the entire project's complexity.

the resource allocation and prioritization of multiple IT disciplines (application integration, help desk, operations engineering, data center operations, and network operations). Each is a project (or portion thereof) that resides in some segment of the IT portfolio. Sustaining activities cannot be cast aside and treated as exceptions to the portfolio management process. The 70% of the IT budget that is spent on sustaining the installed base is too big to be an exception to the portfolio management process.

Depending on the size and structure of the organization, it may make sense to use the same PMT to govern both new and sustaining spending, or to establish one or more separate lower-level PMTs to govern the sustaining spending. However, the most important guideline is to ensure that some PMT is accountable for sustaining the existing installed base. We can divide the sustaining IT segments into three sub-segments, each having its own nuances and need to be governed in its own way:

- Infrastructure portfolios
- Support (service-level) portfolios
- Application preservation portfolios

Infrastructure Portfolios

Although many people do not view infrastructure (data center, server, and network operations and engineering) activities as projects per se, they are best managed as projects in an infrastructure portfolio. For example, IT operations needs to be managed to achieve some service-level objective (availability, performance, etc.), and infrastructure enhancement initiatives need to achieve improvements in service level or unit cost. The portfolio management process governs these activities. If infrastructure decisions are made discretely, then the PMT loses situational awareness of interdependent projects in the IT portfolio. The PMT is best able to govern infrastructure service objectives and performance to ensure that they remain aligned with business needs.

The PMT needs to account for the ongoing cost of infrastructure management, but it needs to balance supply and demand for IT services when doing so. For example, most commercial organizations grow 3% to 10% per year. This growth typically involves new people in new or expanded offices, and typically requires infrastructure expansion. However, few organizations factor in the increased IT infrastructure cost when they plan for growth. They tell the IT department to "absorb" the growth. Doing so requires the IT department rob Peter to pay Paul. Growth is funded at the cost of quality: cutting IT service improvement initiatives or cutting corners. Cutting improvement initiatives breaks the reinforcing cycle of improvements funding further improvements. Cutting corners affects the service level (cycle time, quantity, or quality) or drives up long-term costs. Instead, organizations should fund growth directly but challenge IT service providers to devise a plan to drive down service unit cost year-over-year via continuous improvement. These sustainable cash flow savings can then be "returned" to the PMT and reallocated appropriately. Just as one might reinvest dividends from personal investments, the PMT should reinvest the savings, thus compounding the benefits.

Infrastructure projects fall into a number of categories, each with its own idiosyncrasies:

- *Recapitalization projects:* Replacing or retiring assets
- *Upgrade projects:* Applying commercial off-the-shelf (COTS) software releases to increase capacity, functionality, or performance
- *Enhancement projects:* Modifying software to provide increased capacity, functionality, or performance
- *New IT service launches:* Introducing a new business capability
- *Maintenance projects:* Repairing and expanding existing capabilities
- *Continuous improvement projects:* Improving IT service provision cost-effectiveness

Recapitalization

Recapitalization projects replace or retire infrastructure assets. Infrastructure assets have an intended lifespan, and best-in-class IT managers replace the assets near the end of that lifespan to avoid higher operating costs and outages. Recapitalization is a predictable cost of doing business that should be scheduled at the time the asset is deployed. It shows poor planning to surprise the organization by calculating investment costs on the fly year after year. So, for example, when deploying an asset with a three-year life in 2003, the project puts a placeholder into the portfolio plan to replace or upgrade that asset in late 2005. The asset life should correlate with the depreciation schedule. In this way, managers can keep expenses relatively flat and minimize negative impacts on the balance sheet. With sufficient planning, the PMT need only determine *when* to replace rather than *whether* to replace. In other words, the PMT focuses on scheduling rather than business case evaluation.

Upgrade and Enhancement

Upgrade and enhancement projects are application changes that provide increased performance (service level or cost), increased capacity (volume), or increased functionality (quality or customer service). Upgrades include installation of commercial off-the-shelf (COTS) software application releases. Enhancements include application customization or configuration changes. Many upgrades require configuration, and if an organization has modified a COTS software application, then an upgrade may also require customization. For this reason, the level of effort for upgrades is often underestimated.

Diminishing returns are realized when modifying the installed technology base. Organizations face an inflection point when they reach a certain amount of IT enablement. Diminishing returns from mere technology enablement do not achieve bottom-line performance improvement without holistic transformations requiring a fusion of people, policy, process, and technology changes. Without sufficient situational awareness regarding business operations, often the only way senior leaders recognize the inflection point is when IT projects cease to deliver sufficient value to satisfy expectations.

The value from infrastructure changes is often a function of the organization's technology adoption rate as determined by the industry, culture, and economic conditions. An organization more inclined to be on the leading edge will pursue infrastructure changes more aggressively. A more frugal organization might wait until the last possible moment to change, even risking the need to change during an economic downturn.

Because of the uncertainties involved here, senior leaders need to regulate the amount spent on change requests, just as they do for general and administrative expenses. Many middle managers lack the perspective and objectivity to judge whether changes are justified, given the organization's overall mission and resource constraints. Some changes are justified, such as those that support business expansion and new business endeavors. Too often, however, change requests are justified based merely on alleged improvements in organizational productivity or effectiveness. Productivity and effectiveness translate into bottom-line value when they affect the organization's mission. Yet many changes result in the organization only doing the wrong things more productively or effectively. For example, increasing the number of payables that a department can process per day may not be valuable unless it improves cash flow, cost, supplier leverage, or some other metric. A better investment might be to automate or outsource the accounts payable process entirely and reduce cost, but the payables manager may lack the perspective, initiative, or knowledge to suggest such a project.

Advance planning invariably makes the investment decision easier. If the CFO has a two- to five-year line of sight for the investment schedule, then he or she can ensure that the financial forecast accommodates the investment. The timing of the investment can be aligned with the economic cycle to fund investments at a time when the organization has money to invest. Perhaps now is not the time for a major investment. Perhaps the investment is better postponed until economic conditions change. A savvy organization can time the investment concurrent with recapitalization, which simplifies the investment's funding decision. On the other hand, when the CFO is notified of the investment only 12 to 18 months in advance, the investment has to retrofit into financial forecasts that have already been released to the financial community, often resulting in the need for the organization to "absorb" the investment by cutting others. It becomes a zero-sum game in which somebody has to lose.

Infrastructure changes present some of the most complex portfolio decisions—politically and financially—because of their cost function and organizational impact. Infrastructure changes often provide a step function rather than a linear increase in performance or capacity. The organization may then need to acquire more performance or capacity than initially required, often at a higher cost than it desires. When these costs affect only one stakeholder it is easy for the organization to de-

How Much Security Is Enough?

One problem that many organizations face is how much to invest in security. How much security is enough? In one organization struggling with this dilemma, the IT staff identified hundreds of vulnerabilities as well as solutions to them. The cost of deploying that much security was prohibitive in the current economic environment. The organization established a portfolio management process for projects to address security vulnerabilities. In so doing, they were able to structure the decision-making process regarding security. They standardized risk and probability assessments to ensure that the same heuristics were used in assessing all vulnerabilities. IT management was able to base investment decisions on risk analysis and the probability that a vulnerability would be exploited. It was able to review the criticality (probability, risk, etc.) of each vulnerability relative to that of other known ones. The IT management team had greater situational awareness as to its overall information assurance posture. Whereas vulnerabilities had previously not been addressed in a timely fashion, now IT managers had a consistent, repeatable method for making security investment decisions. They could more easily allocate available funding among the various security investments. When it could not afford to invest in new technology, the organization was able to mitigate risk via brute force, by modifying its information assurance operational processes and responsibilities. IT managers were also better positioned to make a case to senior management for whether additional security investments were required and what the potential business risks were of not addressing the gaps. Overall, the cycle time for decision making decreased by more than 50%, and the percentage of IT management and senior leadership mindshare that the security topic consumed was dramatically reduced.

termine the priority. More often, though, infrastructure changes affect multiple projects, departments, divisions, and even customers.

Infrastructure changes are especially challenging for diversified corporations consisting of business units that differ in their technology adoption rate. Infrastructure investment costs are typically allocated to all business units. What if only one business unit needs the investment? What if all business units don't want to pay for the infrastructure change? What if one business unit operates a low-cost, low-margin business while another operates a high-margin, high-innovation business that benefits from leading-edge technologies? Do the needs of one business unit outweigh the needs of all? Sometimes yes, sometimes no. It may be difficult or impossible to find a win-win solution, but the investment should pay off in the aggregate. The aggregate incremental value to the organization should outweigh the aggregate incremental cost. Sometimes, in extremely diverse corporations, the only equitable answer is to separate business units that lag behind technologically from early-adopter business units, or have the parent company absorb the incremental cost forced upon the frugal business units by the more affluent ones. The "right" answer depends on the implementation alternatives and the aggregate business case. In such situations, it is especially important that an apolitical PMT make the decision based on an objective review of all the options and implications.

New IT Services

New IT service launches introduce a new enterprise application or capability (like a corporate directory) to the organization, and are often treated as "infrastructure" upgrades because they tend to be foundational versus business-specific. The introduction of new enterprise services can be a struggle for some organizations. If a particular department requests the new service, it might be able to justify the cost for itself. However, establishing a new service that can be scaled to support a whole corporation is often more expensive than providing this service for one department. Enterprise-wide solutions are, by nature, initially more costly to deploy than workgroup solutions. In the long run, however, a hodgepodge of workgroup solutions will not serve the needs of the enterprise. As with upgrades, the value of launching a new service is partially dependent on the importance the organization places on technology as an enabler of business value and growth. For example, when organizations first implemented e-mail it required a leap of faith that the improvement in communication would pay off down the road in terms of greater collaboration and faster cycle times. Yet even today, it is difficult for the layperson to isolate and measure the incremental value associated with the e-mail investment. The same issues will apply to wireless and multimedia solutions. For some, it is obvious how to integrate a new service (capability) into business activities to improve cycle time, quality, and innovation. For others, the value is less obvious. Often the decision will hinge on your specific industry's technology adoption rate as well as the current versus desired competitive situation—that is, how important is it for you to retain technological parity with the competition? This question is one the PMT decides.

Maintenance

Maintenance projects include repair and expansion of existing functionality. Maintenance projects are a cost of doing business. They should have been cost-justified and factored into the total cost of ownership (TCO) of the infrastructure when it was initially deployed. Hardware maintenance (preventative and impromptu), for example, is a predictable expense that should be budgeted at the time the organization acquires the infrastructure. If so, the maintenance dollars are already allocated and the PMT need only manage variances to the plan and efficiency goals. If you have the misfortune not to have planned for ongoing maintenance, then you should remedy this oversight by establishing the life cycle plan for the foreseeable remaining life of the infrastructure. (Note that the maintenance life cycle plan is based on the *infrastructure life cycle*, not the asset life cycle, which will likely be recapitalized every 3 to 5 years. Maintenance is an ongoing cost that may change over time as assets turn over, but it never goes away until the infrastructure is decommissioned.) Again, we see no reason to surprise the financial community by calculating maintenance costs on the fly year-over-year. The PMT needs to ensure that the planning is done right. (Also see the discussion of Application Preservation Portfolios.)

Continuous Improvement

Continuous improvement projects are activities that improve IT service provision cost-effectiveness (price for performance). Continuous improvement projects share objectives that drive a noticeable improvement in cost (expense), service capability (functionality), service level (performance), or some combination thereof. In many instances, the organization requires these projects to be self-funding (payback within one fiscal year). Sometimes, an organization is willing to invest proactively in these projects provided they result in a positive NPV. Each organization has its own tolerance for investment in this category. Note that if your organization has neglected spending on continuous improvement, it is likely that your IT service delivery performance suffers as a result. If you are in "catch-up" mode after neglecting continuous improvement, your organization will need to make some hard decisions about how you are going to fund and achieve breakthrough improvements. Hopefully you can address this issue during the next economic upturn. Commercial third-party IT service providers build these continuous improvement costs into their budgets. Many reinvest efficiency savings in continuous improvement. Internal IT departments should do the same. Organizations that manage IT as a cost center struggle to find funding for continuous improvement, which is why we treat it as a separate portfolio segment. Neglecting continuous improvement projects is *not* an option. The PMT needs to ensure adequate funding is available for them.

Support (Service-Level) Portfolios

An organization's expectations about IT support heavily influence its cost. Provision of service and end-user support is a cost of doing business, but it is a cost that can and should be managed by the PMT. In the lifespan of most industries, information technology is relatively new. Most IT has been in existence for only a decade or two, whereas most industries have been around for 50 to 100 years. Thus we are just nearing the time when the use of IT is becoming second nature to the majority of the workforce. The new workforce "grew up with" the technology. Most of the mature workforce has integrated IT into its normal work routine. Unfortunately, the need for computer support over the past decades created a self-propagating effect. Employees of most U.S.-based organizations have become accustomed to having an IT organization at their beck and call, from which they often can obtain real-time computer assistance. Yet every call to a help desk costs $10 to $20. A deskside visit from a support agent costs $25 to $100. Some of this support is required, but a lot of it can be avoided. Although it costs money for users to become self-sufficient, user self-sufficiency provides benefits beyond mere cost savings. As users learn, the propensity for innovation grows and IT asset utilization increases. In time, these benefits increase return on IT investment. The PMT can influence this behavior, the IT service provider cannot. Do not expect the IT department to reduce user demand for IT services any more than you would expect the accounting department to reduce operating expenses.

The PMT needs to select a level of service commensurate with the organization's cost structure and desired culture. Service cost correlates with service level. Providing faster service, for example, requires more staffing or greater automation. These increases in turn raise costs. Organizations that outsource their IT support should be forced to sign a service-level agreement (SLA) spelling out price and performance expectations. If the vendor is managed appropriately, the organization gets what it pays for—no less, but no more. It is a rare vendor that exceeds expectations across the board. Unfortunately, internal IT service providers do not always follow suit, for the most part because they want to be "good corporate citizens" and do whatever is needed for the good of the cause. These good intentions end up undermining the internal market economy for services. The organization's IT consumers (users) become accustomed to getting whatever they want whenever they want it. The IT department obtains a reputation for being too expensive, and the business has little incentive to become self-sufficient. Without proper service accounting (cost accounting) the business is not aware of how its behavior affects expenses. The business demands more and more while the CFO beats on the IT department to cut costs. The same situation may result when IT service delivery is outsourced but corporate retains the cost rather than passing it through to the divisions. This situation is rampant throughout corporate America and is one of the leading causes of dissatisfaction with IT service providers.

We measure cost performance as the cost to the organization of providing an incremental unit of service at a predetermined level of performance. Cost performance pressure (or price performance pressure, if IT service is outsourced) is what maintains the equilibrium in the internal market economy for IT service delivery. This fundamental metric aligns IT with organizational goals. Using the same principles of economics as pertain in external markets, it puts pressure on the

PMT to balance supply and demand for IT services. It puts pressure on the supplier to improve the cost (price) of services over time. All things remaining constant (capacity, performance levels, functionality, etc.), the service delivery price should decline as service delivery processes improve and hardware costs decline. Even if the PMT chooses to use cost improvements to fund increased functionality or capacity, at least customers observe improvement somewhere.

IT service-level management is not complex, especially if you stick with some basic commercial paradigms. A service is any end-to-end workflow that delivers value to the IT consumer (user) or customer (buyer). For example, we do not consider operating a data center to be a service, because it is only one element of the workflow that provides value to the consumer. We would rather consider the service to be application hosting, or better yet application provision. If a PMT establishes an SLA for provision of a particular application, such as order management or general ledger, it knows what value that application provides to the organization. It may not be able to assign a dollar value, but at least it has some intuitive understanding. The same is true for desktop/notebook computer provision, telephone service provision, e-mail service provision, and so on. For these same reasons, we do not recommend treating the intermediary activities (network engineering, maintenance, etc.) as discrete services. They are elements that make up a service, but the PMT typically has trouble valuing the activity. You also do not want the PMT dictating how much network engineering it wants to buy or how much it should cost. You want the PMT to focus on defining the application service level it requires, and then to enable the IT service provider to determine the amount of network engineering required to achieve that service level.

One of the challenges faced by an internal IT service provider is a lack of cost accounting capabilities. This problem dates back to the IT function's origins within the organization. Most organizations set up internal IT service providers as cost centers. As such, they have good financial accounting capabilities but virtually no cost accounting capabilities. Fewer than 50% of companies provide their IT departments with cost accounting and activity-based financial management tools. They also have relatively little ability to fund applications that measure operational performance. Few internal IT service providers have applications that measure service levels, which is a real-time aggregation of operational performance and cost accounting information. In contrast, most commercial IT service providers have all these applications, which is what gives them the edge in providing better performance at a lower price. No reputable commercial IT service provider would set up shop without them. Just as manufacturing organizations have been using cost accounting and performance metrics to drive continuous improvement, so have commercial IT providers for the past decades. Commercial service providers are then able to invest profits from these services into continuous improvements, giving them a competitive advantage. So are we saying that everyone should outsource their IT services? No. Most large IT organizations have sufficient size and scale to provide as good or better service as commercial IT service providers and many small businesses can make do with a few savvy IT generalists. We're simply saying that the PMT needs to understand the economics of IT service delivery. It needs to understand that improved service costs money. If it is getting the improved service "for free," then someone is robbing Peter to pay Paul. The PMT needs to know what it is asking for and understand the consequences of its actions.

Service-level requirements may vary by department, job function, or position. Even though users need to become more self-sufficient, we also need to factor in resource constraints. Organizations need to utilize employees with specialized skills or knowledge. For constrained resources, productivity needs to be maximized, even at the expense of increased innovation and higher service cost. IT service level management is becoming more sophisticated as PMTs segment computer users and define service-level requirements for each. Some user segments will receive high-touch, rapid service levels. Other user segments should make do with a less responsive service level. Some applications drive revenue or cost efficiencies in real time, so they require exceptional service levels. Other applications have a less direct impact on the bottom line and can therefore endure less availability. At the end of the day, it may be an inconvenience when the human resource (HR) application goes down, but does the HR application require the same service level as the order management application? The PMT must decide.

Ideally, the PMT is the final approver of all SLAs. It is accountable for the expense, even when the IT service provider is responsible for drafting the SLA. The PMT may delegate to middle managers in the organization responsibility for ensuring that the SLA reflects their requirements, but the PMT is accountable for the final approval of service levels and their associated costs. The PMT is also accountable for establishing reasonable stretch goals to continuously improve IT service delivery cost and performance over time. Most commercial service providers can offer 5% to 10% cost improvements year-over-year, provided that all variables (capacity, volume, performance, etc.) remain constant. If the variables change, then the organization must use traditional cost accounting variance analysis to establish stretch goals based on the forecast. It is not enough for the PMT to pressure the IT service provider to improve. The PMT must understand the cost structure and drivers as well as how these will affect consumer and provider behaviors. The PMT must be the Alan Greenspan of the organization's IT market economy.

Application Preservation Portfolios

Application preservation portfolio segments are another area for the PMT to monitor. Left to their own devices, middle managers may lump all application expenses in one big "development" budget. The problem is that such changes actually are a mishmash. Many development projects do not reduce cost or add bottom-line value. To describe them correctly, application preservation projects are more similar to infrastructure projects than to new application development projects. The four types of application preservation projects are:

- Bug fixes (correcting errors)
- Upgrades (applying vendor code)
- Enhancements (adding features)
- Operations (keeping the lights on and the system running)

Bug fixes are repairs (a.k.a. "break-fix") due to mistakes or shortcuts that the organization should have addressed but overlooked when implementing the application. Bug fixes include missed requirements (e.g., someone forgot to document some functionality that the application was supposed to have), software defects (errors in the application or configuration that were not caught during testing), and breakage (unanticipated downstream failure caused by a change to something else upstream). Bug fixes are a cost of poor quality and should be avoided to the extent feasible. Some bug fixes are not mission-critical and can be bundled with other preservation projects in order to save time and money. Other bug fixes must be addressed immediately. The PMT is accountable for ensuring that some governance of the bug fixes exists to achieve cost-effectiveness and a zero-defect approach to IT implementation.

Upgrades are periodic new software releases from vendors of COTS software applications. Eventually an organization must install these releases in order to retain support from the vendor and compatibility with new operating systems and other integrated software applications. Upgrading too often can be costly. Not upgrading often enough can result in more bug fixes. The cost of continual upgrades should have been accounted for in the TCO analysis and long-range financial forecasts. The PMT is accountable for ensuring the proper TCO analysis is performed before the application is acquired, including a determination of the proper frequency of upgrades.

Enhancements are new application requirements identified by the organization in response to changing business needs. These true business needs require some modifications of applications, such as reconfiguration and perhaps even programming changes (although both of these tasks are becoming less frequent as best-in-class, user-configurable architectures are increasingly utilized). Often, as a business becomes more familiar with an application's capabilities, managers will want to change (reconfigure or customize) the application to better automate the workflow. These business "wants" may be discretionary in nature, devised to alleviate the pain of workers or middle managers. The PMT is accountable for ensuring that some distinction is made between wants and needs, and for deciding how much funding to allocate for each. The PMT must be careful not to separate the workflow decision making from the software decision making, since they typically are interdependent. Separating them introduces inefficiency into the decision-making process by requiring the organization to iterate these decisions until the two are aligned. We cannot decide to change the workflow unless we accommodate the changes in the software, and vice versa.

Operations activities are ongoing manual interventions required to sustain an application. They are not really enhancements, but are most often lumped into this category because the activities are often performed by the same staff who enhance the applications. The most common form of operations activity is database administration, where someone maintains database integrity via periodic cleanup tasks. The amount of application operations tasks required depends on how the application is designed. Unfortunately, too many developers consider operational costs too late in the development process. A good design will minimize operational requirements, but few developers consider these during the design phase. Operations are a predictable, ongoing expense that should be calculated up front during the TCO analysis and budgeted in the long-range financial forecasts. Operations expenditures are not discretionary. The PMT's role is to challenge the organization to proactively prevent operational costs by designing for efficient operations during the design/acquisition phase of the application life cycle, and to deal with unexpected surprises when the TCO analysis does not properly anticipate the expense.

Organizations need to decide how to best govern infrastructure, support, and application preservation portfolios. Some organizations do so by establishing a departmental PMT to handle decisions across the various special types of portfolios, which allows senior PMTs to delegate tactical responsibilities to middle managers. Other organizations govern each special portfolio type at the level of the senior PMT. The "right" answer may be different for each organization, depending on the issues each faces. The answer might also change as the organization matures. Often decision making is retained at a higher level until the portfolio process stabilizes and spending is aligned with business needs, at which point the senior PMT begins to delegate responsibility for decisions.

Key Themes

- The IT portfolio management process demands accountability for IT investment decisions from the senior management team in particular, and builds it into the process itself.
- Five particular areas in which executive accountability needs to be exercised in the IT portfolio management process include portfolio strategy, project strategy, resource management, fiscal management, and service quality.
- Portfolio segmentation influences the effectiveness and efficiency of the portfolio management process by changing the way the organization makes trade-off decisions and aligns project scope with the organization's mission.
- The most common IT project segments are financial improvement projects, mission-critical projects, enabling projects, and foundational projects.
- Portfolio segmentation enables delegation of decision making for a particular segment of IT projects to a subset of managers. Portfolio decision rights concern the "who" and "how" of portfolio decision making.
- The portfolio management team (PMT) is ultimately accountable for ensuring optimum return on a portfolio of IT investments. The PMT is a senior leadership team consisting of organizational leaders who have been delegated the authority to make portfolio decisions.
- How PMTs are structured, and how they carry out their responsibilities, will vary from one organizational context to the next. Functional, process, and divisional PMTs, for example, are variations on the basic structure of a PMT governing projects in an organization's various departments.
- The allocation of decision-making authority between the PMT and other actors such as project management teams, functional teams, and so forth is what the issue of IT portfolio "decision rights" is ultimately all about. Portfolio decision making has two dimensions, horizontal and vertical. The most effective PMTs are those that are cross-disciplinary.
- Although certain principles guide the PMT through the process of structuring and allocating decision rights for the

IT portfolio, no single right answer resolves the question of which decisions are made by the PMT versus other groups. The trick is to take advantage of the PMT's senior perspective and authority, while not burdening it with micromanaging projects. In determining decision rights for situations with no necessity for cross-organizational decision making, the key question is whether to delegate.

- Because 70% of most organizations' IT budgets is spent operating, maintaining, enhancing, and supporting the installed base, it is necessary to ensure that some PMT is accountable for the performance of the existing system. The existing system can be divided into infrastructure portfolios, support (service-level) portfolios, and application preservation portfolios—each of which needs to be governed in its own way.

Workflow Design

Method goes far to prevent trouble in business: for it makes the task easy, hinders confusion, saves abundance of time, and instructs those that have business depending, both what to do and what to hope.

—William Penn, *Some Fruits of Solitude*

In designing the workflow for the IT portfolio management process, we need to take account of two factors: the activities (work streams) required by the process itself and the interdependencies between the portfolio management process and other IT management processes. In this chapter, we consider each of these factors in turn.

The Four Work Streams of Portfolio Management

For most organizations, the IT budget process drives the IT portfolio management process. For many organizations, the portfolio process is the 30- to 60-day fire drill people go through every year to prepare for the annual IT budget submission. The budget is relatively static from year to year, based on the previous year's budget plus or minus some percentage. This approach, called *snowplow budgeting* because it takes last year's budget and piles more on top of it, has little to do with business strategy. When CFOs want to reduce it, they just skim off the top. The stuff on the bottom rarely sees the light of day. Portfolio planning occurs at the middle manager level. This kind of process may allow no methodical way to translate business strategy into IT projects. Well-intentioned IT staff attempt to make the translation by soliciting and proposing new ideas (project concepts). They continue to collect ideas until they reach or exceed the budget ceiling. In effect, they plan and build the portfolio from the bottom up. Some middle managers perform project definition and business case analysis. Some don't. Most

131

organizations see relatively little assessment of business performance; show little attempt to translate business performance gaps into improvement initiatives; have no methodical way to translate improvement initiatives into IT implications (project concepts); fail to optimize the portfolio to deliver the business results that the company requires to be successful; and have no way to assess the organizational impact of new projects, by either their number or their type, to determine whether the business can absorb them. If, after all the new projects have been proposed, the resulting portfolio cost exceeds the budget, IT managers mediate or arbitrate to shave the portfolio down to a level commensurate with the budget. Senior leadership, for the most part, delegates responsibility for this activity to the IT managers and middle managers. In the end, the project inventory often contains projects and enhancements that provide only marginal bottom-line value. The total value returned by the portfolio may even be less than the cost (resulting in a net loss on the balance sheet). The portfolio may or may not support the business strategy, because the middle managers may or may not understand the strategy and how to achieve it. At the end of the year, the project portfolio does not get the company where it needed to go and senior leadership is disappointed with the value returned from its IT investments.

An organization proceeding in this way will execute some type of portfolio management process, but it may not achieve the organization's strategy, it may not deliver bottom-line results, and it may not serve the needs of senior leadership. It likely will serve the needs of the people who participate, namely middle managers who have designed the process to address their needs and those of their staff. Middle managers will fill the portfolio with a lot of really good ideas, but most of these improvements will not improve cash flows or provide bottom-line value. Most of these ideas will make jobs easier or employees happier, but may not improve organizational effectiveness. Many of these ideas may also turn into projects that add new applications that, in turn, increase operating expenses for the foreseeable future, adding fixed cost. Some of these projects have merit and should be executed. Some of these projects should be deferred. A few of them should be terminated. A good portfolio management process terminates low-value projects and ensures high-value projects have the resources they need to be successful.

This principle is easy to state, but how do we put it into practice? The IT portfolio management process includes a series of tasks designed to let organizations make the link between the IT portfolio and the organization's strategic objectives and performance goals. If you look at portfolio management as an ongoing process or cycle, it has four major work streams:

- *Inventory and calibration:* Collecting and validating project business case and status information, ensuring that the PMT has an accurate picture of existing (in process) and proposed (in concept) projects
- *Strategic analysis:* Translating the organization's strategic plans and performance targets into missing capabilities, and assuring that the project inventory adequately provides new capabilities and performance levels
- *Decision making:* Facilitating the PMT through changing project scopes and charters, and allocating resources (labor, budget, assets)
- *Chartering:* Communicating the PMT's decisions to the organization, ensuring that the decisions are properly executed and result in the appropriate allocation, or de-allocation, of resources

Portfolio Management Workflow (Dynamic View)

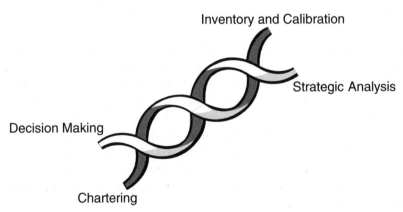

Portfolio Management Workflow (Linear View)

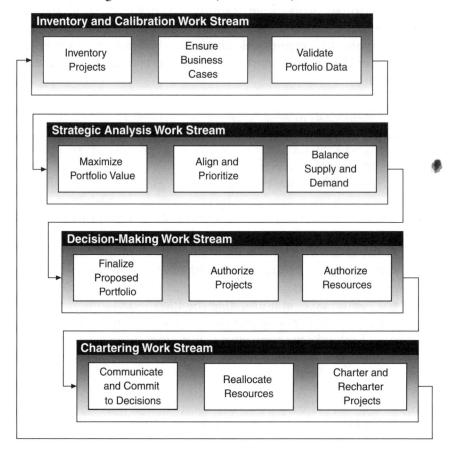

IT portfolio management has increasingly become a dynamic and ongoing process in which the organization executes these work streams in tandem. Business planning occurs continuously rather than cyclically. The portfolio needs to be regularly monitored and adjusted. The greater the risk or uncertainty inherent in the organization or the projects, the more portfolio management must be dynamic. Most organizations make major budget allocation decisions annually, but the portfolio needs to be monitored and adjusted quarterly or monthly. A portfolio management software application comes in handy here. If the organization can get project managers to enter their project information and status on a timely basis, then the organization can preprogram the analysis into the application and obtain near real-time decision-support information. This level of automation makes it easier to rapidly identify trends and business fluctuations, make midcourse corrections to the portfolio and its priorities, and then broadcast these changes to constituents. We will have more to say about software in the next chapter, on *Enablers*.

Inventory and Calibration Work Stream

Spilled water is hard to collect.

    —Chinese proverb

During the inventory and calibration phase, the organization collects information from all existing projects as well as about every proposed new project concept. Project concepts include all projects that the organization would be doing if it had unlimited time and resources. The purpose of documenting project concepts is to understand the *opportunity cost* of the existing portfolio. By better understanding what the organization is not able to do, you can better evaluate whether the organization should keep doing what it's doing or reallocate resources.

    The inventory and calibration phase can be greatly simplified and expedited if the organization is crystal clear on its data collection requirements and definitions. For ongoing projects, most of this information should already exist. If projects utilize good project management methodology, all the information required is out there somewhere. If it isn't, the organization likely has a gap in its project management capabilities. The challenge is to collect the information and put it in a usable format for subsequent analysis. Unfortunately, the information has likely been stored inconsistently and may not be easy to extract. For example, most project managers store project charter and business case information in the form of presentations, documents, and spreadsheets. Few organizations mandate that project managers use a consistent format or a central database. As a result, the organization may find it difficult to roll up information to aggregate it at the portfolio level. Because the organization will need to perform this rollup on an ongoing basis, it should align project management templates and tools to facilitate the portfolio project inventory. Once the portfolio process is operational (steady-state), all the organization has to do is update this information to reflect changes. If project management and portfolio management processes are well integrated, the incremental level of effort required from project managers will be minimal. If project management is less structured or not integrated with portfolio management, the organization will find that the inventory and calibration phase requires considerable effort from project managers.

It is important that strategic analysis phase activities (see the following section) be defined before disrupting project managers' lives in the way that the inventory and calibration phase will. Until the organization knows what analysis to perform, it won't know what data to collect from project managers. Some organizations run off and start collecting data at the outset of their process design, only to find later that they've missed some critical information. Then they need to go back to the project managers and collect more information. After the second or third request for project information, the project managers are going to start to rebel. The quality of the information submitted will deteriorate. The facilitation effort required to obtain the information will increase. Suddenly, project managers start to view the portfolio process as inefficient and their level of support and cooperation decreases. That's not a good way to start a new process. Take extra time to consider what the organization is going to do with the information before setting out to collect project data.

Data requirements for new project concepts may differ from requirements for mature projects. Expect the precision of the information for new project concepts to be much lower than for mature projects. Some of the best ideas begin as ambiguous concepts in someone's head. Middle managers propose new project concepts all the time. Some new project concepts may not have a complete business case or plan. New project concepts will have a lower degree of accuracy in terms of cost, benefits, and risk. An incomplete business case is a sign that the project team has inadequate resources (or motivation) to complete it. In these cases, the PMT may need to charter a small project to develop the business case, or freeze the project until the business analysis is completed. The organization may not want to wait for good ideas to mature before assigning resources to them. The organization may want to incubate high-potential new ideas with the right resources that can rapidly identify whether the project has merit. If people begin working on these concepts unofficially "in their spare time," the PMT loses situational awareness. Don't skimp on the front-end business case analysis and planning. The less invested in the early stages of a project, the less the organization will get from it. Also, don't hesitate to require best-guess estimates for new projects; just don't hold people accountable for delivering on these ballpark estimates. (For further discussion of the business case and the function it performs in the portfolio management process, see the appendix "Business Case Analysis.")

Most organizations have unofficial projects, not fully sanctioned and possibly not even formally acknowledged (a.k.a. skunk works, black projects, etc.), usually a sign of an inefficient or ineffective portfolio management process. The whole point of portfolio management is to allocate resources to those projects that have the greatest potential value. If managers need to circumvent the process to meet the needs of the business, or middle managers believe they need to circumvent the process to be innovative, something is wrong with the process. If the PMT feels that some new concept has potential value, then the PMT should stand up a small project team to research the concept and develop a business case. The PMT cannot effectively balance resources when the organization allows projects to operate outside its purview. Sanctioned projects miss their deadlines because assigned resources are working on unsanctioned projects "in their spare time." Project teams exceed budget, miss deadlines, or cut corners because sanctioned projects do not get the resources or mindshare that they require. Eventually the situation becomes a self-perpetuating cycle, once managers perceive that the most efficient way to run a project is to circumvent the portfolio process. Managers become accustomed to initiating projects without PMT approval, which impairs organizational productivity. When the resource allocation to this set of projects grows, it undermines the portfolio management process and its value proposition. As the PMT loses situational awareness and control over resource allocation, low-value projects consume the organization's resources, and overall return on investment declines rapidly.

The portfolio process should be designed to serve the needs of all projects that serve business needs and provide return on investment, from the beginning of their life cycle to the end. Thus it is important to establish a strict guideline that allows for only minimal circumvention of the process. No project should be "exempt" from it. Err on the side of *inclusion* rather than exclusion of activities. This advice is perhaps somewhat counterintuitive, but the process will be much more efficient if designed under the assumption that it will deal with thousands of projects, both large and small. That assumption will force portfolio management process designers to streamline the process, designing efficiency into it. Based on our experience, it is much more difficult to scale up a process to handle more projects than it is to scale down the process to handle fewer projects. Most people want to focus on the few really big projects that represent the big dollar impacts. That's only logical, except thousands of small projects are likely consume a large portion of the IT budget and have the lowest return on investment. The application maintenance, upgrade, and enhancement budget often becomes a slush fund for every middle manager's pet project. The really big IT projects may consume only 10% to 20% of the IT budget and resources. The organization knows that many of these projects are top priorities, so what good is implementing a portfolio process just for them? (Perhaps the organization should revisit the project governance and accountability structure for these top-priority projects if they are failing.) Sometimes the really hard decisions have to do with how to prevent the organization from wasting time and mindshare on seemingly urgent but relatively unimportant IT service requests. Sometimes it is more difficult to dedicate resources to the truly important and strategic projects because the day-to-day needs of the business keep getting in the way, but here is precisely the place where the PMT should begin to focus its attention.

Don't let special projects operate outside the portfolio management process either. Special projects may require special PMTs, but they don't justify circumventing the process. Highly confidential projects may require an executive PMT. Security projects might require that the PMT be composed of executives with proper security clearances. However, none of these reasons justify circumventing the process. The only way to maintain transparency in projects, priorities, and objectives is to ensure that all projects follow the process.

Despite the need to be inclusive, do not obsess about every project when first launching the portfolio management process. It's okay if a few fall between the cracks at first, as long as the PMT plans to catch them later. Sometimes it is easier and faster to get the organization to adopt the process if it deals with 80% of the IT projects first and worries about the rest later. The process must be designed to easily accommodate 100% of them in the end.

Another aspect to consider, one that is also relevant to the next chapter that discusses strategic analysis, is how often the organization should revisit the portfolio. Different portfolio segments might require different refresh cycles, and some might need a way to trigger portfolio review based on business trends or events. For example, an organization might assess infrastructure segments once or twice a year but might need to assess its strategic application investments on a quarterly or monthly basis. As organizational needs change throughout the year, the portfolio should adjust accordingly. In some instances, the organization may need to trigger interim portfolio reviews based on events or trends. For example, when a company decides to acquire another company it should immediately reassess its portfolio to curtail investments in systems that might be affected by the acquisition (e.g., financial and HR systems) until the full acquisition integration plan is better understood. Deferring these investments could improve corporate financial performance, especially if the system changes can be performed as part of the acquisition integration effort. Hence, the organization will need a way to inventory and calibrate the portfolio periodically, but also on-demand.

Strategic Analysis Work Stream

Life is like a dogsled team. If you ain't the lead dog, the scenery never changes.

—Lewis Grizzard

Whereas the inventory and calibration phase is routine and focused on control, the strategic analysis phase should be exploratory and focused on value. The inventory and calibration phase adds value by ensuring transparency in the portfolio. The strategic analysis phase adds value by maximizing the expected value of the portfolio. In this phase, the PMT needs to ask two questions:

- Is the organization working on the right business problems (doing the right things)?
- Is the organization optimally scoping each project (doing things right)?

The answer to the first question will be relative. It depends on what the opportunity cost of the current portfolio is—that is, what other things could the organization do with its IT resources (people, funds, assets) if they were not otherwise committed? Could it deploy resources to other projects that might be of greater value to the organization? The highest-value projects typically span organizational boundaries, change responsibilities and accountabilities, and generally disrupt the status quo. High-value projects are often uncomfortable, risky, and threatening. It is no surprise that they don't often make it onto the to-do lists created by middle managers. Most middle managers don't even think of suggesting them. Middle managers may also be unwilling to shut down lesser-value projects, where the organization has invested a lot of mindshare and resources, built a coalition of senior executive sponsors, and made claims and promises, even though that may be the best course of action. Don't expect middle managers to jeopardize their reputations or careers by speaking out against popular opinion. Use the portfolio process to make those decisions for them.

What if the organization could manage this front-end process better? What if it could better understand the broadest set of all possible project concepts before decision makers become too committed? What if it could systematically screen project concepts early, before too many resources are expended? What if it could objectively compare and contrast the value proposition of each project? What if the organization could do these things with a minimal investment of resources? The strategic analysis phase should enable it to accomplish all these tasks.

Strategic analysis allows an organization to manage important drivers of behavior in the IT market economy. For example, the organization might hold the maintenance budget flat and force a 5% to 10% annual productivity improvement. This requirement would drive IT implementers to design efficiencies into their applications and processes to achieve this goal in the long run. This shift, in turn, might motivate IT managers to consider additional criteria when evaluating application concepts, such as asset utilization and projected annual maintenance cost, putting pressure on the organization to simplify the application architecture and minimize the number of new platforms. In just this one simple example (one that is perhaps a little optimistic in its assumptions), one can begin to see how portfolio strategy affects all aspects of the IT ecosystem. Hence, even though the organization may evaluate portfolio segments separately, it needs to manage them holistically. The maintenance segment, for example, affects and is affected by the new-development segment. All segments are the responsibility of the PMT, even though most PMTs seem to obsess only about the new-development segment.

Execution of strategic analysis can be done in two ways: top-down and bottom-up. It is possible to use both approaches simultaneously. The bottom-up approach is more commonplace and easier to accomplish, but may provide less value. The bottom-up approach requires the organization to gather all current projects and project concepts and force-rank them within a segment based on estimated value. It is relatively simple in its execution. The hardest part is achieving some degree of consensus or aggregation of rankings. The weakness of the bottom-up approach is that it may not really support the organization's strategy. Middle managers may not address—or even consider—the gap between the strategic objectives and the portfolio's expected outcome. Often, middle managers will aggregate projects in some way to make them meaningful to executives. They may cluster them by strategic goal, for example. This approach may provide the illusion of organizational alignment, but this bottom-up approach works effectively only when project concepts deliver capabilities to meet organizational objectives. It presupposes that managers proposing projects have a sufficiently broad, unbiased perspective and understanding of strategic business needs, which is not always the case.

To make the strategic analysis phase more effective, consider using a top-down approach. The top-down approach begins by clearly articulating the organization's *strategy* to answer three questions:

1. *Where are we going?* Define the long-term goals of the organization. Try to be as quantitative or explicit as possible.
2. *What will make us successful?* Define the capabilities the organization must have to meet its goals. Try to be as specific as possible.
3. *How will we get there?* Define the architecture and set of initiatives (projects) required to deliver these organizational capabilities. The project list should be comprehensive, including projects that address technology, processes, and people.

Most organizations have a vision and have spent some time understanding their strategic goals. If so, then the organization probably has the answer to the first question. If not, then it has quite a bit of strategic thinking to do before it can begin to optimize the portfolio. After all, if the organization does not know where it is going, then how can it optimize the IT portfolio? Entire books are devoted to answering the first question, so we won't dwell on it here. The only team that can validate the answer to the first question is the seniormost leadership team. Only it has the authority to decide where the organization is going. The PMT can facilitate this decision by raising the question in the context of the IT portfolio management process. It might even help by documenting an implicit statement of direction. It is unreasonable, however, to expect to answer the question completely in the context of an IT alignment exercise, even though it is what many organizations do expect.

With the vision and strategic goals as the *desired state,* the organization can proceed to answer the second question: *What will make us successful?* Another way of putting the question is to say that the organization needs to decide what *organizational capabilities* (product, service, and performance) are required to achieve the desired state. Then it must perform a gap assessment by comparing current organizational capabilities against those required to achieve the desired state.

Comprehensive IT Portfolio Strategy

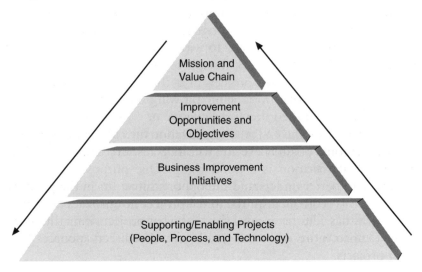

The gaps or shortfalls identified should provide the organization with a summary of missing capabilities for achieving its strategic plan. Note that any overachievement in particular areas may indicate that the organization is overspending on IT in those areas. Specify each of these findings in business (not IT) terms, looking at products, services, process performance, and other relevant factors.

Next, the organization should propose business initiatives (not IT initiatives) to cultivate missing capabilities. Many of the business initiatives will require software applications and infrastructure enablers. Identify these needs, group them into IT project concepts, and add them to your portfolio inventory. The resulting set of current and proposed initiatives is the *core strategic portfolio* (CSP). The CSP establishes the link between business strategy and the IT portfolio. Defining the CSP provides an alternative set of projects to compare with the existing portfolio. An organization might even develop multiple sets of alternatives. It may find multiple ways of achieving the strategy and, hence, various possible CSPs. Each CSP represents one set of projects that the organization could pursue. Ideally, the organization calculates a NPV for each set and selects the one with the highest value. Alternatively, the organization can qualitatively assess each set of projects in terms of how well it achieves the overall mission, given the overall cost and resource impact. The risk of each scenario must be factored into the quantitative or qualitative analysis. (We say more about the subject of risk later in this chapter. See also the discussion of risk analysis as a function of the business case in the Appendix "Business Case Analysis.") In putting together a CSP, keep in mind that a successful strategy has more to do with ability to execute than with brilliant ideas. If the CSP is not feasible or the organization is not able to successfully carry out the projects in it, then the CSP itself is worthless (or even worse than worthless, if it will potentially cost the organization more than the value it delivers).

After defining the CSP, the organization now likely has more projects than it could possibly execute within its resource and budget constraints. That situation is a good thing. One purpose of the CSP exercise is to better understand the opportunity costs in the portfolio even after this refinement of the initial project inventory. The organization now has a better appreciation for what projects it might do if it either (a) had more resources, or (b) could redirect resources from other projects.

This top-down approach to strategic analysis is more time-consuming and difficult than the bottom-up approach, but it is well worth the effort. When properly institutionalized into the planning and budgeting cycle, this top-down approach becomes, with practice, much more efficient and effective than the bottom-up one. It becomes the organization's way of doing business. The top-down approach requires greater involvement by senior leaders and subject-matter experts. Despite its simplicity, few companies invest sufficient time to complete the exercise. Most companies never get past question 1. Questions 2 and 3 require the organization to contemplate doing something other than executing its status quo business processes to achieve its goals. They require the organization consider changing the way it does business.

Regardless of which approach is used, top-down or bottom-up, once the organization has gathered all the projects in the portfolio that it might want in the CSP, it is time to align and prioritize. Before turning this task into a zero-sum game by threatening to cut projects (with winners and losers), first make sure that all the projects are scoped optimally. For example:

- Alter project scope to satisfy multiple departments' needs.
- Bundle maintenance updates and enhancements to reduce release and change management overhead.
- Reduce the scope of any project that costs too much to enable it to proceed, even at the price of reduced application functionality.
- Look across divisions and combine similar endeavors.
- Implement a new process without the underlying software application or with a quick and dirty solution, then add the software next year.

A given organization may not view these suggestions as "optimal," but sometimes they may be the best approach for an organization with limited resources. Organizations are accustomed to project approval being an all-or-nothing game. It doesn't need to be. Sometimes the only way to optimize the whole is to suboptimize the parts.

Once the organization has done everything it can to optimize and consolidate the CSP, the final strategic analysis step is for the PMT to rationalize it, balancing the supply of funding and resources with the demand for projects. Typically decision makers are left with no choice

From Business Strategy to the CSP

A large manufacturing company revamped its strategic planning process to incorporate development of a CSP on a periodic basis. It used a cascading planning process. The business strategy identified the top-level goals. These goals were then applied to each segment of the value chain. Each segment of the value chain, in turn, determined the capabilities it required for success. For example, it was determined that a 10% improvement in supply chain costs would translate into specific business improvements for procurement, order management, and manufacturing. These business improvements would then form the basis for business improvement initiatives such as warehouse consolidation and strategic sourcing. Finally, the PMT evaluated each business initiative, including IT requirements. The PMT selected, redirected, or rejected each business initiative based on the risk-adjusted expected value for the project. The final set of projects was rationalized against resource supply and the organization's capacity for change. The resulting portfolio of business and IT initiatives was then chartered.

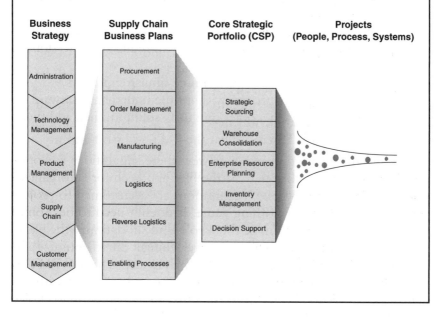

but to defer, cancel, or reject some projects. The trick in using this method in a nonpolitical manner is to assess projects relatively instead of absolutely. Remember that a project concept is the result of someone's idea. Criticize the project and you criticize the idea. In an era where people value innovation, all ideas are good. However, some ideas are more valuable than others. Assess the *relative expected value* of each idea through one of two methods used most often:

- Defining the efficient frontier of projects—the one set of projects that together provide the greatest value, while meeting all the business constraints (budget, resources, etc.). This analysis can be performed many ways, ranging from a simple ranked list of projects based on their value drivers, to pairwise trade-off analysis, to more complex analytical methods.
- Selecting from among several sets of projects, with each representing an alternate portfolio scenario that fits all the business constraints, such as multiple CSPs. Then compare these scenarios and select the one that best fits the organization's needs. This method may be required when a number of highly interdependent projects are in the portfolio. For example, canceling an infrastructure project might require canceling all dependent business projects.

In the early stages of portfolio implementation, agreement on the value drivers used to evaluate projects is more important than the method used for portfolio rationalization. If the PMT buys in to the assessment of the value drivers, it is more likely to support whatever rationalization method is presented to it. If the PMT disagrees with the valuation, the organization will never even get around to using the methodology. So pick a method that the PMT will trust and support. The organization can use multiple methods together. Software utilities are available to help with the analysis, and many of the fully integrated project and portfolio management applications support both types of analysis. Some organizations are more comfortable with a simple ranking while others may embrace a more complex approach. Start simple and continuously improve, after the organization becomes comfortable with its new portfolio management process. Don't try to take too big a step right away.

After the rationalization process just described, it is time to use the value drivers previously discussed to determine how the IT portfolio will be structured to maximize value. Rate each project against its contribution of value to determine which projects have the greatest merit. Because of its imprecision, however, valuation is difficult. A project valuation at the onset is a forecast, not a fact. The business case cannot be calculated factually until the end of the project, once the costs and benefits are realized. Some costs can be forecast with a great deal of accuracy, but the benefits are highly speculative. Everyone has seen or heard of business cases that look good on paper but don't pan out in real life. Studies have shown that more than 50% of financial business cases are highly subjective or speculative. For complex projects, this subjectivity is not the fault of the person performing the analysis. It is a fact of life. Too much is unknown at the onset of a complex project. The project is likely to encounter difficulties that were unanticipated. Even if the organization continuously improves its business case analysis, constantly honing its templates and incorporating learning from past projects, it still may not get the business case right at the onset. For this reason, we recommend that the business case be revisited at the end of each phase of the project. The PMT can then decide whether they want the project to continue.

In the case of financial measures, it is easy to compare metrics across projects, but is that comparison meaningful? Financial analysis too often provides the illusion of accuracy. Organizations that require precision in their benefits forecast can use sophisticated financial investment models, but at the end of the day it will still be a forecast. Each organization needs to decide how much rigor they want to build into the business case analysis. For example, if NPV is a value driver, then it is easy to compare NPV across projects. But what if financial measures are not the only value drivers considered? What if the organization cannot calculate NPV because the projects are too far removed from the bottom line? Or what if financial benefits are only one of several critical metrics, such as in a not-for-profit or governmental organization? What if the organization simply doesn't trust the numbers? In these situations, the organization may need to rate each project against more subjective measures, and introduce human intelligence into the strategic analysis.

For example, let's compare two projects:

- *C2C:* A supply chain project that hopes to reduce cash-to-cash cycle time by 20%, promising an ROI greater than 60% and an NPV of $10 million

- *Sat30:* A customer-service project that hopes to improve customer satisfaction by 30%, promising an ROI greater than 55% and an NPV of $11 million

It becomes immediately evident in this case that the PMT cannot use financial measures alone to rate the projects under consideration, because the numbers are too close. Estimation error could be the sole cause for the differences. The organization needs additional measures of value. So, for example, it may want to understand the breakdown of investment requirements and sources of benefits. The Sat30 project benefits are supposed to come from revenue enhancement. The PMT would need to understand how the Sat30 project team translated a 30% improvement in customer satisfaction into increased revenue. Some degree of speculation is needed in this calculation. However, the same may be true for the C2C project, where the projected benefits come from cost reduction. It looks like the organization should add some type of confidence interval into the value analysis. What assumptions did each team make in terms of organizational consolidation and process change? Is the organization ready and willing to make the required change? Perhaps the team assumed a major consolidation of departments and changes to delegations of authority. Is the organization ready to make those changes? Can the organization make the changes as fast as the team thinks it will? The PMT needs answers to these questions, and the project teams will need to provide this type of information in their business cases. If the project teams have not considered these questions, they need to go back and complete their homework.

We could go on for many pages defining all sorts of metrics that might be used in the strategic analysis phase of the portfolio management workflow design, but do not try to come up with every possible metric that your organization *might* use. When first rolling out the process, stick to a small set of balanced metrics that allow the PMT to triangulate on the right decision by looking at the problem from multiple perspectives. These perspectives might include the following:

- *Financial:* What will the project do to the bottom line? Metrics include cash flow, capital investment, NPV, and payback period.
- *Desired customer experience:* How will the project affect customer satisfaction? Metrics include sales impact, customer churn, customer satisfaction, and market share.

- *Organizational impact:* What is the resource and cultural impact? Metrics include resources requirements, business disruption, and degree of change (process, policy, delegation of authority, organization, etc.).
- *Risk:* Do we understand the expected value, given the likelihood of risks? Metrics include controllable risk, uncontrollable risk, technology risk, schedule risk, change risk, and vendor risk.
- *Interdependencies:* Is the project dependent on other projects or activities? Metrics include impact on other projects if this project fails, and impact on this project if another project fails.

As your portfolio management process matures, add metrics that help to dissect the investment decision-making process. Don't try to create some type of artificial intelligence application that completely automates it. Most organizations will at first be suspicious of the metrics if they previously made decisions subjectively. The more ad hoc the current process, the less comfortable the PMT may be with a highly structured approach. At first, the PMT may distrust the accuracy of the metrics and resist mechanizing the decision-making process. Although it will be hard at first to get a consistent set of accurate metrics from the project managers, they will become accustomed to calculating the metrics and calibrating across projects throughout the organization. The organization needs to become comfortable with the process and the decision-making methods it entails. Even with the right variables, it will be difficult to get all the senior leaders to make the hard decisions. Keep it simple at first.

Decision-Making Work Stream

If one does not decide when one should, one will suffer the consequences.

—Chinese proverb

The decision-making phase of the portfolio management workflow design should be straightforward, if the organization has done its homework in the first two phases. If not, then decision making can be the death of the new portfolio management process. PMT decision makers will likely evaluate the viability of the process based solely on this phase, because they engage the most at this point. If the analysis and recommendations presented to it are not logical, or if the organization does not support the analysis, the PMT may start to question the analysis, and the entire decision-making process can unravel.

A good decision meeting holds no surprises, for the presenters or the PMT. Therefore, in addition to performing all the analysis, the organization also needs to prep the PMT so it knows what to expect when it walks into the decision meeting. Distribute meeting material far enough in advance so that the organization has time to brief each PMT member and answer any questions he or she may have. Each PMT member should have plenty of time to talk with any of the project managers to understand the situation better. If the organization attempts to rush the decision making, then either the PMT will stonewall the decisions or will not sufficiently engage. A decision stonewalled by the PMT may spin off into a never-ending cycle of rehashing the same decisions over and over. If the PMT does not sufficiently engage, then it starts down a slippery slope of abdicating accountability. If PMT members are to be accountable for making the decisions, they deserve sufficient time to consider the inputs to those decisions.

In the first few iterations of a new portfolio management process, someone trained in portfolio management should schedule one-on-one meetings with each PMT member. Take the time to walk each PMT member though the analysis and recommendations. Ask questions to ensure understanding and buy-in. Be sure to leave time for both education and discussion. During the initial few cycles of the portfolio management process, educate the PMT members on the process. Tell them what decisions they need to make and when they need to make them. Explain their responsibilities. Don't expect them to remember how the process works. PMT members are typically senior leadership team members and they have a lot on their minds. In time they will learn the process. Until they learn and institutionalize the process, however, the organization needs to provide a coach or facilitator. (For more detail on how to help prepare PMT members for meetings, see the section on "Decision Support" in the *Enablers* chapter.)

Structuring the PMT meeting helps make it successful. Some people think that good meetings happen if you have well-intentioned people. They don't. Bad meetings happen to good people, too. Most people assume that senior managers naturally run effective and efficient meetings. After all, they are in meetings all day; you'd think they would have learned how to meet. Wrong. They haven't. More often than not, their meetings are disorganized, inefficient, and ineffective. Most people also assume that any manager can facilitate well. Wrong. Facilitation is a skill rarely taught in any management training class. Worse yet, if several different managers attempt to control the meeting, it may not achieve its objectives. A favorite game managers like to play when they don't want to make a decision is to derail the meeting. You need to be ready to prevent all these possibilities. Don't be afraid to add structure. Establish clear meeting objectives, an agenda, and ground rules. Review the objectives, agenda, and ground rules with the PMT at the opening of the meeting and provide the opportunity for the PMT to buy in to them. Then make sure you have a good facilitator at the meeting. In the long run, most good senior executives will value a resolute but diplomatic facilitator. Good facilitators know when to dictate and when to guide the team to the right answer via subtle questions (*guided discovery*).

It is also helpful to conspire with the PMT chairperson before the meeting, to agree on the approach and meeting objectives, agenda, and ground rules. Clarify the expectations and roles. Decide who will facilitate. Discuss how the chairperson wants to handle significant disagreements among the team members. If the chairperson is more senior, he or she may be comfortable arbitrating when the PMT does not achieve consensus. However, the chairperson may not want to dominate the meeting, and might require the facilitator to have a contingency approach (such as structured dispute resolution). For the first few meetings, organizations might want to bring in a professional executive facilitator with experience in keeping senior executives on track and driving them to consensus. Keep in mind that the choice of an executive facilitator can be, shall we say, "career-determining," and make every effort to find the right person for the job.

The PMT chairperson needs to ensure that each member is represented at the meeting. Decide whether the PMT will allow delegates. If so, then delegates must be empowered to decide on behalf of their respective PMT members. If PMT members miss a meeting, then the chairperson cannot allow absent members to blame bad decisions on their peers. This behavior can become dysfunctional and erodes accountability. Along these lines, it is also a best practice to schedule extra time for the initial PMT meetings. Figure out how much time you think they will need and then double it. If the meeting runs over and a follow-on meeting is scheduled, PMT members may forget what transpired or, worse yet, not attend the follow-up meeting. It might take months to schedule a follow-up meeting with everyone present.

The types of decisions made by the PMT will likely depend on how comfortable it is with the portfolio management process. A less mature organization will likely start with some basic decisions. A more mature organization might be able to move through the basic decisions quickly, allowing time to focus on more strategic ones. The progression followed often looks something like this[1]:

Creating Investment Awareness

• What projects are in process?
• What new projects are in queue?
• Who is the business sponsor for each?
• Who is the project manager for each?
• How much are we currently spending on each?
• What is overall IT budget breakdown by element of expense? By department? By capital spending?
• Where are resources currently allocated?
• How will we staff new projects?

Building the Investment Foundation

• How do the projects link to business initiatives?
• What is the prioritization of the business initiatives?
• What are the costs and benefits of each project? How do we objectively identify and assess qualitative benefits?
• What is the risk of each project? How do we objectively break down and assess risk?
• How do the projects rank in NPVterms? In qualitative terms?

Developing a Complete Portfolio

• Have level 1 and 2 questions been answered not only for business application-related projects but for *all* projects (maintenance, operations, service improvement, infrastructure, etc.)?

---

[1] United States General Accounting Office IT Investment Management Maturity Stages.

- Do projects incorporate not only IT tasks but all activities required to make them successful, including process, organizational, and facilities tasks?
- Do all projects have a complete business plan that addresses strategic alignment, governance, organizational change management, and risk mitigation plans?
- What is our unit cost variance (improvement or deterioration in IT service unit costs for the same service levels and volumes)? What corrective action is needed?
- What is our service-level variance (improvement in performance metrics at same unit costs and volumes)? What corrective action is needed?
- What is our volume variance (unanticipated excess or shortfall in business demand for IT services)? What corrective action is needed?

Improving the Investment Process

- Is the PMT fully empowered to make all portfolio decisions? If not, how do we overcome or mitigate the obstacles?
- How can we improve our decision-support information (transparency and situational awareness) to make more effective portfolio decisions?
- How can we improve the IT portfolio management process to make it more efficient?
- How can we improve the integration of IT portfolio management with the other management processes to make the management system more efficient and effective?

Leveraging IT for Strategic Outcomes

- How do we need to adjust overall spending to accommodate the anticipated economic climate? How will spending adjustments be allocated to each portfolio segment in the form of constraints or augmentation?
- What is our CSP? (Where are we going? What will make us successful? How will we get there?)
- How does each project fit into the desired-state enterprise architecture?

- What unit cost and service-level efficiencies have been achieved? How do our unit costs for IT service delivery compare with those of commercial third parties, industry peers, and competitors (benchmarking)? What corrective action is needed?

Chartering Work Stream

Good speech need not be behind other's backs.

—Chinese proverb

In the final, chartering phase of the process, the PMT needs to come up with a list of decisions and action items, and determine how that information will be disseminated after the meeting. Clear decisions are easy to document. A good indication that decisions are vague occurs when it is difficult to articulate them. Project teams need to know not only the decisions made but also why and how these decisions will affect their projects. Delays or ambiguity in furnishing critical information can send the organization into a tailspin as people try to interpret the decisions. Multiple interpretations can turn into conflict, cause follow-up meetings, and create additional confusion. Too much uncertainty will render the portfolio process ineffective.

Commit to carrying out the PMT's decisions as a matter of honor as soon as the decisions are final. The more public the commitment, the harder it is for the organization to reverse or resist the decisions. It is also important to tie the decisions to the budget and financial management processes. As resources are reallocated, budgets should change accordingly to reinforce accountability. If projects promise benefits, then financial planning projections should be adjusted to account for those benefits. To ensure optimal return on project investments, require the PMT members to sign up for the revenue and cost improvements at the time they charter a project and approve the business case, which in turn will drive accountability for results. If a CRM application promises to increase revenue or decrease cost, then adjust the financial plan at the time the PMT approves the business case. This adjustment ensures senior management accountability for *results,* which will motivate it to take greater care when making decisions. The PMT cannot allow a project to fail without obtaining the desired improvement some other way. If it cancels the project, it can change the forecast or use the funds another way. A lot of people ask how to track the results of IT and project investments. Don't track them. Book them! Build the expected benefits into the financial forecast or resource plan. This approach avoids the need to track them separately. Tracking is an overhead cost and does not really establish accountability. More importantly, booking the results at the time the PMT approves the business case ensures senior management accountability for achieving project benefits. Once the PMT commits to the forecast, it is difficult for team members to change it without shutting down the project.

Interdependencies

Our technology forces us to live mythically, but we continue to think fragmentarily, and on single, separate planes.
— Marshall McLuhan, *The Medium Is the Message*

IT portfolio management is part of the enterprise IT management system. (For a diagram of the whole IT management system and the place of IT portfolio management within it, see the chapter on *IT Portfolio Management: What It Can Do and How It Works.*) As such, it naturally intersects with a number of other IT management processes and needs to be managed in conjunction with them. This section briefly outlines those IT management processes that have the greatest interdependence with IT portfolio management and considers the relationships between the former and the latter.

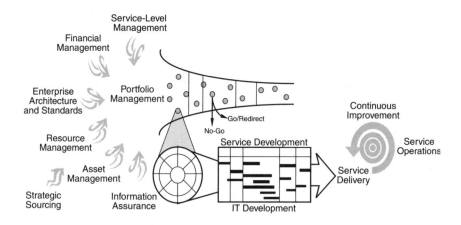

Service Development Process

We already discussed the need to integrate service development project information (as well as information connected with other IT management processes) with portfolio management to avoid redundant data. (See *IT Portfolio Management: What It Can Do and How It Works.*) Doing so will not only avoid inefficiencies but also enable the organization to act more quickly on new information, providing managers with shared situational awareness. We also discussed the need to align project and portfolio decision making, to keep projects aligned with ever-changing business conditions. The easiest way to integrate such elements of the IT management system with portfolio decision making is to hold the PMT accountable and responsible for results: the PMT makes concept phase and business case decisions as well as the "go/no-go" decision at the end of the plan/design phase of a project. Once the PMT approves the concept and business case for a service development project, the PMT can delegate *execution accountability* to the project's governance team (e.g., a project steering committee). As long as the project does not vary significantly from the business case (cost and benefits), and business conditions do not require a change in objectives (results), the PMT does not need to reengage in project-level decisions. In effect, both the project team and the PMT agree to a contract. The project team agrees to execute the plan and deliver on commitments in exchange for the resources (people, funding, assets) identified by the plan. The PMT agrees to provide the resources in the plan in exchange for deliverables provided on time and within budget. Some organizations go as far as to establish a real paper contract. After all, if the IT project were outsourced the vendor would require one. Why not ensure the same level of commitment internally that you would establish with a total stranger?

With proper planning, the PMT can approve the business case and charter (or recharter) the project during periodic PMT meetings. Contrary to common practice, organizations don't need four-hour meetings to review a project. If everyone does their homework in advance, the decision itself does not take long. Some organizations fear that the PMT decision-making cycle will increase delays in starting new projects. It may at first, but it is not healthy to obsess about time-to-start until the process matures. For organizations with less mature processes, the important metric is *time-to-results*. Many a project would benefit from a little more thought prior to chartering. How many projects receive a scope change that could have been avoided if the organization had not been so hasty in starting the project?

Effective and aligned portfolio and service development processes force the organization to create and follow better plans and give it an ability to make better decisions, which results in faster time-to-results. Forcing project review by the PMT prior to chartering also requires middle managers to plan ahead. The need for most projects can be anticipated if the business and IT managers plan ahead. Within a year of implementing a robust portfolio management process, the number of projects initiated at the eleventh hour should be less than 1%, a number small enough to handle via an exception procedure. In the interim, it is good to put a spotlight on these rush projects, analyzing them to determine how best to *prevent* them in the future. Don't make it too easy for exceptions, lest the organization have no motivation for changing its poor planning behavior. Most rush projects are the result of a breakdown somewhere else in the IT management system. More often than not they are due to poor business planning, which means that the PMT didn't do a good enough job during the strategic analysis phase. Perhaps it used the bottom-up approach instead of the top-down approach. The PMT will need to strike a balance between being responsive to business needs and establishing a cadence for decision making. Remember that quality processes are free. It is the poor-quality processes that cause the organization to waste time and money. Keep the organization focused on removing the systemic causes of failure.

Integration of Portfolio, Project, and Service Development Management

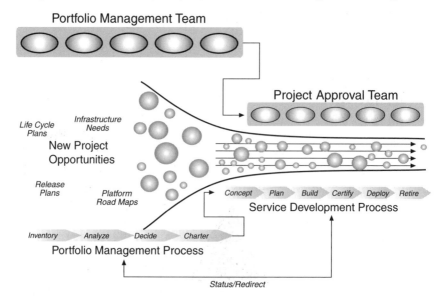

Resource Management

IT portfolio management is an investment management process, and resources represent a significant percentage of IT investment. Typically, more than 60% of IT costs are labor-related. In a perfect world, resources would be completely fungible, but that is not the reality. Resources are not generic. Resources are people and people have different skills and aptitudes. In the long run you can develop new capabilities in employees, but in the short term consider their skill sets to be fixed. Contract labor on a short-term basis may offer more flexibility, but it typically comes at a premium price. Even outsourced resources are not completely fungible. For example, do not expect to hold an outsourcer accountable for business stability (operations and maintenance) and at the same time tell the outsourcer that you want ultimate resource flexibility. Business stability requires a degree of resource stability. Effective resource management requires an understanding of long-term (12-month) resource and skill needs, critical skill requirements, and emerging skill needs.

At some level, portfolio management and resource management need to be integrated. You cannot make portfolio decisions without

Workforce Management

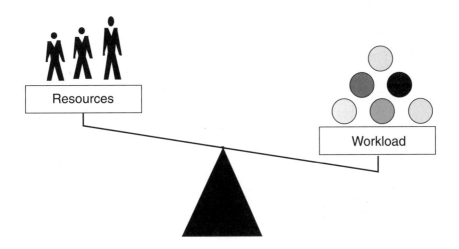

allocating resources. If the PMT does not understand the resource requirements for a project and does not know whether those resources exist, then the PMT cannot ensure the success of the project. Chartering a new project with known resource risks is not a good practice. Resource risk is a controllable risk that the PMT is responsible for mitigating, not exacerbating.

Portfolio management supports various resource management approaches, ranging from aggregate resource management (headcount management) to named-resource assignment. Aggregate resource management will require that resource discussions take place ex ante. Resource decisions are made in advance of PMT meetings, contingent on certain projects being approved. Therefore, in advance of the PMT meeting, the organization must perform what-if analysis on each possible scenario, and check back with the resource "owners" to ensure that the resourcing scenarios are feasible. This approach works best if project decisions can be made well in advance of the project launch, to allow time to transition resource assignments and recruit the right staff. Organizations that have three or four months' line-of-sight to new projects and can make resource decisions that far in advance are able to use aggregate resource management. This approach does have inherent inefficiencies, because the PMT is likely to reject some recommendations, which will periodically throw your resource managers into a tizzy as they try to accommodate portfolio decisions. The worst-case scenario is that the PMT makes decisions that are impractical, which results either in the need for a follow-up PMT meeting or in decisions that don't stick. Or the organization suffers (trying to do too much with too little) because middle managers are afraid to speak up and tell the PMT members that they have messed up. The other weakness of this approach is that it allows the PMT to abdicate responsibility for addressing resource constraints (balance demand with supply) at the outset. If the PMT does not have to address real resource assignments, then it has no appreciation for how much productivity might be lost by assigning the wrong resources to the right projects.

Named-resource management, where you schedule and track each staff member, is a more disciplined process. If your current resource management process is ad hoc (informal), trying to implement a new portfolio management process and a new resource management process might be too much change for your organization to handle. For some organizations, taking project and resource decisions out of the hands of middle managers may be too much for process designers, senior leaders, and middle managers to handle. Process designers may not have the experience and capacity to redesign and implement both portfolio and named-resource management processes. If the process is not robust, senior leaders might not have adequate visibility into resource capabilities and skill requirements, thereby prohibiting them from making informed decisions.

Few organizations are prepared to enable a central PMT to assign resources. Few organizations have the project planning discipline required to provide an accurate forecast of resources. Inaccuracy in resource planning will result in inaccurate portfolio decisions, which will cause the organization to iterate portfolio decisions. Then cultural (political) issues must be considered. What's in it for the managers? What manager will voluntarily give up resource assignment authority? Resources are the lifeblood of the organization. If you control resources, you have organizational power. You can sit around and debate project priorities, but if you don't have any resources to execute the projects, the discussion is futile. If middle managers are to be accountable for project results, they want to control their resources, because resources are the tool they use to drive success. Besides, managers are typically compensated based on the number of resources they control. The amount of resources you controlled last year is likely to determine the amount of resources you will control this year, plus or minus. Hence, middle managers prefer to make decisions within their functional silos, rather than risk losing their resources.

What most process designers fail to appreciate is that a fundamental change in resource accountability and responsibility is implicit in going to a new resource management model. If middle managers do not select projects (the purview of the PMT) and they do not assign resources (also the purview of the PMT), then what do they do? In the past, they focused on managing project managers and developing resources. However, good portfolio, project, and resource management practices ensure that anyone staffed on a project is successful because the processes ensure success. In effect, they move the organization to a commercial IT service provider model where portfolio, project, and resource decision-making roles are matrixed into the organization. IT organizations should thus begin to separate resource ownership from compensation decisions. They should begin valuing project and service management skills over functional management skills. Managing a large implementation project and managing service quality are far more valuable skills than performing administrative tasks. Too often functional, project, and service management roles are combined into individual job descriptions, which is too much for any manager to handle effectively.

The senior executive team might want to change, but it might not appreciate that changing the role of middle managers requires behavioral changes at all levels of the organization. Resources need to understand what is expected of them. Middle managers need to learn how to lead through process, instead of using a command-and-control leadership style. In addition, senior leaders need to invest the time, money, and patience to enable this transition to occur. A strong organization might absorb all this change at once, but other organizations might want to consider phasing them in over time. If you do not already have a strong resource management process, then plan to loosely couple portfolio and resource management using the aggregate approach, allowing extra time during the analysis and decision-making phases to consult resource managers. You can improve resource management over time, as the portfolio management process matures and the organization becomes more confident. An organization with strong portfolio and service development processes can live with some inefficiency in resource management. An organization with weak portfolio and service development processes may never stop firefighting, which may appear to be a resource management problem. In fact, implementing better resource management will not put out the fires, but only enable you to dispatch the firefighters faster. Have you ever calculated the productivity of firefighters? They spend a lot of time waiting for fires and going from fire to fire, but what percentage of their time do they spend fighting them? It might be a good model for emergency response, but when used for IT service delivery it is very expensive.

For further discussion on resource management, see the discussion of portfolio throughput and optimized resources in the chapter *Articulating—and Achieving—Benefits of IT Portfolio Management.*

Enterprise Architecture and Standards

Enterprise architecture and standards (EA&S) provide shared situational awareness to the entire organization's operating model and enable the PMT and functional review teams to manage by exception.

Traditional IT practitioners will equate the term *architecture* with a representation of hardware and software. Enterprise architecture, however, includes the technical architecture as well as the process and organizational views. It is a broader scope that becomes increasingly necessary as organizations achieve diminishing returns from technology investments and must combine process and organizational changes with technology to obtain greater value from investments.

The purpose of any architecture is integration: to ensure that each component of the system operates efficiently and effectively with other components. The purpose of IT architecture is to ensure that each application and hardware component operates in harmony with—or is properly isolated from—other components. The purpose of *enterprise architecture* is to ensure that processes, technology, and organizational responsibilities operate in concert. Enterprise architecture provides the PMT and other decision makers with situational awareness of how the organization operates. In the absence of an enterprise architecture rendering, each decision maker has a different perception of how the organization operates. It is like the proverbial blind men trying to develop common understanding of what an elephant looks like. They might be able to piece together their individual impressions over time and arrive at a shared picture, but wouldn't it be better if every senior leader had a common view of the whole elephant from the beginning? Enterprise architecture renderings show how each project fits into the bigger picture. They provide traceability from the business workflow requirements through to the IT infrastructure requirements. This feature allows designers to take a 360-degree look at what an application might affect (people, process, and technology) if changed, providing IT practitioners better contextual awareness of their actions, and helping business and IT managers understand the complexity involved in changing critical components (workflow, technology, policy, and roles). Finally, they help the PMT better understand the business implications of a project.

Like resource management, EA&S needs to be integrated into the portfolio management process. The PMT determines the cost structure of the organization. In so doing, it creates incentives (or disincentives) for efficient designs of process and systems. If the PMT values a better understanding of the enterprise architecture, it may sponsor its documentation or at least require some chief architect to learn the architecture and advise the PMT. If the organization wants to standardize, it had better get the PMT to understand, buy in to (accept accountability for), and enforce the standards. If the PMT is oblivious to the full effect of its decisions on the enterprise architecture, then it leaves to chance the possibility of achieving any benefits from EA&S. Consequently, huge investments in EA&S will not return significant value without the PMT on board and the EA&S activities integrated with the portfolio management decision making.

Contrary to popular belief, EA&S is not supposed to constrain the organization but to enable it. Projects with designs that comply with EA&S guidelines should move through the portfolio management processes without difficulty. The organization manages the design decisions by exception, trapping only those designs that do not comply with EA&S. The PMT or project governance team stops projects that do not comply to enable the organization to evaluate whether the enterprise architecture is flawed, the standards are obsolete, or the project design is unsuitable. Failure to trap noncompliant projects removes the teeth from the EA&S process.

The PMT is accountable for EA&S standards decisions. The enterprise architecture process consists of analysis (design) and decision-making (governance) activities. Enterprise architecture decisions are *business decisions* that must be made by the PMT in the context of the strategic plan and the bottom line. After the PMT buys in to the enterprise architecture, then standards (for technology, process, facilities, human resources, etc.) can be established by the functional disciplines to facilitate the transition to the desired state. In the absence of an accepted future-state enterprise architecture rendering, technical standards decisions are made without a well-understood and agreed-upon roadmap (a time-sequenced list of required initiatives) that defines how the organization will make the transition from the current state to the desired state. Hence, for example, one manager thinks that standardization is the right answer while another thinks that decentralized autonomy is. One manager thinks that growth is most important while another thinks that cost containment is. Both may be the right answer, depending on what part of the business from which one is viewing things. Most staff functions strive for efficiency while most customer-facing functions strive for growth. As long as these parts of the organization hold conflicting visions, the effect of EA&S will be marginal at best. Rather than arguing such points, the organization as a whole is better served by creating the desired-state enterprise architecture rendering, and making all decisions in terms of how effectively and efficiently the standards effect a transition to the desired enterprise architecture.

Conflicting Visions

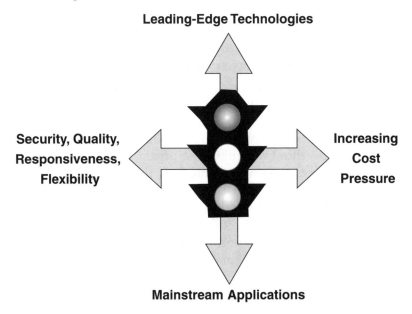

Because the objective of enterprise architecture is to gain common situational awareness of the desired state of the organization—including responsibilities, processes, and technology—the differences between creating an actionable enterprise architecture and one that sits on a shelf include the following:

- Understanding who is accountable for the outcome
- Determining which responsibilities those who are accountable are willing to delegate to a subteam
- Determining who will represent the organization on that subteam

Enterprise architecture is not exclusively an IT activity, because the most critical enterprise architecture decisions are workflow decisions, which are typically not IT decisions at all. Too often the organization will charter the IT department to go off, develop the architecture, and come back with a drawing. In part, this conception arises because the term *architecture* has a legacy rooted in technical activities (technology, engineering, construction, etc.). Business leaders

are not as comfortable with enterprise architecture, whereas IT organizations have dealt with architecture issues for decades. Given the increasing number of transformational efforts requiring synchronized
changes to processes, organizational structure, and technology, however, business leaders must learn to manage EA&S and take a proactive role in its definition.

It follows then that the primary reason EA&S efforts fail is often
insufficient participation by the business functions. More than 50% of
architecture projects are overseen by IT managers with little or no
business involvement. The enterprise architecture project degenerates
into a technology architecture exercise. Another common reason for
EA&S project failure is that the EA&S team attempts to get the design right the first time. Although this intention may sound efficient,
it is not particularly effective. Few organizations have a common understanding of the current-state architecture and issues. So, it is not
reasonable to expect people to agree from the start about what the desired state should look like.

To be successful, the EA&S team must establish common situational awareness of the current-state issues and root causes as well as
buy-in to the desired-state enterprise architecture. Accomplishing this
buy-in often requires an iterative approach that brings the organization along step-by-step. The thought leaders may be three steps ahead
of the rest of the organization, but it is not likely that the organization
will just accept their expert opinion and move on from there. Thought
leaders need to be patient and lead the organization through each step
in the thought process. They need to guide the organization to the
right answer, not cram it down their throat. Achieving buy-in may also
require compromise. If the EA&S team develops a perfect architecture, from an engineering perspective, but the key decision makers do
not truly support the vision, then the EA&S effort has failed. The
EA&S team may need to compromise technical efficiency to accommodate political differences or real financial constraints. This concept
is a difficult one for technologists and engineers to accept. It might
take the organization several iterations over several years before the key
stakeholders see the wisdom of the "perfect" architecture and are willing to support it. On the other hand, they may decide that the organization is inherently imperfect and, hence, cannot support the perfect
architecture. In enterprise architecture, as in life, the best choice is not
always the ideal answer.

Yet another reason EA&S efforts fail is that the project team suffers from *documentation paralysis:* it becomes maniacally focused on creating drawings and loses sight of the project objective. The best enterprise architecture can be written on a napkin if such a basic representation is what it takes to get the organization to buy in. More likely, the team will get caught in the trap of building complex models. These models have value in highly complex applications, but they take a considerable amount of time to build and often are not easily understood by the decision makers. They are often time-consuming to maintain. Unfortunately, most of the tools are designed for analysis, not presentation of the enterprise architecture renderings to senior leadership. This focus causes the EA&S team to create even more documentation to communicate to management and the rest of the organization. Before you know it, the team is devoting more time to documentation than it is to making meaningful recommendations. The team becomes resistant to change, because it is so time-consuming to make those changes. The effort it takes to maintain the models becomes prohibitive, the team becomes obstinate, the PMT loses patience, and a lot of resources are wasted.

Enterprise architecture is most effective when performed iteratively. Like all models, enterprise architecture models should start out simple and imperfect, and improve over time as the organization learns. Begin by notionally sketching out the processes, technologies, and responsibilities using simple block diagrams. Then the EA&S team can add more detail once a conceptual understanding of, and consensus on, the desired state is achieved. As the EA&S team drills down, it will need to involve additional decision makers. The senior leadership is not going to make detailed design decisions, so approval teams for each discipline are needed to make the detailed decisions. The pace of the EA&S team should match the rate at which the organization can learn. If the EA&S team gets too far out ahead of the organization, the EA&S team will have to slow its pace to obtain consensus. Think of an EA&S effort as a marathon in which the EA&S team needs to stay just in front of the rest of the pack. If it gets too far out in front, it will burn itself out before the race is finished. The marathon is long and runs on a track, each lap representing an increasing level of detail. The challenge in this marathon is that the pack has a tendency to get bored and wander off. The EA&S team will need to keep them sufficiently motivated and on track.

Why Standardization Is a Business Decision

Consider one mid-sized manufacturer of electrical components that standardized its ERP and CRM systems on Oracle
software. The firm spent hundreds of hours researching the options and driving the organization to consensus. All that time was
wasted when it decided to implement Siebel in its call center. The
call center management argued that the Siebel software was better suited to its needs. Later, the organization decided to integrate its call center software with its order management software,
so that call center agents could provide customers with estimated
ship dates. The TCO—which now included the considerable cost
of integrating Oracle and Siebel compounded by the ongoing
maintenance cost of two application platforms plus integration—
more than offset any incremental value that Siebel offered in the
first place.

Large organizations spend millions of dollars and thousands of
hours of their top technologists' time establishing standards and technology architectures. The goal of these efforts has typically been to reduce the future installed-base complexity. However, creating standards
in a business strategy and enterprise architecture vacuum is a waste of
time and money. More often than not, the time invested in standards
development is wasted when the business decides it "needs" a particular application that adds complexity to the installed base.

Financial Management

We made the point previously that IT portfolio decisions and funding
decisions go hand in hand. The relationship between portfolio management and IT financial management is obviously a crucial interdependency that the portfolio management process must take into
account. Traditional IT budgeting approaches are not especially effective. An organization that invested heavily in IT last year may not war-

rant the same level of investment this year. Budget allocations are typically based more on history than on project merit. At the other end of the spectrum, zero-based budgeting, where managers must justify every dollar spent, is too time-consuming and prone to human error. Most managers do not have a good enough understanding of their cost structure to predict their budget needs from the ground up with a high degree of accuracy.

Implemented properly, a well-integrated portfolio and financial management process will transform IT budgeting methods. Together portfolio and financial management enable the organization to understand and predict IT expenses. They provide senior leadership with a method for driving down fixed costs over time. The traditional snowplow budgeting method is archaic in comparison. Discussions of service levels and project priorities replace budget discussions. Discretionary investments (budgets) are determined via the portfolio management process. The PMT evaluates investments based on merit and assigns resources, or not. This method allows the PMT to more rapidly move resources (funds, labor, and assets) from lower-priority projects to higher-priority ones, within or across organizations, as merited. This approach helps the organization focus on its priorities, and provides tremendous financial flexibility by reallocating or releasing funds previously held captive in stovepiped budgets.

Portfolio-based budgeting also allows shifts in resources between different types of projects (customer-facing, internal improvement, etc.). Ideally, all resources are virtually pooled by portfolio segment. As the PMT is able to shift more and more resources into the discretionary investment pool, away from fixed operating expenses, the organization increases its flexibility in shifting the allocation of resources among priorities within a segment as well as across the various segments. The PMT can more easily make a strategic decision to shift the mix of investments in response to market and economic conditions. It includes the option to withhold funds when business turns down, as well as to temporarily infuse the organization with funds when business turns up. Perhaps the biggest benefit of portfolio-based budgeting is its implicit increase in organizational accountability for properly scrutinizing investments prior to allocating funds. We take away the age-old excuse ("But we've always done it that way") of allocating resources a certain way.

Notional Timing of Portfolio Management and Budgeting Cycles

IT strategy and budget are aligned via an iterative process

IT Portfolio and Roadmap Planning

| Solicit customer input | Develop next period's portfolio | Approve road map and project priorities |

Financial Planning (Budgeting)

| Review prior year's budget | Set financial targets/ constraints | Propose budgets and allocations | Approve financial plans |

July   Oct.

© Copyright 2004 Pittiglio Rabin Todd & McGrath, Inc. Used with permission.

Comprehensive IT Financial Management

Comprehensive IT financial management consists of three dimensions: financial accounting, cost accounting, and cost allocation. *Financial accounting* is the most commonplace of the three financial dimensions, being the same for IT as for other types of expense. The IT department needs to deal with the same procurement and accounting issues as other departments. IT depreciation and amortization can be somewhat tricky only because IT assets can be copious, distributed, and relatively difficult to track. Assets need to depreciate (amortize) as fast as, or faster than, their useful life; otherwise, the organization's annual expenses are inflated compared to the value received from those assets.

The extreme scenario is when assets remain on the books long after they cease to create value (such as a PC depreciated over 5 years when it is only used for 3 years). Many IT managers struggle with inflated budgets because depreciation expenses remain long after an asset has been redeployed or retired. In theory, these expenses are written off when the asset is retired, but because it is difficult to track the thousands of IT assets on the books, many accounting departments have chosen to leave them there until they are fully depreciated. IT asset management can be a source of frustration for IT managers, especially when they often are accountable for the expense but may not have made the initial investment decision and may not have authority for managing the devices distributed throughout the organization. These maintenance and depreciation expenses are a problem because they affect cost accounting and allocations for IT service.

Cost accounting is perhaps the most important and most neglected IT management practice. *IT cost accounting* tracks how expense items are utilized to deliver services. Departmental IT financial ledgers provide insight into *how much* is spent, but do not provide transparency into *why* the money was spent—where those expenses are going. The only way to manage IT service provision efficiently is to manage service cost. The only way to understand service cost is through cost accounting. No reputable commercial IT service provider would operate without cost accounting, just as no reputable supply chain manager would operate without it. Nevertheless, most in-house IT service providers lack cost accounting capabilities. Most IT managers get into trouble year after year because they cannot differentiate among increases in cost due to volume (growth, usage), quality (functionality, service level), and operations. Many CFOs require that IT service providers fund volume and quality improvements through operating cost efficiencies, yet most internal IT departments cannot track these levers, so they are unable to explain cost fluctuations in terms that the CFO can understand. Some IT departments attempt to reverse-engineer the information, but they lose credibility if the CFO believes the information is contrived because it did not come directly from the financial applications. At the end of the day, it is difficult to determine definitively what caused expense increases, making it difficult to assign the incremental expense to services and, ultimately, to the business unit that should incur the service allocation cost.

Cost allocation is critical to maintaining equilibrium in the IT market economy. When IT is outsourced, the outsourcer tracks demand and supply for services, and then invoices each customer for the amount of IT services used by that customer. Competitive market pressure forces the IT service provider to keep prices (and expenses) competitive. Customers use only those services they can afford. Equilibrium arises out of the value that the customer places on the IT services. To the internal IT service provider, cost allocation becomes a proxy for direct charges to the customer. Like an outsourcer, internal IT service providers have multiple customers, namely the business units and staff departments. Ideally, cost allocation is based on actual services consumed by each internal customer. Any other form of cost allocation invariably causes dysfunctional behavior, inefficiencies, and interdepartmental bickering. For cost allocation to be effective, the IT department requires cost accounting (by service) as well as tracking of service utilization (service units used) by each customer. In concept, the *cost allocation* for an internal customer is equal to the cost of providing a unit of service at a predetermined service level (unit cost) multiplied by the number of units delivered to that business unit. Most organizations allocate costs for infrastructure services, such as desktop management, based on a standard rate, even though each user might require a slightly different level of service. In practice the allocation formulas can become quite complex.

A good IT department will align cost allocation formulas with service-level agreements, reporting both cost and performance to the business department (customer) on a monthly basis when reporting these allocations to the finance department. Regrettably, the CFO typically controls cost allocations. Most CFOs want to simplify cost allocation, while the complexity of IT service delivery calls for complex allocation schemes that match service-level agreements. The problem is further compounded by the fact that most business unit executives like these allocations to be predictable and consistent on a month-to-month basis so that they can forecast their financial performance, whereas a usage-based allocation varies as the business's use of IT services fluctuates. Unfortunately, few CFOs truly understand that in the absence of effective cost allocation, the organization is dependent on well-intentioned employees doing what they think is right and spending what they think is appropriate. However, when everyone has different opinions and perspectives, even the best-intentioned employees become dysfunctional.

What does all this accounting information have to do with portfolio management? Everything! The PMT needs to understand the full implications of every project, service level, or architecture change that it approves. The only way to understand the implications is when business case analysis is based on actual changes, modeled from the perspectives of financial accounting (corporate profit and loss), cost accounting (incremental service expense), and cost allocation (business unit incremental expense). Only then can you understand the true impact of a decision on IT budgets.

When a PMT makes a portfolio decision, the decision affects not only the work priority but also the financial structure. When the PMT charters a project to implement a new application, it commits the organization to the cost allocation associated with the cost of operating, maintaining, and supporting that application indefinitely. It commits the organization to the increase in application support services. It commits the organization to the addition of assets. It commits the organization to an increase in help desk telephone calls, and so on and so forth.

The PMT too often fails to appreciate the implications of its decisions. Suppose the PMT authorizes a project to implement a new application, which in turn requires an infrastructure upgrade (desktop, operating system, and network). Not only is the PMT committing to the total cost of ownership of the new application, it is increasing the annual cost of every computer impacted by the infrastructure upgrade. The cost of upgrading the operating system (e.g., Microsoft Windows) can be smoothed out if the upgrade is staged over time, but when a new application forces an organization to upgrade rapidly, the one-time costs can be highly visible on the balance sheet. Major infrastructure upgrades are like trying to repair or replace the foundation of a building that touches every element of the architecture.

IT Governance Processes

The cause is hidden; the effect is visible to all.
                        —Ovid (Publius Ovidius Naso), *Metamorphoses*

IT governance is the set of processes used by the organization to *manage* information technology. IT portfolio management decisions are inextricably linked to other governance decisions, and vice versa. The processes are not discrete. They are systemically connected.

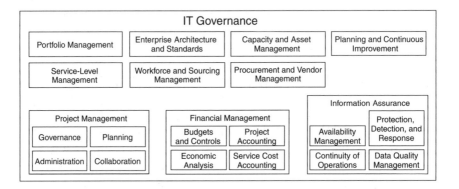

If an organization does not govern IT services, then it cannot hope to govern IT investments. Information technology investments and assets are managed by governing the IT services that perform the acquisition, implementation, ongoing operations, and maintenance activities. Organizations can outsource IT service provision, but when they abdicate responsibility for IT service governance, they are asking for trouble. *CIO Insight* magazine's 2002 Strategic Alignment Research Study found that more than 50% of companies lacked a process to review IT service performance relative to enterprise strategic goals and initiatives. It doesn't matter who employs the IT staff—the organization must manage service requirements and service performance. It is possible that a good service provider might exceed expectations, but more often than not, the service provider falls short of them. An organization can either wait for these situations to happen and then react, or it can work proactively with the service provider to avoid them. The level of required involvement depends on the service provider and the organization's needs. The better the service provider, the more it will understand and look out for its customers' concerns, and the less the customer must become involved. The more complex or unique the organization's needs, or the less mature the service provider, the more the organization will need to be actively involved in managing service levels to ensure proper decisions are made. The organization does not need to do the service provider's work—that is, it doesn't need to micromanage the service provision. However, it does need to establish service-level requirements and retain transparency at the major control points via performance metrics.

If an organization does not effectively govern IT investments, then it cannot manage IT services. If the organization makes poor investment decisions, it will affect IT expenses for the rest of the technology's life. These IT expenses are commonly referred to as the total cost of ownership (TCO). As we already observed, making effective IT investment decisions requires the organization to understand not only the investment and operating expenses but also the total impact on all interdependent applications and networks for the full investment life cycle. It is difficult to implement a new software application without affecting some IT service. Many investment decisions are made myopically, without total awareness of the implications and organizational impact. Many financial analysts just don't understand how all-encompassing their IT financial analysis needs to be. Hence, many IT investment decisions are made without visibility into the cradle-to-grave costs and implications.

IT has a maturity curve that every manager involved with service and portfolio management must understand if he or she truly wants to optimize investments. In the beginning, when technology is less mature, it may be more prone to failure or instability. Less mature IT tends to be more difficult or costly to support, and is often not cost-effectively scalable to serve a large population. However, it is important to note that this does not make new technology "bad" per se. In some situations, applying new technology is most appropriate. These situations tend to occur when the consumer (user) population is sufficiently mature to address the issues that new technology may bring. New technology may also provide a temporary competitive advantage.

New IT should be managed more cautiously than mature technology. As IT matures, it is readily adopted by large numbers of people. Various enhancements and add-ons increase its value and make it easier to deploy and support. Standards emerge. IT support matures. Maturity brings efficiencies and economies of scale that drive down the technology's operations and maintenance (O&M) cost. When the first wireless networks emerged in the 1990s, they presented security risks. This aspect caused challenges for mainstream corporate and government organizations that couldn't afford the security risk and didn't want to be bothered with the business disruption from technology quirks. The value of the technology was not negated, however. Plenty of consumers with niche needs valued the freedom that the wireless technology offered. The early adopters fueled research and development, which produced better and more secure wireless network capabilities.

At peak maturity, the technology *itself* ceases to provide much competitive advantage. If the technology is standard and accessible by most everyone, then competitors can adopt it. When anyone can adopt the technology, the competitive advantage it affords in and of itself is minimal.

As technology matures, organizations must blend business process changes with technology in order to retain or obtain competitive advantage. An organization requires innovation at this point. Simply deploying the technology provides an organization with *competitive parity,* at best. If the organization wants a competitive advantage, it needs to find a way to use the technology better, faster, or cheaper than the competition. Sometimes the technology becomes a catalyst for process change. Additional innovation then comes from process changes, enabled by the technology. An innovative organization might even find ways to innovate with processes that do not require new technology investment. In any event, the period of competitive advantage obtained by bringing new capabilities to the market provides value to technology leaders. However, technology fast-followers can learn from technology leaders, and may be able to retain a competitive position at a lower cost. Organizations must choose where they want to be technology leaders and where they want to be technology followers. It is like a decathlon. You don't need to excel at every event, but you need to excel at certain ones. The organization's mission and strategy determine which events it needs to win. The relevance of particular technologies to winning these few critical events determines where the investments should be made.

Maturing IT, Declining Competitive Advantage

A major food and beverage company deployed its first-generation handheld devices for collecting and reporting in-store inventory in the 1980s. The devices provided competitive advantage in the form of rapid situational awareness of in-store sales. The company had the presence of mind to recognize that the return on this increased level of decision-support would more than compensate for the higher investment cost. Compared to today's handheld computers, the devices appear primitive and specialized, but they served their purpose. They enhanced the firm's profitability.

As its competitors found innovative ways to transmit sales data back to headquarters, the competitive advantage that the company had gained from its handheld devices began to diminish. It was not the fault of either the company or its technology. The technology was still valuable and continued to provide the same functionality as before, but the competition had begun to catch up. As often happens when innovative technologies mature, this one had become "needed to play" rather than an inherent source of competitive advantage. In effect, the technology and associated decision-support processes upped the ante for competitors to perform at the leader's level. Eventually the company will need to decide whether its salesforce automation should and could continue to be an area of competitive advantage. To retain salesforce automation as a strategic advantage, the company will have to enhance the technology and processes with new capabilities that provide increasing market advantage. Yet this strategy will create an obligation to invest at a level that provides market leadership on an ongoing basis, which becomes a financial burden to an organization. On the other hand, should the company decide that innovations in this area are not justified, it can decide to forgo research and development in lieu of other more valuable investments. Under these conditions, it would put the salesforce automation technologies into a "maintenance mode," investing only what it would take to sustain the current business capabilities.

At the end of the IT asset life cycle, IT presents new challenges. IT never actually becomes obsolete. IT typically continues to serve its intended purpose if maintained properly and left unchanged. New business processes, market environments, or technologies render IT obsolete. New IT assets that do not coexist well with the aging installed base cause the old IT to fail. It is not really the fault of the old technology or vendor. It is our own management decisions that render IT obsolete. *We do it to ourselves!* Isolate and maintain the technology, and it will continue to operate until the hardware physically fails beyond repair. Introduce new technologies and the old ones will become obsolete. It is a systemic loop. IT service managers must consider the increased cost of providing services to customers with old IT, where decline in demand concurrent with the increase in complexity might make support cost-prohibitive. Remember, the next time you decide to upgrade an application or piece of hardware, every upgrade decision will likely cause something in the interconnected enterprise to fail (i.e., be incompatible with something else). As more new technology is added, the probability that some additional cost for technology failure will be hidden somewhere in the project increases. If the organization slows the adoption of new technology, it reduces the interdependencies it must manage. If an organization doesn't want to invest a lot of money in new technology, it should stop adding it.

When an organization decides to install new IT that is not compatible with its existing (legacy) IT, managers must factor the cost of replacing or enhancing the obsolete applications into the cost of introducing the new IT. If we modify or isolate the older IT to avoid conflicts with the new IT, we must also anticipate that the O&M cost may increase. Testing every piece of new IT with all the installed IT to ensure compatibility can become quite expensive. The most seemingly innocuous step, like upgrading a desktop computer, can cause mission-critical software applications to fail. For that reason, most organizations retest all existing applications with each major desktop operating system upgrade. Most organizations have dozens of platforms, many with more than one configuration. Some organizations retain their hardware and software for 5 to 10 years. As the number of applications grows and the number of operating systems grows, the multiplicative effect makes testing increasingly complex and labor-intensive. When the number of platforms grows out of hand and the organization cannot afford to test all the applications, then an upgrade or deployment degenerates into an exercise in trial and error. Either cost or quality suffers. If each department or division selects its own platforms, it is even more difficult to deploy global IT upgrades. The next time you are tempted to complain that an operating system upgrade is taking too long, add up the number of generations of hardware, the number of operating system configurations, and the number of applications. Multiply the three numbers and that will give you an idea of the number of possible points of failure during the deployment.

Large organizations must deal with added complexity when one division wants to upgrade its technology but another does not. If the desired rate of technology adoption in one division is faster than in another, it can cause added strife within the organization. What is peculiar is that most people will blame the technology for this strife, when it is actually the fault of having multiple business models (cost structures, product margins, profitability, risk tolerance, etc.) as part of a single operating entity. In many cases, a company's diversification is the crux of the problem. One would think that it would be a perfect opportunity for senior executives to step in and mitigate the strife. Unfortunately, few executives have the insight to see this relationship. They view it as a problem that middle management should resolve or as an IT problem that the CIO should resolve. However, it is not an IT problem—it is a business problem that arises when technology reaches the end of its life cycle in one division while still remaining viable in another.

The adoption of COTS software adds additional complexity to the IT life cycle challenges. COTS software vendors typically release software maintenance updates several times a year, mostly containing bug fixes and minor enhancements. They release larger upgrades with new functionality (platform upgrades) on a periodic basis, such as every 12 to 24 months. Back in the days when organizations developed their software in-house, they controlled the frequency of updates and upgrades. Many organizations limited application changes to those that were mission-critical. In so doing, some organizations were able to minimize their O&M costs. Now COTS software vendors control the frequency of updates and upgrades. Vendors increasingly design new IT to work harmoniously with old IT, but it costs more to include this compatibility. Vendors cannot afford to sustain backward compatibility with all the old releases of hardware and software. Too many old releases make this accommodation impractical. Eventually, vendors discontinue support for the older IT to provide customers with a reasonable price. IT staff members have a propensity for installing updates and upgrades sooner rather than later, in an attempt to provide the latest features and functionality to application users and to proactively avoid software incompatibilities.

In effect, the vendors shortened the software life cycle, as compared to the home-grown applications of the prior era. Managers complain that they are at the mercy of the vendors. They are not. Updates and upgrades do not need to be installed as soon as they are released. Organizations can choose to be early adopters, followers, or laggards. It is management's decision to introduce new IT into the organization. If you don't add anything new, then the existing IT continues to operate as intended. Vendors typically support old releases for 2 to 3 years, so managers have some wiggle-room to schedule these investments. If, however, other situations cause the organization to introduce new IT, then it may have to install upgrades and updates more frequently. The further behind an organization falls in its installation of vendor releases, the greater the risk a problem may result from introducing new IT assets. If an organization is far behind in its updating of applications, it can overly complicate new application implementations. Organizations that modify COTS applications complicate the issue even further. When they modify a COTS application, it increases the cost, complexity, and risk of upgrading the same software. As a result, all the time pressure of vendor upgrades is compounded by the added responsibility of repeating these software modifications and tests every time the vendor releases an upgrade.

Managers are fooling themselves if they think that they can separate the IT investment process from the ongoing IT governance processes. Before investing in new IT, managers must understand the impact on TCO. New IT platform deployments might cause considerable increases in TCO. The purchase and installation cost of some particular piece of software may be reasonable on the surface, but the hidden TCO may be substantial. Even though the addition of one application may be marginal, the multiplicative effect of adding one application at a time over the course of many years is quite substantial. Managers cannot arbitrarily cut TCO. They must reduce user demand for these services or reduce the cost of service provision (through greater efficiency or simplicity). The work of operating and maintaining IT does not go away just because the CFO doesn't like the price tag.

Governance Across the IT Life Cycle: The Case of the Help Desk

When supporting new IT, a help desk must have a system that enables it to innovate and learn from every new telephone call. As users uncover new questions and concerns, IT support staff must capture the issue and its resolution lest they be doomed to solve the same problems repeatedly. Tight collaboration is required between call-takers, technical support staff, and engineering in order to provide rapid resolution for callers. However, once IT technical support and engineering answers a few thousand phone calls, it has encountered more than 80% of the technical issues that are likely to arise. Put this knowledge into the hands of call-takers on a just-in-time basis and the average agent with relatively little training can resolve 80% of customer calls. The average call center agent costs at least 30% less than a technical support agent and approximately 50% less than an engineer; therefore, organizations save money by shifting call resolution to a lesser-skilled workforce.

As IT is mainstreamed, services need to be scaled and become more efficient lest the cost for providing these services increases linearly—or worse yet geometrically—with each new customer. The same arguments can be made regardless of which IT services we are considering. The theory holds true for application development services, desktop maintenance services, and data center services.

At the end of the IT life cycle, new problems arise as support questions become fewer and farther between. As agents leave the organization, knowledge diminishes, and application users reach a point where they know more about the application than does the IT support staff. As issues arise from introducing new IT that does not work well with these old applications, the IT support staff is increasingly incapable of resolving the issues. The support staff's knowledge base does not contain these answers to previously unencountered problems. IT support brings in technical support, and tech support, in turn, brings in IT engineers to

(continued)

troubleshoot the problem. Often the IT engineers need to modify the application coding or configuration to resolve the issue. Perhaps they need to upgrade the application. O&M costs immediately increase. If the number of application users is simultaneously declining, it has a compounding effect on the metrics. When hundreds of consumers use an application, the O&M cost per user is relatively low. As the number of consumers declines, the O&M cost per user increases proportionately. If the cost increases and the number of users decreases, the cost per user seemingly skyrockets.

From a management perspective, at the beginning of the IT life cycle, the cost per call of IT support appears high due to the small number of application users and the efforts required to research and resolve each question. Eventually, the knowledge base contains 80% of the answers and the cost per call should begin to drop. As IT matures the absolute cost peaks (due to a higher call volume), but the cost per call might fall to its lowest point (the denominator increases as the numerator decreases). Later, cost per call grows slightly as the technology nears the end of its life cycle and the number of consumers declines. At the end of the life cycle, the cost per call might peak again as experienced users begin to experience new compatibility issues with emerging IT.

All bets are off, however, if a support organization does not store the answers in a knowledge base. Lack of a knowledge base prevents an organization from leveling the learning curve. Without a knowledge base, each agent must relearn the answer to every question. An agent may need to answer 2,000 calls before he or she encounters 80% of consumer issues, which means that it might take a well-trained agent 4 to 6 months to traverse the learning curve. When organizations properly deploy a knowledge base, these same agents need only learn how to use it, which should take only a week or two.

Finally, it is worth noting while considering the interdependency between IT portfolio management and IT governance that one needn't be a technologist to manage IT investments. Some of the best IT managers come from a manufacturing environment, because they think of IT in manufacturing terms. IT assets "manufacture" information. Greater commonality among IT assets reduces O&M costs. If the assets use standard parts, they are cheaper to maintain. Underutilized assets are a waste of capital, but the converse is not always true. Just because the asset is heavily utilized, it does not directly follow that the resulting *inventory* of data produced is valuable. In fact, a surplus of data may be costly to warehouse. It is another point well worth considering when fielding requests from applications users for some new piece of technology.

Six Sigma

Six Sigma originated as a method and set of tools for incremental process improvement. It is especially valuable for taking waste out of repeatable, labor- or asset-intensive processes. Six Sigma proposes a five-phase method for process improvement: define, measure, analyze, improve, and control (DMAIC). Organizations can use the DMAIC method as a phase-gate process, reviewing the project at the end of each phase, for business process improvements as well as pure IT implementations. In establishing the phase-gate process, the organization must decide how much governance to build into it. Some organizations prefer to allow grassroots efforts to bloom and fade on their own, driven by employee initiative. Others find the "thousand flowers blooming" approach to be a bit too chaotic and a drain on resources. These organizations instill stronger investment management controls. Portfolio management complements Six Sigma by providing these controls.

Portfolio management teams review a Six Sigma project the same way that they review any other project. A common approach is for the portfolio management team to review projects at the end of the "define" phase. Some organizations struggle at this early phase of the project life cycle because they know so few details, but it is no different from reviewing any other project concept at the outset. The organization has only an order-of-magnitude business case at this point. The team can typically estimate the level of investment and expected improvement. If the business case changes significantly, the PMT can reengage to determine whether to redirect, terminate, or authorize the project to proceed.

Key Themes

- The IT portfolio management process includes a series of tasks designed to let organizations make the link between the IT portfolio and the organization's strategic objectives and performance goals. The process has four major work streams: inventory and calibration, strategic analysis, decision making, and chartering.
- The inventory and calibration work stream involves collecting and validating project business case and status information, and ensuring that the PMT has an accurate picture of existing and proposed projects.
- The strategic analysis work stream translates the organization's strategic plans and performance targets into missing capabilities, and assures that the project inventory adequately provides new capabilities and performance levels.
- The decision-making work stream facilitates the PMT through changing project scopes and charters, and allocating resources.
- The chartering work stream communicates the PMT's decisions to the organization and ensures that the decisions are properly executed and result in the appropriate allocation, or de-allocation, of resources.
- IT portfolio management has increasingly become a dynamic and ongoing process in which the organization executes the four work streams in tandem. Business planning occurs continuously rather than cyclically.
- As part of the enterprise IT management system, IT portfolio management naturally intersects with a number of other IT management processes and needs to be managed in conjunction with them.
- Crucial interdependencies to be managed include those between the IT portfolio management process and service development, resource management, enterprise architecture and standards, financial management, and other IT governance processes.
- Effective and aligned portfolio and service development processes force the organization to create and follow better

plans and give it an ability to make better decisions, which results in faster time-to-results.

- Because portfolio decisions cannot be made without allocating resources, portfolio management and resource management need to be integrated. Portfolio management supports various resource management approaches, ranging from aggregate resource management to named-resource assignment.

- The PMT is accountable for decisions about enterprise architecture and standards. These decisions are business decisions that must be made by the PMT in the context of the strategic plan and the bottom line.

- Because portfolio decisions affect an organization's financial structure, the PMT needs to understand the financial implications of every project, service level, or architecture change that it approves. The only way to understand the implications is to base the business case analysis on actual changes, modeled from the perspectives of financial accounting, cost accounting, and cost allocation.

- If an organization does not govern IT services, then it cannot hope to govern IT investments. Information technology investments and assets are managed by governing the IT services that perform the acquisition, implementation, ongoing operations, and maintenance activities.

- For organizations that want to utilize strong investment management controls, portfolio management complements Six Sigma by providing these controls.

Enablers

A good End cannot sanctifie evil Means; nor must we ever do Evil, that Good may come of it.

—William Penn, *Some Fruits of Solitude*

The use of process enablers in the IT portfolio management process is discretionary, although highly desirable. Enablers such as decision-support, performance metrics, software, and other best practices make the portfolio process more efficient, make decision making more effective, and sometimes help to ensure the process "sticks" once it is implemented. Organizations do not need sophisticated, expensive enablers to implement a robust portfolio management process. More sophistication doesn't necessarily translate to better enablers. When it comes to enablers, you don't always get what you pay for. Sometimes improving a standard template, for example, is the only thing needed to address inconsistencies. If the organization needs to expend a lot of effort to keep the process going, then it is not going to be sustainable. The organization needs to integrate process execution into the management staff's way of doing business. Be careful here! If you actually empower the broad organization—in the truest sense—it might exceed your expectations. Then what would you have to complain about?

The best way to ensure that a process will stick once implemented is to increase accountability and drive continuous improvement. Accountability motivates improvement. In time, continuous improvement may become part of the organization's culture (specifically, its behavioral norms), but not without accountability. As noted many times, it is essential that the senior leadership team be accountable for the efficiency and effectiveness of the process. Increase accountability by increasing transparency in organizational performance. Ensure that a scorecard with metrics measures the process's efficiency and

187

effectiveness as well as that of the portfolio. Automate these metrics, so that the organization is not dependent on someone "doing their job right" to report them. Publish these metrics to the organization to increase common situational awareness of performance.

When introducing metrics, it is crucial to build process assessments and improvement into the organization's regular planning process. Teach the entire organization to recognize and focus on value drivers, throughput, and cost. Give the entire organization the tools it needs to define, measure, analyze, improve, and control its processes. The goal of process improvement is to take waste out of the system and increase value. The whole point of implementing a process-based management approach is to provide a foundation for continuous improvement. Be forewarned, however, that diminishing returns are typical of process improvement. If the management team starts to question improvements or process-related expenditures, then consider whether the enablers are adding sufficient value. What the management team is likely trying to convey is that it is not seeing sufficient results for the level of effort and mindshare being invested. When enablers do not contribute sufficiently to process efficiency or effectiveness, they become overhead. Process improvements need not be huge projects with dozens of dedicated resources. Often facilitators are all that is needed.

Decision Support

How can one beam alone support a house?

—Chinese proverb

Decision-support includes all the effort required to make effective decisions efficiently. Decision-support tools include the data, queries, reports, and charts necessary to assist with decision making. Decision-support also includes all the effort necessary to integrate across the organization's portfolios. Failure to roll up and assess investments across the organization severely lessens the value of a portfolio management process. The tools are just the apparatus, and do not by themselves ensure effective decisions. They are merely different lenses, which means that they don't change the facts being observed. Rose-colored lenses may make the portfolio look better to senior leadership, but they won't improve its value. At the end of the year, the PMT will still be on the hook to optimize the portfolio *results*. The process does require reasonably accurate and complete data to be effective. Note that we say *reasonably* accurate and complete. Some people in an organization will be compulsive and attempt to collect perfect data. The world is not perfect, so do not expect your data to be. Data are just one way of providing situational awareness. They do not replace the need for interpersonal communication and good judgment.

A fair amount of validation and decision-support preparation goes into an effective portfolio review. The inventory and calibration phase of the portfolio management process collects the data required for decision-support. Value drivers make up a large portion of the required data. You will also need information on project status (variance-to-plan for schedule, cost, resources, expectations, and deliverables). Project information needs to be timely and defined as clearly as possible to avoid bad decision making caused by ambiguous information. Decision makers will require the information to be consistently tabulated and consistently formatted. It is distracting when the information contains inconsistencies that raise doubts about the entire portfolio's integrity. Good decisions made with bad information can result in something worse than your present situation, and the portfolio management process may lose credibility if the organization cannot trust the data. Those preparing the analysis will need to calibrate information across projects to ensure apples-to-apples comparisons. For example, one team might rate its project as high-risk while another team might rate its project as medium-risk, even though both projects really have the same risk level. If we don't have standardized templates, one TCO calculation might be different from the others. Hence the need for standardized data definitions and templates. (For more on this topic, refer back to the discussion of the design principle "Focus on Transparency" in *IT Portfolio Management: What It Can Do and How It Works*.)

Common terminology and templates provide the following benefits:

- Improved communication among stakeholders
- Improved decision-support (charts, graphs, etc.)
- Apples-to-apples comparisons

In the strategic analysis phase of the portfolio management process, decision-support can be useful for developing scenarios and recommendations. Senior decision makers will likely require that a lot of the analysis be performed in advance of meetings. Many PMTs charter a working team of middle managers to front-load the strategic analysis with a set of recommendations. These recommendations comprise the bulk of decision-support for this phase. If you attempt to get a PMT of senior leaders, who probably already work more than 60 hours per week, to perform all the analysis itself, then you are likely to see your portfolio management initiative die on the vine. Most senior leaders are accustomed to reviewing a set of recommended options (scenarios, alternatives). When you provide recommendations for the PMT, it can then either make a decision or redirect the analysis. If the decision-making process is likely to be highly contentious, or if a high degree of mistrust is present in the organization, you might use a cross-functional working team to do the analysis, similar in membership to the PMT. For example, if the PMT includes the division heads, then the working team would include one representative from each of those divisions, each appointed by his or her respective division head. If the decisions are less likely to result in contentiousness, you might assign the decision-support analysis to an objective project management office (PMO).

In the decision-making phase of the process, decision-support can be used to build consensus. If strategic analysis has been delegated to a PMO, it is critically important that the responsibilities of the PMO are clear. The PMO does not make decisions, because it has neither the perspective nor the authority to do so. Decisions are the purview of the PMT. The PMO is a workgroup that validates and calibrates data, performs analysis, and draws conclusions in the form of recommendations to the PMT. In the absence of a sophisticated portfolio management software application, a PMO can prepare the information for PMT decision meetings. (In effect, in this situation the PMO is a cost of not having a robust portfolio management software application.) This initial preparation enables the PMT to focus during its meetings on making decisions. The PMT can actually spend most of its meeting time on the more ambiguous decisions, handling the routine ones mechanically (e.g., by scoring, ranking, etc.). In situations with multiple (tiered) PMTs, the seniormost PMT challenges the organization with high-level stretch goals during the strategic analysis phase. Then the analysis rolls up through each lower-level PMT to the seniormost team. The job of the seniormost PMT is not to second-guess the decisions made by the more junior PMTs but to hold those PMTs accountable for making good decisions and aggregating an understanding of the big picture. The seniormost PMT would intervene if it judges that the whole could be less than the sum of the parts.

As the portfolio management process matures, the PMT members will become more comfortable with the analysis presented to it and may even want to begin to perform some of it themselves. Don't expect this confidence to happen on day 1. At a minimum, the PMT will require a condensed tabular listing of projects that summarizes the risk-adjusted cost, value, impact, and interdependencies of each one. Although it may be necessary to use a presentation format to facilitate the PMT through the first few meetings, be careful of creating too much overhead. Eventually, you want the PMT to become a working management team, accustomed to reviewing reports and charts rather than expecting a canned presentation. Taking weeks to create a PMT presentation will cause a bottleneck in the process, which will impede the agility of the organization's decision making. Eventually, the PMT needs to become accustomed to, and comfortable with, seeing raw project data, metrics, and templates. The trick, at first, is to give the PMT greater situational awareness and educate it on the process without overwhelming team members with new jargon and an overly complex or cumbersome process. The PMT is the primary audience for portfolio information, because it is accountable for the portfolio's performance. It is not the only audience, however. Middle managers use portfolio information to manage resources. Project managers use portfolio information to communicate status and create situational awareness for large project teams. IT customers within an organization use portfolio information to better understand and prioritize their own requests.

Sample Portfolio Management Reports

	Project Priority	Forecasted Benefits (Aggregate)	TCO One-time (Aggregate)	TCO Ongoing (Aggregate)	Projected Net Benefit (Present Value)	Project Risk
A—Major Projects		$ 15,000,000	$ 2,250,000	$ 1,250,000	$ 7,500,000	
Project #1	1	$ 10,000,000	$ 1,500,000	$ 1,000,000	$ 5,000,000	High
Project #2	2	$ 5,000,000	$ 750,000	$ 250,000	$ 2,500,000	Medium
B—Medium to Large Projects		$ 625,000	$ 515,000	$ 310,000	$ 340,000	
Project #3	1	$ -	$ 50,000	$ 10,000	$ -	Low
Project #4	2	$ 500,000	$ 250,000	$ 250,000	$ 250,000	High
Project #5	3	$ -	$ 150,000	$ 50,000	$ -	Medium
Project #6	4	$ 125,000	$ 65,000	$ -	$ 90,000	Low
C—Continuous Improvement Summary		$ 50,000	$ 150,000	$ 15,000	$ 150,000	
D—Break/Fix and Maintenance Summary		$ -	$ 350,000	$ -	$ 350,000	

Qualitative Benefits

Customer-Facing Improvements   Internal Improvements

	Project Priority	Quote-to-Order Cycle Time	Order-to-Installation Cycle Time	Product Mix & Offering	Customer Satisfaction	Customer Support	Employee Dev. & Satisfaction	Employee Productivity	Corporate Growth	Decision-Support, Planning, & Forecasting	Infrastructure & Life Cycle
A—Major Projects											
Project #1	1	X	X				X				
Project #2	2				X	X					
B—Medium to Large Projects											
Project #3	1									X	X
Project #4	2							X	X		
Project #5	3										X
Project #6	4			X		X					
C—Continuous Improvement Summary											
D—Break/Fix and Maintenance Summary											

In addition to tabular listings of project information, a variety of graphs can be used to model the portfolio for analytical purposes. The most popular format is a "bubble chart," because it allows the PMT to view projects in three dimensions. (Most managers use the size of the bubbles to illustrate project cost.) The four most popular x-axis and y-axis comparisons, illustrated by the following graphs, include:

- Risk versus value
- Value against time to project completion
- Project priority against project phase
- Skill supply versus demand

Sample Portfolio Analysis Decision-Support Graphs

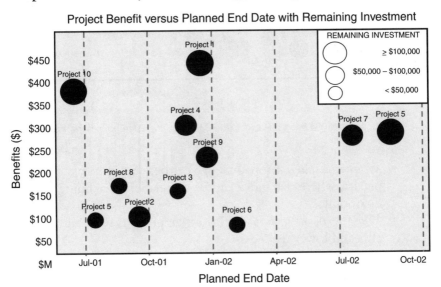

Project Benefit versus Planned End Date with Remaining Investment

- *What it displays:* Individual project benefits vs. project planned end date by remaining investment
- *What decisions it supports:* Portfolio prioritization; rationalization of the pipeline, including justification to cancel projects with unacceptable return on investment

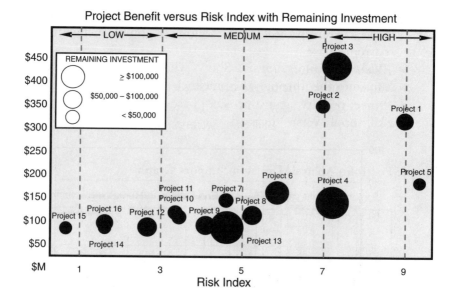

Project Benefit versus Risk Index with Remaining Investment

- *What it displays:* Individual project benefits vs. project complexity, where risk index can be calculated by defining a risk taxonomy
- *What decisions it supports:* Prioritize projects with higher benefits and lower risk

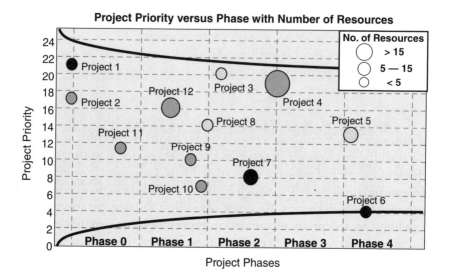

Project Priority versus Phase with Number of Resources

- *What it displays:* All active and pending projects in the portfolio; current project phases; degree of completion within current phase
- *What decisions it supports:* Shows whether projects are moving smoothly through the pipeline

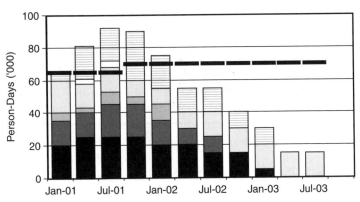

- *What it displays:* All planned project resource needs by project type; resource gap; resource capacity
- *What decisions it supports:* Acceleration or delay of existing projects to meet capacity constraints; contract resource requirements

Furthermore, if an organization is accustomed to a high degree of automation, it can buy software applications that enable it to identify the efficient frontier of projects as a means of decision support. The efficient frontier of projects is calculated based on predetermined value drivers and business rules, which include not only yes/no decisions but also more/less decisions. Be forewarned that the organization may be unwilling to accept an automated interpretation, or may not have the discipline to agree on the relative importance of the various value drivers in a portfolio. In either case, it will need backup information to support decision making. The trick is not to become so enamored of creating graphs that the PMT becomes overloaded with superfluous details. Once organizations finally obtain portfolio information, it is common for them to become so excited about having it that people overload the PMT and overly burden the project teams. Too much information is confusing. At first, the working team may become more familiar with the data than the PMT, so it is easy to underestimate how overwhelming the data can be when viewed for the first time. The queries and graphs are primarily for analytical purposes. Present them to the PMT only if they are necessary to support a particular recommendation. Pick no more than a handful of basic tables and graphs at first to present to the PMT. Add to them as the process matures. As the PMT becomes more comfortable with the process, it will likely request that certain analyses be provided. The facilitator and process designer's role is to educate the PMT on what questions to ask, and then impress team members with how easy it is to answer their questions.

Decision-support is an area where portfolio management software applications add tremendous value. Dynamic (ongoing) portfolio management absolutely requires automation. Keeping information current requires distributing responsibility to project managers to enter their information on a periodic basis. With the right tools, updates to status and plans also update the analysis and decision-support. The more dynamic the portfolio, the more vital it will be to keep the information current. Once the PMT becomes comfortable with the process, it may even want to use the tools itself to monitor and assess the portfolio in real time. Many PMT members eventually request some type of dashboard or early warning notification so that they can monitor projects and manage by exception. Do not, however, allow the portfolio management application to distort the focus of portfolio management. The application is meant to achieve greater efficiency and effectiveness within the process. The risk is that an organization will become so captivated by the software that people will become distracted from their primary portfolio management accountabilities and responsibilities.

The PMT shouldn't see the information that it will use to make decisions for the first time at the PMT review meetings. Different managers have different decision-making styles. Some managers may require time to contemplate the information before reaching a conclusion. Others make decisions on the spot. Some of these spot decisions are good, but many are not. The PMT is more prone to make bad decisions if it does not have sufficient time to consider the relevant information. Your organization will be better served if it gives PMT members time to study the information in advance of meetings. To ensure a smooth PMT meeting, try to provide all background information and decision-support charts at least one full week before the review. Someone familiar with the analysis should sit with each PMT member before the PMT meeting, review the analysis with him or her, highlight any issues, and answer any questions that have straightforward answers. Educate and inform all the PMT members offline, before meetings. Coach PMT members to deal with individual questions and specific issues in advance of PMT meetings. It is easier to resolve specific issues or uncertainties one-on-one, in a private setting. The PMT may require further details on projects and ask, for example, to review a project's business case information in detail. Although this approach may at first seem inefficient, it is a best practice to obtain as much consensus as possible before the actual meeting. PMT members should be armed with sufficient insight to make the trade-off decisions before they walk into the meeting. Use the face-to-face meetings of the whole PMT to focus on discussions that concern the majority of PMT members. It is difficult to find time when all PMT members can meet face-to-face, so dealing with individual issues and uncertainties *before* the meeting allows the PMT to focus on real decision making *during* the meeting, and prevents having to schedule follow-up meetings. If these issues are handled well, everyone will walk away from the PMT meetings with a greater feeling of success.

Performance Metrics

Whether dealing with monkeys, rats, or human beings . . . organisms seek information concerning what activities are rewarded, and then seek to do (or at least pretend to do) those things, often to the virtual exclusion of activities not rewarded.

—Steven Kerr, *On the Folly of Rewarding A, While Hoping for B*

IT practitioners used to believe that the way to evaluate the performance of an IT department was to poll the business units. Then they realized that this was a lazy man's way of measuring performance. Surveys are yet another example of how organizations mismanage IT. IT is a link in the value chain, and thus part of an organization's effort to deliver value to customers or other constituents. IT deserves more precise measurement than a merely subjective customer satisfaction poll. We wouldn't evaluate engineering performance based on how the salesforce "feels" the engineering department is performing. We wouldn't evaluate the finance department merely based on the business units' view of how it is performing. Why measure IT that way? If the business units are dissatisfied with IT service delivery, then their managers should revisit service-level performance and requirements. If the PMT is dissatisfied with IT service development, it should improve the portfolio management process. If organizations don't have the information to objectively review IT performance, then it is high time they implemented an IT performance measurement system.

One of the most frustrating things about working with an IT department is that most of the data out there is not stored in a way that facilitates IT *management* reporting. IT management reporting requires real information (facts and trends) based on aggregated data. Unfortunately, most organizations are loaded with data but don't have much information. *Water, water, everywhere, but not a drop to drink.* Most IT departments face the same problem. Most IT applications provide operational data (statistics), the kind of data that are useful to technicians who troubleshoot application failures. Each application pumps out its own statistics, in its own format, designed for the people who manage that component. This information is less valuable to managers trying to monitor portfolio performance. The information is too fragmented. It is not what the PMT requires.

The IT performance measurement system needs to provide indicators of portfolio cost-effectiveness. *Portfolio cost-effectiveness* is an indication of a portfolio's efficiency (cost) and value (effectiveness). The PMT requires measures of end-to-end cost-effectiveness that aggregate component statistics to illustrate process performance. The measurement system needs to motivate continuous improvement and provide a catalyst for learning. It needs to affect not only the IT department but also everyone accountable or responsible for IT management. The measurement system needs to enable the PMT to make informed decisions based on facts.

Is it sufficient to evaluate the effectiveness of the portfolio management process based on whether the PMT is satisfied? If the PMT and the leadership team are both satisfied then that might be sufficient, assuming that both are tuned in to the IT portfolio. However, a lot of executives were "satisfied" during the late 1990s because they were sitting fat and happy on piles of money. They didn't realize how much was out of alignment until the market turned down. Now, a lot of executives are unhappy with the IT portfolio, but they won't take the time or spend the money to find out why and fix it. These executives are not satisfied, but they can't explain why. They never implemented performance metrics, and don't have the appetite to start now. Their evaluations of IT performance are subjective, based on personal perceptions and intuition. Executives that harangue IT managers over every little thing demoralize the IT staff and promote a defensive and defeatist attitude at a time when what is required is a constructive, nurturing environment. It is quite common for this situation to escalate until a CxO brings in outside help to "assess" the situation. Many organizations could have saved a lot of money on these assessments if they had implemented a good performance measurement system in the first place. It may be insufficient to use PMT satisfaction as an effective measure.

Most IT departments are measured primarily on cost. As noted previously, the measurements used are typically based on financial accounting instead of cost accounting. A debate about the absolute cost of components is only marginally productive. It is rarely the case that an organization is paying a lot more for the same components than another organization is, because most procurement organizations have matured to the point where that issue is not a major problem. A debate about the amount of IT procured is only marginally better. Do you need 200 servers or 225? Benchmarking spending levels might be one way to gauge order-of-magnitude spending, but we wouldn't base any major decisions on it. Most organizations are already in the ballpark. What does it mean if one company spends 10% to 20% more on supply chain applications than another company? It just means they spend more on supply chain applications. So what? To make a meaningful decision, one needs to understand *why* they spend more. Odds are that their process or business model is different. Odds are that one company has optimized its business processes and information. Odds

4

are that this optimal configuration of process and information affects the level of IT spending. Perhaps the optimization drives down IT expense. Perhaps it is more expensive to operate. Because it is impossible to know such things, raw data cannot be used to make IT rationalization decisions. Besides, benchmarking was invented to help organizations learn, not to evaluate spending.

The cost-effectiveness of the portfolio management process can be monitored using five sets of *tiered measures*. Each measure represents a summary of lower-level metrics. The beauty of tiered measures is that, when implemented properly, they allow the PMT to drill down into increasing levels of detail to see which metrics are causing performance to suffer. Tiered measures link performance from the bottom of the organization to the top. Every staff member involved in an IT project or service can see how his or her performance affects overall portfolio performance.

The five measures of IT portfolio management process cost-effectiveness are:

1. Schedule variance
2. Service-level variance
3. Standard cost variance
4. Resource capacity variance
5. Service development variance

Schedule variance: Schedule variance is a measurement of the percentage of times projects do not deliver when planned. Both project schedule underruns and overruns are important. If we want to optimize efficiency and effectiveness, we need to learn how to deliver on time. Projects that take longer than planned are an indication that we need to plan better. Odds are that some other project or department was counting on the project being completed on time. Somewhere are resources counting on the project's deliverables. Now those resources can't do what they planned to do when they planned to do it. In some cases this situation wastes money. Delivering too soon may also waste money. Projects that deliver too far ahead of schedule create an opportunity cost. Perhaps the project resources concerned would have better served the organization by postponing the project in favor of a more urgent one. If a project delivers an application far in advance of when it is needed, the risk is that the business will change its requirements before the application can be deployed. Another risk is that someone will damage the project deliverables (hardware or software) while they sit idle. Schedule variance can be caused by many factors, all of which indicate an opportunity for process improvement in the IT management system. It may be that the team underestimated the work requirements. It may mean that the PMT overloaded resources. It may mean that the PMT prioritized improperly. It may mean that the PMT lacks sufficient workforce scheduling capabilities. It may mean that the process lacks sufficient planning heuristics.

Service-level variance: Service-level variance is a measure of the percentage of time predetermined service levels are not met. Every IT service should have a specified service level defined. The service level is based on business requirements. If business requirements for service performance are met all the time, then the service level is 100%. The service-level variance is 0%. Service levels are typically based on a combination of performance requirements (supply) and business expectations for volume (demand). For example, an IT service provider may commit to provide e-mail application services for 500 to 550 employees, seven days a week between the hours of 6:00 a.m. and 2:00 a.m., available 99.9% of the time (less than six hours of total unscheduled downtime per year). If the IT service provider is unable to supply this level of service, the organization can investigate the reason. A variance from the specified range in the demand for the service would trigger a discussion. Perhaps the cost would increase. Perhaps the service level would decrease. The measure provides a trigger for taking action.

Standard cost variance: Standard cost variance measures the range in what it costs the organization to deliver a unit of service. Each IT service component (development, integration, help desk, network management, data center operations, maintenance, etc.) has a unit cost. Unit cost is the cost of providing one unit of service at predetermined service levels. Examples include cost per call, cost per connection, and so on. The specific units used are less important than is measuring each service's variance from the standard cost. Using cost accounting, organizations should set a *standard cost per unit* for each service and project, based on the expected cost of providing an incremental unit of service. Organizations should base this cost on the expected *standard volume,* the volume of units they expect customers to demand, which may also be determined by service-level discussions. Then they should measure the variance. The variance should be reported in terms of *volume variance* (caused by increased/decreased usage), *cost variance* (caused by higher/lower operating costs), and *service-level variance* (caused by the need to provide a higher or lower service level). The type of variance provides the PMT with insight into where the organization needs to improve.

Resource capacity variance: Resource capacity variance is a measure of whether actual staffing capacity (supply) meets the needs (demand) of the organization. One might think that this measurement is actually a secondary metric that should be manifested in schedule and cost variance. Yet for many organizations, 60% of their IT budget is labor cost, which warrants an emphasis on resource capacity. Resource capacity variance is calculated by subtracting the resource supply from the resource demand. Resource supply should be calculated based on the workload that the average staff member can handle. For example, most organizations spend 30% on overhead activities including management reporting, time reporting, staff meetings, sick leave, and vacation. Hence, one staff member only contributes approximately 1,400 hours per year. Loading resources at 100% burns the staff members out and does not permit the organization to absorb day-to-day spikes in demand. If resource capacity is set at 100%, the organization is set up for failure. Also, don't forget to calculate the time that will be spent supporting and maintaining hardware and software. This operational capacity should be either allocated to the service delivery and operations portfolio or, at a minimum, excluded from the service development portfolio. It should not surprise managers to find out that the average service development programmer spends only 40% of his or her time developing new applications after accounting for overhead and operations support responsibilities. For this reason, more and more IT managers are establishing separate organizations to handle maintenance and support activities.

Service development variance: This measure looks at the percentage of projects that do not deliver fully according to predetermined requirements. It is perhaps the hardest measure to calculate. Many CFOs would prefer to calculate it in terms of whether the project achieved the desired improvement in NPV. However, as we discussed previously, if the IT project benefits are not measured in financial terms, it makes it impossible to measure comprehensive service development variance. The CFO should hold the leadership team accountable for financial improvements. The project team is responsible for delivering according to plan. The PMT or project governance team approves the service requirements, and the project team should deliver a service that meets those requirements. The project team is accountable for performing a thorough requirements definition. If a service does not meet expectations because the requirements were incomplete, the project team is at fault. If the service does not deliver fully against the approved requirements, again the project team is at fault. Approved requirements are those that the PMT authorized and funded. If the PMT constrained the requirements to save money, for example, it is not the project team's fault. In any event, the scope of requirements should address not only features and functionality but also end-to-end system performance, reliability, availability, interoperability, accessibility, and ease of use. The reason for holding the project team accountable for requirements variance is that poorly defined requirements are a leading cause for project failure. This measure addresses this shortcoming by creating a disincentive for shortcutting the requirements definition activities.

When initially deploying the portfolio management process, it may also be helpful to adopt other metrics that measure the process itself. These metrics do not measure portfolio cost-effectiveness per se; they are indicators of how efficient the portfolio management process is. We list some of them here because they may be helpful as an organization initially deploys its process. Be careful not to focus so much on these metrics that you deemphasize bottom-line performance measures. At the end of the day, it is results that count.

Consider these suggested process metrics:

- *Portfolio inclusion ratio:* Percentage of IT budget addressed by the portfolio management process
- *Strategic allocation:* Percentage of IT budget allocated to truly strategic endeavors
- *Governance allocation:* Percentage of IT budget allocated to service governance activities

- *D&O allocation:* Percentage of IT budget allocated to service delivery plus service operations
- *Decision-support waste:* Number of hours spent compiling and reformatting data to prepare for a PMT meeting plus facilitation hours
- *PMT meeting efficiency:* Number of hours PMT meetings run beyond scheduled hours (including the need to reconvene because of insufficient time to complete the agenda)
- *Time-to-decision:* Average lag between need identification (request) and concept review (decision)
- *Process survey:* Participant survey feedback on process efficiency and effectiveness
- *Review index:* Actual on-time phase reviews divided by requisite phase reviews
- *Contract integrity:* Number of project phase contract violations (time, cost, or quality)
- *Wasted expense:* Total budget variance after plan phase of a project (including total cost for projects cancelled after plan phase and sunk cost from projects redirected after plan phase)

Best Practices

If history repeats itself, and the unexpected always happens, how incapable must Man be of learning from experience.
—George Bernard Shaw, *Maxims for Revolutionists*

Portfolio management is difficult enough to implement without having to think at the same time about improving the whole IT management system. Once implemented, however, IT portfolio management can be a catalyst for continuously improving overall IT management and performance. Imagine, if you can, the following results from a successful implementation of portfolio management:

- IT-enabled transformation projects are evaluated by the firm's thought leaders in a few hours. No longer will such projects require months of time wasted deliberating over strategic direction.

- Innovative concepts that are buried among the rank-and-file, kept submerged by the fear of well-intentioned employees, suddenly have a mechanism to allow them to surface. No longer do transformation concepts have to percolate up through layers of management. They go from concept directly to the team best equipped to evaluate and incubate them.
- The quality of decision making increases tenfold. No longer are decisions made based on gut feelings and popular opinion.
- Collaboration among senior managers increases. Personal coalitions expand across functional silos and organizational barriers erode, which in turn creates an environment that promotes teamwork and cross-pollination of ideas.
- Senior leaders suddenly have a mechanism for separating the wheat from the chaff within the organization. The gifted employees who will ultimately make the organization successful rise to the top while the overachievers and the fearful fall by the wayside.

Sound too good to be true? It is not. Our experience confirms that companies with mediocre performance tend to be controlled by politically savvy decision makers, not leaders in their field. These managers rose to the top based on their ability to manage upwards, not based on their ability to manage a business. Senior managers, who are leaders in their field, repeatedly demonstrate an interest in best practices and are personally motivated to continuously improve lead companies with consistently high performance.

Many best practices can be integrated with a strong portfolio management process. Sometimes it is actually easy to implement them in tandem with improving a portfolio management process. We list some of them here for consideration:

- *Business case analysis:* A strong financial analysis that evaluates projects in terms of value can help to remove subjectivity from decision making. Many strategic projects have quantifiable benefits. The more the organization is challenged to think about how IT projects affect the bottom line, the more they will think strategically in support of the business. (For a more detailed treatment of business case analysis, see the appendix on this subject.)

- *Financial worksheets:* Organizations that have a strong financial management discipline utilize worksheets to ensure that they continuously improve their analytics. They rarely begin analysis with a clean sheet of paper. Every financial analysis is based on a template (worksheet) that is continuously improved. TCO is not reinvented each time it is calculated, it is determined based on heuristics and prior analysis.
- *High-caliber teams:* A high-caliber team can go a long way toward assuring the success of a project, even in the face of IT management process deficiencies. However, in most organizations, only a critical few are capable of leading initiatives. Senior leaders are not forced to recognize at the outset that they are compromising when they stand up a new project with insufficient leadership.
- *Iterative development:* Risky or ambiguous projects call for special methods for mitigating risk, and iterative development is one such method. As opposed to using a big-bang approach to implementing new applications, the general principle behind iterative development is to develop or implement a new application incrementally. Each capability and functionality is tested and proven before the organization invests further. The project can be redirected or terminated at any time.
- *Phase-based reviews:* As noted in *IT Portfolio Management: What It Can Do; How It Works,* most projects follow a six-phase life cycle concept, plan/design, build/integrate/test, certify, deploy, and retire. Sometimes, as with large or risky endeavors, every phase of the cycle from plan/design thru deploy is repeated several times, with new increments of functionality (releases) each time. The best-governed organizations approve the budget for a project but make funds available on a phase-by-phase basis. They do not grant access to the entire budget at the outset. Project managers commit to a contract at the beginning of each phase in exchange for the current phase of funding. Then the team must deliver per the terms of its contract (as to objectives, deliverables, etc.) before the next phase of funding is granted. Any significant mid-phase variance to plan triggers an interim review. In absence of a variance, the project is self-managed (assuming a high-caliber team and a good governance team).

- *Project governance teams:* A governance team (a.k.a. steering committee) picks up where the PMT leaves off. The governance team ultimately decides how much authority will be delegated to the project team, and to what extent the project team must go to the governance team for decisions. With high-caliber teams, the governance team, on average, need devote only a few hours every month to its work. If the project team is not as strong, the governance team may need to retain much of the decision authority, delegating to the project team only responsibility for making recommendations and executing the project plan. The PMT holds the governance team accountable for results. The governance team, in turn, holds the project team accountable for planning and execution activities. The governance team provides the month-to-month leadership perspective to the project team. The governance team members ensure that their peer management team members are sufficiently engaged to achieve the desired results.

- *Risk mitigation and contingency plans:* Any organization serious about mitigating risk must build actionable mitigation and contingency plans into the master schedule. Use risk identification techniques like decision tree analysis or Monte Carlo simulation to document and assess risk likelihood. Develop mitigation plans that include actions to prevent risky situations. Contingency plans spell out exactly what will be done in the event that expected risk is encountered. For example, if technology immaturity is a risk, then develop a plan to test the technology early in the project life cycle, deferring major expense commitments until the technology proves sufficiently mature. Should the technology prove too immature, plan how the project will substitute another technology.

- *Roadmaps and release plans:* Everyone agrees that the optimal project size and duration is 3 to 9 months. Longer projects incur agency costs. Large initiatives can be carved into smaller efforts. An overall roadmap or release plan determines what functionality will be deployed, and when. A best-in-class roadmap incorporates all aspects of a project: people, processes, and technology. The roadmap itself effectively becomes a subportfolio.

- *Technology introduction methodology:* Most organizations struggle with the introduction of new platforms and major upgrades (desktop operating systems, network operating systems, databases, and enterprise application upgrades). Most of these same organizations don't use a standard process for introducing new IT. They repeatedly reinvent their technology introduction methodology, doomed to repeat the same mistakes. Why would they ever expect to get it right? You have an applications implementation methodology, so why not a technology introduction methodology?

- *Workflow reengineering and application integration methodologies:* The PMT is accountable for results, so it is responsible for ensuring that the organization employs the right methods for reengineering, application integration, and so forth. If you want the organization to adopt a standard methodology, then raise the hurdle for exceptions. If a reengineering or integration project team feels it requires a special dispensation to circumvent the standard methods, make them explain their reasons to the PMT. If the issue is not sufficiently important to be sent to the PMT, then the exception is probably not justified. If too many exceptions arise, then the methodology needs to be changed.

- *Voice of the customer (VOC):* Few organizations are adept at deriving requirements for IT-enabled solutions. This step is repeatedly identified as one of the most important in any project, because it codifies the intent and value proposition, and is especially important for complex transformation initiatives (comprised of people, process, and technology changes). Nevertheless, most organizations perform this activity superficially via ad hoc methods; they begin with a solution bias and reverse engineer confirming business requirements; or they sample a limit set of stakeholders. The consequences are mismanaged expectations, overspending, and stovepipe solutions. A best-in-class VOC process begins with business issues/problems, defines the business context, derives and validates business requirements, generates multiple solution concepts that fulfill business requirements, and then selects the optimal solution based on objective decision criteria.

Software Tools

There are no days in life so memorable as those which vibrated to some stroke of the imagination.
—Ralph Waldo Emerson, *Beauty, The Conduct of Life*

Why have we left the discussion of portfolio management software until the end? Because you might not have read the rest of the book had we started with a discussion of software. We've seen best-in-class portfolio management processes implemented on a shoestring software budget, using spreadsheets and document templates. We've also seen worst-in-class practices implemented with million-dollar portfolio management applications. The value from portfolio management will not come from software alone. Some vendors claim that their software will improve the return on IT investments. The software may entice someone to look at the data and make a better decision, but the software will not make people make decisions. The software will not hold senior leaders accountable for IT management. The software will enable the CIO to make some decisions, and may arm the CIO with better information to use in facilitating the business leaders through a portfolio management process. Performing trade-off analysis will identify the highest-valued projects, but a lot of the analysis is so subjective that it does no good unless the organization buys in to the data and is willing to stop investing in lesser-valued projects. The analysis and software might help shed light on the problem by providing greater situational awareness, but it won't make the problem go away, because it won't address the people and process aspects of IT portfolio management.

Software tools may enable a more efficient portfolio management process. Some things are more difficult to do with improvised tools—tasks including dynamic data collection, aggregation (rollup), and real-time analysis (decision-support). Software tools can help institutionalize procedures, if they automate workflow, and in this way help make the process stick. If the staff has no choice but to use the tool, then the tool might guide the process. If the tool makes it easier for the staff to do its job—if using the tool is the path of least resistance—then the staff might be motivated to use the tool, and consequently follow the process.

Software tools *will:*	Software tools will *not:*
• Automate . . . provided that people use the tool • Institutionalize procedures . . . provided that people use the tool • Enable consolidation . . . provided that people use the tool	• Provide leadership • Ensure alignment • Ensure information integrity • Ensure that decisions stick

Don't get so caught up in the tool's implementation as to forget the people and process changes required to achieve real bottom-line results. It is easy to become enamored of the technology. Software vendors need to sell software. Some may lead you to believe that their software doesn't need a process, or should be chosen in advance of the process. These promises are short-lived. Understand the vendor's motivations. Most vendors achieve their objective—sales—the day you purchase the software. The vendor may claim it seeks satisfied customers, and the sales staff may genuinely be concerned for their customers' satisfaction. Still, at the end of the fiscal period, they need to sell software. We've seen no portfolio application that will provide a return on investment unless an organization is willing and able to make the portfolio decisions. Organizations that have a lot of low-hanging fruit (low-value projects) probably don't even need commercial software at the outset. Robust portfolio management applications really pay off when they enable the organization to move to the next stage of performance.

Numerous IT organizations fail to follow their application implementation methodology when implementing portfolio management software, which is why so many portfolio software efforts fail. Failed efforts start with a request for information (RFI) and become so embroiled in vendor discussions that the entire initiative derails. It may be helpful to issue an RFI to gain insight into portfolio management best practices, but don't let the vendors short-circuit your transformation effort.

Develop shared awareness and buy-in to portfolio management objectives before investing in software. Without clarity on the business case for portfolio management, clarity on the business case for portfolio management software is not possible. If the process changes have not been carefully designed, automation requirements are uncertain. Do you *need* a Porsche? Or just a Hyundai? We know you'd rather have the Porsche, but is that what is right for your business? If the organization does not buy in to the process, it is not ready to talk to software vendors. Is the organization pushing to buy software? Great—use that momentum to gain buy-in to some fundamental process changes.

A best-in-class portfolio management process requires best-in-class portfolio management application software. Most organizations cannot afford to develop their own best-in-class applications with all the functionality of the top COTS portfolio management applications. If an organization is just looking for a way to enter some status information and roll up the portfolio, perhaps a home-grown application may suffice. It all comes down to requirements. What are the business requirements? Is the organization looking for breakthrough improvements in performance or a bandage solution? Is the organization buying a short-term fix or investing in IT that will become a core enabler of the portfolio management process? Will the organization accept automation of the portfolio management process, or is it not ready to go there yet? If people in your organization are not ready to change, you're not ready to convince them to change, or senior management isn't ready to take accountability for change, then don't invest a lot of money in software.

Portfolio management software offers a broad range of capabilities (functionality), including:

- *Investment and prioritization management:* Project concept submission and approval, inventory, decision-support graphs, scenario analysis, ranking analysis (to define the efficient frontier), what-if analysis, etc.
- *Resource management:* Forecasting demand for resources based on project and service requests and plans, allocation of named resources to projects, tracking time against assignments, analysis of variance-to-plan, forecast of skill requirements, etc.
- *Project management:* Work breakdown planning, tracking, status reporting, monitoring variance-to-plan (schedule and cost), etc.
- *Financial management:* Project-based and service-level cost accounting as well as integration with purchasing, vendor

management, financial accounting and budgeting, application life cycle accounting (total cost of ownership), asset management systems, etc.

- *Service management:* Service level monitoring, reporting, variance analysis, etc.
- *Collaboration management:* Project portals, document management, team collaboration, etc.

These needs can be addressed with a set of small, simple applications or point solutions. Point solutions, however, may not combine to deliver the same value as one integrated solution. The whole may be less than the sum of the parts. A mishmash of loosely coupled point solutions will not deliver the value of one comprehensive and integrated IT management system. The challenge is that the smaller point solutions may be cheaper to buy and maintain. Also, each smaller point solution may offer better features than one integrated solution, because integrated solutions rarely can sustain best-in-class feature sets for all capabilities. The organization may need to choose between best-in-class features and best-in-class integration. It is so important to consider longer-term needs before buying portfolio management software, which is another reason we put this discussion at the end of the book. Many IT managers find themselves in a predicament after building or buying a bunch of point solutions, then finding that they cannot deliver the information required by the organization to manage IT holistically. Decision makers need all the data in one integrated system so that they can correlate resource, project, and funding information when making portfolio decisions. After spending thousands of dollars on IT management systems, they find that they have the information but still cannot make effective decisions because they do not have the decision-support capabilities of an integrated dataset.

If your organization is confident it is ready to invest in software, then make an effort to understand what level of automation the next stage will require. The first step in determining what software to buy is to define requirements. The three levels of requirements are *business, functional,* and *IT.*

- *Business requirements* help formulate the problem statement. Business requirements provide shared situational awareness for the acquisition. The objective is not to acquire software.

The objective is to solve the problem and achieve the benefits outlined in the business case.

- *Functional requirements* identify specific functionality and service levels necessary to meet business requirements. (Note that functionality is not synonymous with features, which we will consider in a moment.) Functional requirements address people, process, and technical capabilities. Functional requirements are a good reality check for holes in the process design, so some prefer to define functional requirements in parallel with the process design. Functional requirements detail what capabilities are required (e.g., weekly refreshing of resource allocation changes in a central repository) without prescribing how to deliver those capabilities. For the most part, functional requirements are agnostic when it comes to technology.

- *IT requirements* define requisite application features and operational specifications. If acquiring COTS applications, it may not be necessary to specify IT requirements to the same extent as for home-grown applications. However, many COTS applications are highly configurable and can be integrated with others (financial, HR, etc.), so it is appropriate to at least define IT requirements for interfaces and configuration. It is also appropriate to note performance targets that may be unique to your organization due to its size, geographic distribution, connectivity limitations, or other characteristic.

A good COTS request for proposal (RFP) includes business, functional, and IT requirements. Anything less gives the vendor an incomplete understanding of what the organization is trying to accomplish. Anything more will add clarity. Engineer people, process, and technology requirements concurrently, as one integrated solution. For example, if the process calls for data entry and analysis to be performed by a distributed workforce (project managers in the field) and the organization needs to improve productivity by entering the data only once, then the software will need to support a distributed workforce. If project managers perform most of their data entry offline, then the software will need to support some type of replication or import-export capability. Asking project managers to duplicate data entry builds inefficiency into the process. Requiring project managers to enter the information online changes the project management methodology, which could have its own repercussions. Also consider operational parameters. If only a few people will use the application, then more solutions are likely to be found out there than if thousands of users will use it. Scalability is an issue for many of the cheaper portfolio applications.

We have intentionally omitted a discussion of specific vendors offering software for automating the portfolio management process, because the information would have become obsolete by the time this book went to print. The portfolio management software market is evolving rapidly. At this time, it is highly fragmented, with dozens of vendors claiming to sell portfolio management applications. The increased competition is healthy, but it makes the future somewhat uncertain, and so adds uncontrollable risk to any sizeable investment. The good news is that many of these applications have a payback of one to two years, provided they are used to automate a robust portfolio management process. The bad news is that your management will not want to hear that its brand new software application may have a useful life of only a few years. Ask the vendors where they plan to concentrate development efforts in the future. What functionality do they plan in future releases? They won't promise you anything, but at least you will be able to get a feel for their focus. Note the current customer profile (installed base) of any software you may be considering purchasing. Customer demand is a strong driver of future software features. If the organization's needs are not aligned with those of the vendor's other customers, then the organization may be disappointed with future releases.

Ultimately, every organization requires an integrated IT management process that allows it to manage a portfolio of projects and services. The robust portfolio applications may be deficient in service-level management, and vice versa. Deficiencies are okay as long as the organization designs around them. An organization may require three different applications today (portfolio, service, and financial management). Just make sure the three are interoperable.

Obtain a current market analysis when you are ready to create a RFI/RFP. IT analysts can provide current evaluations of project, portfolio, and resource management applications. In a nutshell, the market is comprised of vendors that have entered the portfolio software market from different perspectives:

- Developers of professional services software (consulting, applications integration, etc.)
- Developers of project management software (work breakdown structure, critical path analysis, etc.)
- Developers of research and development software (combination of the preceding types, but initial releases were designed for product development)
- Developers of IT performance management software (for service levels, monitoring, etc.)

Each historic origin provides a bias. Each origin brings with it a different legacy of features designed for a particular market. Some may be more or less suited to a particular organization's needs, depending on the requirements. As your organization begins to explore the applications, it will see for itself which ones add the most value.

Key Themes

- Enablers—decision support, performance metrics, best practices, and software tools—make the portfolio management process more efficient, make decision making more effective, and sometimes help to ensure the process "sticks" once it is implemented.
- Organizations do not need sophisticated, expensive enablers to implement a robust portfolio management process.
- Decision-support tools include the data, queries, reports, and charts necessary to assist with decision making. Decision support is especially valuable for the strategic analysis and decision-making phases of the portfolio management process.
- The IT performance measurement system needs to provide indicators of portfolio cost-effectiveness. The cost-effectiveness of the portfolio management process can be monitored using five sets of *tiered measures:* schedule variance, standard cost variance, service-level variance, resource capacity variance, and service development variance.
- Many best practices can be integrated with a strong portfolio management process, including business case analysis, high-caliber teams; project governance teams, iterative development, phase-based reviews, risk mitigation and contingency plans, roadmaps and release plans, workflow reengineering and application integration methodologies, financial worksheets, and technology introduction methodology.
- The value from portfolio management will not come from software. Software tools may, however, enable a more efficient portfolio management process.

Articulating—and Achieving—the Benefits of IT Portfolio Management

It is much more difficult to measure nonperformance than performance.

—Harold S. Geneen, on why management sometimes accepts underachievement

A disciplined portfolio management process takes the waste out of the IT management system and reinvests time and effort in solving business problems. As we noted in *IT Portfolio Management: What It Can Do; How It Works,* every organization manages IT investments, at least in the sense that everyone decides—either implicitly or explicitly—how and where to spend the IT budget. Whether an organization's portfolio management system tends to be ad hoc and informal or planned and structured turns out to have a significant bearing on how efficient and effective the system is.

The following table outlines a simple four-stage model for IT portfolio management practices in terms of their efficiency and effectiveness. *Informal* practices are the least effective and can be especially inefficient in organizations larger than 50 people. *Functional, collaborative,* and *enterprise-wide* practices drive increasingly efficient and effective IT investment management. To compare these four stages with one another, we look at the effectiveness of each stage of practice in six key areas, which together reveal how efficient and effective an organization's overall portfolio management process is:

- In the area of *strategy,* we are concerned with how well integrated IT planning is with the rest of the organization's planning process. We are also concerned here with who takes ownership for IT strategy and planning. In general, the more responsibility that a business abdicates to IT, the less

217

likely it will be that IT strategy and plans are aligned with business needs.

- In the area of *implementation,* we are concerned with whether the PMT can rely on a consistent, repeatable, predictable process to guide projects, or whether it must rely on the heroic efforts of a few select experts to get the job done.
- In the area of *operations,* we are primarily concerned with whether the service level delivered meets business needs, and whether the businesses can rely on the operations processes to deliver the services they need when they need it.
- In the area of *governance,* the highest level of practice is achieved when the IT department and the business functions share accountability for IT-enabled investments, and ownership and delegation of authority are clear, not only for implementation but also for bottom-line results.
- In the area of *metrics,* where it is easy to get bogged down in minutiae, the primary concern is with demonstrating both that performance commitments are being met and that continuous improvement occurs.
- In the area of *organization,* we look to see whether resources are aligned with priorities and fully utilized throughout the enterprise.

IT Portfolio Practices at Various Stages of Adoption

Informal Practices	*Functional Practices*	*Collaborative Practices*	*Enterprise-Wide Practices*
Strategy	**Strategy**	**Strategy**	**Strategy**
• Limited/no planning	• Few/no long-range plans (roadmaps)	• Roadmaps for key platforms	• Planning centers around value chain and core processes, not organizations or applications
• Emphasis on problem-solving results in proliferation of point solutions	• IT function "owns" the portfolio	• Business units "own" their portfolio	
• No team "owns" the portfolio	• Portfolio developed primarily from bottom up	• IT planning synchronized with business planning (corporate) calendar	• Company "owns" the portfolio
• Limited/no visibility into what projects are in the portfolio	• IT planning driven by budgeting timeline		• IT planning embedded in business strategic and annual planning cycles
			• Well defined 3-year enterprise process and system roadmap; planning is ongoing (roadmap adjustment vs. replanning)
Implementation	**Implementation**	**Implementation**	**Implementation**
• Unclear/no repeatable method	• Method emphasizes technology implementation	• Integrated projects responsible for end-to-end business transformation	• Adept at using holistic business transformation (people, processes, technology) to drive increased ROI and rapid payback
		• Integrated projects address people, processes, and technology change	

(*continued*)

IT Portfolio Practices at Various Stages of Adoption (*continued*)

Informal Practices	*Functional Practices*	*Collaborative Practices*	*Enterprise-Wide Practices*
Operations	**Operations**	**Operations**	**Operations**
• Unstable operations • Infrastructure deployed ad hoc	• Stable operations • Infrastructure deployed deliberately • Basic service-level objectives implemented but with limited measurement	• Infrastructure capacity and release plans driven by service-level objectives (SLOs) • SLOs defined by business based on need • Rudimentary service level measures in place	• 99.9% service-level achievement • Service-level reporting well established
Governance	**Governance**	**Governance**	**Governance**
• Teams are structured ad hoc • Practices/tools are informal • Customer-supplier relationship not clearly defined	• Teams comprised mostly of IT staff, with some cross-discipline collaboration • Some use of best practices/tools, primarily by the IT function • Requester-supplier relationship between IT and business	• Strong partnership structure on all projects between IT and business units • Consistent use of best practices/tools by IT and business unit staff • Shared accountability among leadership team for project success • Shared accountability among project team for effective project execution	• Internal market economy drives IT to function like a commercial service provider • Highest level of collaboration between IT and business unit staff • Universal use of integrated best practices/tools across disciplines and organizations • Shared accountability among leadership team for bottom-line mission results • Shared accountability among project team for efficient and effective project execution

(*continued*)

IT Portfolio Practices at Various Stages of Adoption (*continued*)

Informal Practices	*Functional Practices*	*Collaborative Practices*	*Enterprise-Wide Practices*
Metrics	**Metrics**	**Metrics**	**Metrics**
• Limited/no visibility into work-in-process and outstanding demand • Limited/no quantitative performance measurement • Limited knowledge of service provision costs • Limited/no motivation to improve	• Some/limited visibility into IT project status • Some/limited quantitative performance measures, focused on IT department (vs. IT process) • Knowledge of aggregate operating costs • Weak motivation to improve	• Actual vs. plan exception reporting for project status • Performance measures focused on the process (as well as the IT department) • Visibility into unit cost, demand, capacity (supply), and service level • Strong motivation to improve	• Real-time visibility into project status • Performance measures focused on mission success factors (e.g., application performance) • Integrated service-level and cost reporting • Continuous improvement culture fostered by leadership team collaboration to align performance with business need
Organization	**Organization**	**Organization**	**Organization**
• Resources managed informally • Centralized IT resources prioritize based on urgency or first-in, first-out	• Resources optimized within departments • IT allocates resources to business units and prioritizes based on business unit priorities • Limited enterprise-wide resource leverage	• Resources optimized within departments with some cross-departmental teams • Aggregate resource alignment with key projects • Use of third-party providers to lower cost or augment capabilities	• Named-resource management permits real-time shift of resources between projects and across departments • Effective, seamless use of third-party providers to manage cost and service quality

The IT management practices of most organizations are *functional* at best. Few organizations have reached the *enterprise-wide* stage. Not every organization requires enterprise-wide practices. However, in our experience, most large organizations require a minimum of *collaborative* practices to satisfy CxOs.

This way of describing the effects of improved IT portfolio management focuses on the *characteristics* of organizations at various stages of their development from informal to enterprise-wide practices rather than on the ultimate *benefits* to be achieved by this development. What, then, are the concrete benefits, in terms of performance, that an improved portfolio management process offers? We can illustrate the escalating benefits as an organization moves from informal to enterprise-wide portfolio management practices with a graph similar to the one that follows, which shows that step-function improvements (as opposed to the results of continuous improvement) assume a greater magnitude as cross-functional practices become more tightly integrated.

How do you get such step-function improvements in performance? Where should you focus your efforts in order to do so? The step-function improvements illustrated here comprise improvements in three particular areas: increasing throughput, optimizing resources, and expanding what we call the "efficient frontier" of projects.

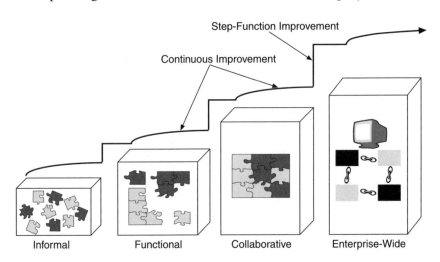

Increasing Throughput

Reduced throughput is one of the leading symptoms of an organization with a weak or ad hoc portfolio management process. Effective and efficient portfolio management increases portfolio throughput. We define *throughput* as the output produced by a given amount of input. More specifically, we define *portfolio throughput* as the number of projects completed successfully (on schedule, at or below budget, and meeting expectations) for a given amount of resources (money, people, and assets).

Portfolio decision making affects throughput by managing two variables: project cycle time and portfolio capacity. *Project cycle time* is the time from concept initiation (the first dollar spent on the notion) through project completion (the last dollar spent on the project prior to the cutover to steady-state operations). *Portfolio capacity* is the rolling average number of projects successfully completed annually (or within any other given period).

Portfolio decision making affects project cycle time by determining the size, charter, and deliverables of projects. Lengthy projects clog up the project pipeline and are more prone to failure. They are complex, tie up resources, and consume organizational mindshare. They are more prone to failure for reasons that parallel manufacturing processes with a lot of work-in-process inventory. The longer incomplete projects remain "in process," the more prone they are to breakdowns (scope changes, version-control problems, business disruptions and divergence, governance distractions, etc.). Project staff is more likely to turn over on longer projects, thereby depleting knowledge and requiring repetition of project work. On long projects the sense of urgency is reduced, because motivation follows a "bathtub" curve (high at first, declining and dropping off in the middle, increasing again near the end).

Portfolio decision making also affects project cycle time by ensuring effective project governance (project assurance, decision making, reporting, etc.). Project teams expend an inordinate amount of time and energy on governance-related deliverables, even in a highly disciplined and well-managed governance process. A cumbersome governance process creates unnecessary overhead in the form of surplus status reporting, circuitous decision making, excess documentation, and redundant quality assurance mechanisms. An ill-defined governance process requires project leadership to guess at what the governance deliverables are, necessitating ever-evolving reporting requirements and redundant briefings, and obscuring who the real decision makers are. A weak governance process fails to force decisions, or causes the organization to revisit decisions, thereby delaying and distracting the entire project team.

Portfolio decision making also affects portfolio capacity. Portfolio managers determine how many resources exist, what skills are required, and how fast to release (launch) new projects. It might seem logical to minimize time-to-start for a new project. Too often, however, portfolio managers try to cram as many projects as possible into the portfolio. Trying to execute too many projects simultaneously decreases throughput and reduces productivity. We call this practice the *peanut butter principle:* spreading critical resources too thin makes them ineffective.

Throughput declines when it takes longer for critical resources to finish a project. Suppose it takes a critical resource 20 days to complete a task. If the people involved dedicate their time to just this one task, their cycle time to complete the task is 20 days. If they split their time evenly between two projects, cycle time effectively doubles. Three projects triple the cycle time, and so on. The longer a task remains open, the greater the potential for error. People forget what they've done. People forget what they intended to do. Someone might redirect the task. Other dependent tasks can get out of sequence. In some instances, productivity declines as resources waste time switching back and forth between tasks, trying to juggle too many demands on their time. They become distracted and ineffectual, unable to focus on the task at hand. Critical resources become a bottleneck. Quality suffers as people start to cut corners. Poor quality creates additional waste in the form of quick fixes and rework. Ultimately, throughput declines.

With a decline in throughput, managers may question resource effectiveness. They are most likely to question the project's management and resource skills, and in some cases will even suspect employee integrity. In almost all assessments, these factors rarely turn out to be the primary cause of reduced throughput. What happens more often is that the leadership team cannot make the hard decisions. It tries to do too much, too fast, with too few resources, too ill-defined a process, and with too little leadership involvement.

The Bottleneck in the Business Unit

A mid-sized insurance company struggled with the problem of reduced throughput. The organization was increasingly dissatisfied with its throughput for IT projects. Senior management felt that "it took the IT department too long" to complete projects. We reviewed the IT department's processes, and although we found some inefficiency, none of it was anything that should have been causing major delays. We then looked at resource allocation in the IT department, which appeared reasonable and not the cause of delay. The last place we looked was at the business resource allocation, which is where we found the bottleneck. Not enough business resources were allocated to the project. The business unit was causing its own delays by not dedicating resources to activities such as leadership, requirements definition, testing, and training. The well-intentioned IT resources attempted to perform these tasks on behalf of the business, but IT staff were not authorized to sign off on them. The business delayed signing off because it wasn't adequately involved. The IT staff, in an attempt to be productive, kept executing the project plan and got too far out in front of the business, which caused rework when the business finally reviewed the plans and redirected the effort. The project delays caused the business to increase pressure on the IT staff to accelerate the timeline—despite the fact that it was not IT staff who had caused the delay. The project was pressured to cut corners, causing quality problems, which in turn caused additional rework. The project fell into a downward spiraling, systemic loop of poor quality, resulting in waste, spending overruns, schedule slippage, dissatisfaction, and shortcuts.

The right thing to do was to tell the business that the project would have to be shut down unless people there got with the program. The right thing to do was to force the organization to balance its supply of resources with its demand for new IT. The right thing to do was to make these hard decisions. This organization didn't do the right thing. Instead, this organization spent millions of dollars each year on rework and other instances of wasted resources. The organization's leadership team dealt with increased frustration and distraction due to apparent IT cost overruns and mismanaged expectations. The bottom-line impact was reduced throughput, because too much focus was spent on time-to-start instead of on successful completion.

Optimizing Resources

In order to maximize portfolio capacity, it is necessary to optimize resources. Some people are under the misconception that *resource productivity* is sufficient. They are wrong. If the organization does not successfully complete an optimal number of projects, then the organization is wasting resources. It may be wasting resources productively. It may be wasting resources efficiently. Yet, time, energy, and money spent on the portfolio without commensurate value are, indeed, merely wasted.

For resources to be optimized:

- *Resources must be busy:* People need to be efficient and devote their time to assigned activities.
- *Resources must be productive:* People need to be competent at their assigned activities.
- *The process must be effective and efficient:* The tasking of resources must be consistent, repeatable, and geared to organizational effectiveness.

Resource Optimization

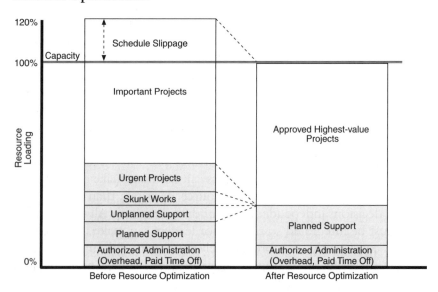

Before Resource Optimization   After Resource Optimization

Portfolio management affects portfolio capacity by managing critical resources. Manufacturing managers are familiar with the principles of capacity constraint. Some of the best IT managers have a strong manufacturing background, and an understanding of how to manage constrained resources. Like manufacturing assets, human resources are not particularly fungible in the short term. It would make life easier if everybody was interchangeable. In the real world, however, individuals too often have specialized capabilities or knowledge, and we cannot exchange one person for another without retraining. Not everyone can be an effective project manager, and subject-matter experts are painfully few. Most likely a small number of organizational resources are critical. Only a small percentage of people might actually have the perspective, experience, and expertise required to make projects successful. Those few become the bottleneck. A good portfolio management process will manage bottlenecks, because it gives portfolio managers visibility into the queue of projects and visibility into the types and numbers of resources required now and in the near future.

Portfolio managers can better flex resource capacity to meet the organization's needs if they have advance knowledge of resource needs. The more lead time they have, the better they can balance the supply of resources with the demand. The portfolio and service development processes provide valuable demand planning information that helps an organization to adjust its skill mix. Managers use this information to predict short-term spikes in resource needs versus steady-state resource requirements, which in turn allows an organization to use its resources more strategically, balancing the number of short-term contract resources and long-term permanent ones. Many organizations choose to treat resource management as a separate process. However, it is easy to see that when it is tightly integrated with the portfolio management process, it makes portfolio managers much more effective. The portfolio process can no more make effective project decisions independently of resource decisions than it can make project decisions independently of funding decisions. All this information must be integrated so that senior leaders can make informed decisions consistently, comprehensively, and with full understanding of how these decisions impact other projects. (For a more detailed discussion of managing the interdependency between portfolio management and resource management, see the section on resource management in the "Interdependencies" portion of *Workflow Design.*)

Expanding the Efficient Frontier of Projects: Doing the Right Things Right

Effective portfolio management expands *the efficient frontier of projects*. Two streams of work are required to expand the efficient frontier:

- Determining what projects to pursue (*doing the right things*)
- Determining what will make the projects successful (*doing things right*)

To do the right things, managers need to understand the difference between IT that provides competitive advantage (*strategic*) and IT that is merely needed-to-play (*critical*).[1] An application may forever be a critical piece of the enterprise architecture, but that quality doesn't make it any more strategic than the roof over your head. Buildings are not strategic, but none of us would want to live without the benefits they provide. IT, like buildings, requires regular maintenance. IT, like buildings, requires modification (enhancement) to accommodate evolving requirements. But most IT applications are not strategic. An integrated financial application is a good example of a mature technology that is critical, but it may not be strategic. Integrated financial applications emerged in the 1980s and became trendy during the ERP software application boom of the late 1990s. Most corporations adopted them. Various flavors (configurations) exist, tailored to meet the needs of different industries. Compared to the old fragmented financial applications, the new ones provide tremendous financial analysis and reporting capability. However, for the most part, these applications no longer offer competitive advantage. They provide competitive parity. Typically, large organizations have already gleaned most of the financial management benefits that stem directly from the software itself. Organizations now must change their business processes to obtain additional improvement. Adding a feature here or improving some function there offers diminishing returns as measured by its impact on organizational performance. Most software capabilities can now be matched by the competition. Hence, diminishing returns are realized with the continued technology

---

[1] For an illustration of this distinction, see the example in the section on *Interdependencies*, under the heading *IT Governance Processes*.

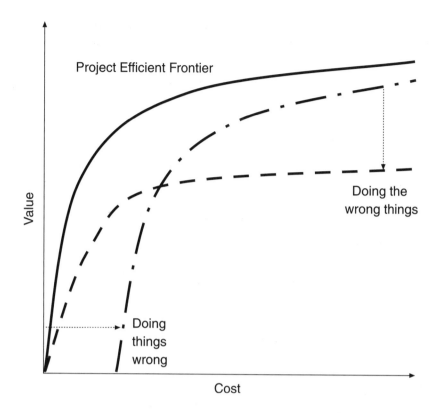

enhancements beyond those required to adapt to evolving operational requirements. An organization needs to scrutinize enhancements to ensure that they are truly required to meet evolving business conditions, or that the enhancement truly provides some type of bottom-line efficiency. Nevertheless, the applications remain mission-critical and must be sustained until the organization or the application ceases to function.

Most portfolio management processes overlook or more or less deliberately neglect the second work stream for expanding the efficient frontier of projects: *doing things right.* In our experience, subtle changes to project scope can increase the value returned or shorten the payback period for a project. Just as minor changes to a commercial product may enable it to better serve multiple market segments, so can slight changes to a software application enable it to serve multiple purposes or return greater value sooner. Without prompting, project teams may not even consider the payback period—the time it takes for an application to actually deliver enough value (benefits) to justify its development costs.

Sometimes simply by adding a focus on faster payback to the list of objectives, a project can dramatically increase its overall return. Sometimes all it takes is to resequence project activities over time—that is, change the road map. Unfortunately, most project teams have enough trouble simply defining the business and IT requirements. By the time they spell out the requirements, the organization is so impatient to move on to implementation that team members don't stop and think about how they prioritize functionality, bundle releases, deploy capabilities, and so on. Did they maximize value or did they prioritize based on criteria such as political correctness, middle manager biases, and the squeaky wheel? (It is easy to focus on appeasing one particular organization or stakeholder with a lot of clout or money.) Perhaps the organization that initiated the project assumed that its needs took higher precedence than those of others, and the IT service provider has marched to that drum because it lacks the political clout to do otherwise and does not have access to a PMT that can intervene. We often find that the particular business need that triggers a project concept in the first place may not be the most important need. Sometimes it is simply the most urgent one. It does not necessarily mean that it should be the top priority. It is the job of the project team to make a recommendation, but it is the job of the PMT to make the right decision, because that decision will affect the entire resource portfolio.

Ultimately, the PMT must approve the way the project team sequences the deployment of functionality to achieve maximum value for the entire organization. Some organizations are inclined to take a big-bang approach to software implementation, trying to deploy the software everywhere at once. For big organizations this tactic can be debilitating. It depletes business and IT resources and impedes the steady-state business productivity. Soon senior leaders are investing more time in managing the application deployment than in managing the business. Such organizations need to determine where and how to deploy software to maximize value returned for each dollar invested. Where is the biggest bang for the buck? Which modules of CRM functionality actually improve the bottom line, which are needed to play, and which are just nice to have? Should the modules be deployed concurrently, at the risk of depleting organizational resources and creating additional schedule risk, or should they be deployed sequentially over time?

Adding Up the Benefits

Overall, effective and efficient portfolio management processes offer the benefits of enabling an organization to do the following:

- Optimize the efficient frontier of projects
- Increase value from the project portfolio (return on investment)
- Cancel lesser-value projects
- Optimize scope of projects for optimal payback period and value
- Reduce scope overlap and redundancy among projects
- Reduce project schedule and budget slippage
- Ensure proper project governance and accountability
- Better manage project interdependencies
- Increase throughput (more output for the same amount of input)
- Balance the supply of resources with demand for resources (dollars, labor, assets, etc.)
  - Less waste (less work-in-process; lower caching)
  - Higher quality (fewer shortcuts)
- Gain earlier visibility into future resource needs
- Engage in better resource planning
  - Right skill mix
  - Right mix of temporary versus long-term resources
  - Right mix of internal versus external resources

While listing the benefits, it is important to emphasize that improving the IT portfolio management process can and should improve the bottom line. Most organizations do not realize just how much they waste through ineffective decision making. Doing the right projects right can increase return on investment and reduce the payback period. Canceling lower-value projects frees up funding for higher-value ones. Also, managing project resource loading reduces project cost and increases the number of projects completed per period. The amount of dollars saved by robust portfolio management can be eye opening. The following table shows typical gains from various aspects of portfolio strategy:

Portfolio Management Benefits

Portfolio Strategy	*Metrics*
Doing the right projects	
Increased value (project benefits)	→ 25% to 50% greater ROI
Shorter payback (results focus)	→ 10% to 25% shorter payback period
Canceling lower-value projects	
Lower investment expense (one-time)	→ 15% to 25% reduced investment (capital) expense
Avoiding operating expense (ongoing)	→ Annual expense = 20% of one-time cost
Managing pipeline overload	
Decreased waste (less work-in-process)	→ 10% to 20% reduced schedule slippage, overruns
Improved throughput and productivity	→ 10% to 20% more projects completed per year
	→ 30% reduction in non-value-added tasks
Strategic sourcing (labor)	→ 5% to 10% lower contract-labor cost
Increased project forecast accuracy	→ Actual project costs delivered within 10% of original forecast

To summarize these gains, we list three ways that IT portfolio management affects the bottom line:

- Increased efficiency
- Increased capacity
- Increased value

Increased efficiency: IT portfolio management makes an organization more productive. We assert that, on average, organizations are 20% more productive after implementing a new portfolio management process. A lot depends on where the organization is starting from and how thoroughly it improves its portfolio management practices. In our experience, going from informal practices to functional practices alone can deliver a 20% productivity improvement. This improvement does not necessarily translate into a 20% decrease in labor expenses, however. If we cannot reallocate and consolidate resource assignments, then we cannot reduce headcount and cannot realize a labor cost reduction. If the net labor expense reduction is greater than zero, however, then we should be able to identify some cost reduction (bottom-line or opportunity cost) in the IT budget. Suppose that through resource reallocation we can see our way clear to eliminating five resources (headcount), at a per-person annual cost of $100,000 (salary plus benefits). That elimination represents a permanent $500,000 annual labor expense reduction, if someone is willing to sign up (be accountable) for achieving the reduction. This calculation is just one example of expense reduction. On the other hand, our goal might be to do more with the resources we have rather than decrease headcount.

Increased capacity: The next benefit to look for from IT portfolio management is an improvement in capacity. Calculating the value of increased labor capacity is somewhat tricky. Not all improvements in labor capacity are usable. For example, if we free up 10 minutes of someone's time, does the organization really benefit? We need to understand what benefit comes from the increased capacity. To understand the benefit, we need to calculate the opportunity cost, the cost of not achieving the capacity increase. Many managers discount opportunity costs, mostly because they are rarely calculated objectively. Our view of organizational resource use may change when we make the proper calculations. In the preceding example, a company achieves a 20% gain in productivity. Suppose they also free up an incremental 20,000 hours. This amount represents 10 full-time equivalent (FTE) resources (one FTE equals 2,000 hours per year). These hours are comprised of bits and pieces of time spread across 30 people. A headcount of 10 represents $1 million, but $1 million is NOT our opportunity cost; because we cannot eliminate bits and pieces of people, we have no way to realize the benefit. We may not even be able to use all the bits and pieces of people's time effectively. On the other hand, suppose we can use 5,000 hours from those bits and pieces to execute two more projects each year than we otherwise would be able to execute. Suppose each average project of that size generates $250,000 in annual savings to the organization. Then the opportunity cost is two projects, or $500,000 achieved year-over-year ($500,000 per year for the near future), if someone signs up for achieving these savings. If we do not implement the portfolio effort, then the forgone opportunity of performing these two additional projects each year represents our opportunity cost.

Increased value: Portfolio value (calculated, in dollar terms, as NPV) is another bottom-line benefit of IT portfolio management. If we replace lower-value projects in the portfolio with higher-value ones, then the net increase in portfolio value is a benefit. It is difficult to calculate this number ex ante because you don't know what "better" projects you'll come up with until you implement the new portfolio management process. It might even take your organization a year or so to learn how to come up with better projects. In our experience, it is common for organizations to see in excess of 2% to 10% increase in portfolio value within one year of implementing a best-in-class portfolio management process. Some have enjoyed greater increases in value, depending on the baseline. These benefits have been achieved year-over-year. If you've implemented portfolio management improvements for only a small portfolio segment, improved portfolio management still likely represents a significant value!

How to Drive Change

Change is one thing, progress is another. "Change" is scientific, "progress" is ethical; change is indubitable, whereas progress is a matter of controversy.

—Bertrand Russell, *Philosophy and Politics*

Portfolio management is a little different from most processes, because it is a management process that affects managers more than their staff members. Trying to get managers to change is tricky. Trying to get managers to change when the process implementers are more junior in the organization is especially tricky. Senior management mandates don't usually achieve the desired result. Managers are adept at passively resisting change. They may appear to accept the proposed changes, but when it comes time to really start to use the process, managers find all sorts of reasons why it isn't ready for implementation. Or managers implement the process and then exploit loopholes and technicalities to serve their personal agendas rather than supporting the original intent. Good managers want to understand the value proposition before they will even consider change, and it is entirely reasonable for them to do so. Change is time-consuming, disruptive, and full of uncertainty. Managers need to understand what the benefits of the new process are going to be. They need to understand how these benefits will translate into organizational value. Managers need to know whether the changes will make their departments' missions easier or more difficult, how the changes will affect their staff members' responsibilities and workload, and how the process will affect their own personal spans of control. Only once the organization has clarified these issues are managers likely to buy in and proactively support the change effort—and this statement presumes that the changes are in their favor.

One of the major challenges of IT portfolio management is that if we genuinely implement a robust portfolio management process, it shifts the power base of an organization. (If it didn't, then the changes in an organization's decision-making process wouldn't be significant enough to impact the bottom line.) Messing with the power relationships in organizations threatens some managers; at a minimum, it unnerves the current decision makers. Some people will not want to change. Enlightened managers will see how the overall benefits to the organization outweigh the potential risks or personal impositions, but most will obsess about the downside risks (e.g., that their span of control will be reduced or that they will be held more accountable for results). Those who previously determined which projects had higher priority than others may no longer have as much control or even influence over the decision-making process. Those who previously were not held accountable for repeated project failures may find increased scrutiny of past decisions.

Messing with the Power Base

At a government agency, a large project that was over budget and way behind schedule was cancelled before we even defined the portfolio management process. Was it the right thing to do? Yes. But being the right thing didn't make it any more palatable for any of the parties involved. The project was behind because the organization was not properly supporting the transformation endeavor. It was nobody's fault. Nonetheless, the program manager and contractor lost credibility. The cancellation became a black mark on their respective records. That outcome was unfortunate, because the organization should never have started the project in the first place. The leadership team had never fully bought into the transformation effort.

When setting out to convince people to change their behavior, it is important to recognize that some type of portfolio management process already exists. It may be ad hoc, but it exists, so that claiming no portfolio process exists or that the process is "broken" might not be the most tactful message. In most organizations, people will admit to potential opportunities for improvement, but the uncertainties involved in transformation projects make people wary of them, which is why managers will push back when you attempt to implement a new process. This resistance, in turn, is why the change needs to be driven from the top down. To avoid the pitfalls inherent in such an approach, portfolio goals need to be constructive, not punitive. The focus needs to be on improving the bottom line. You're not implementing the process because people are not doing their jobs. You're implementing it because you've reached a plateau in performance, and the only way to rise above that plateau is by working collaboratively to maximize the value of the portfolio. Recognize that, when first implementing the process, it is likely to expose issues some managers would prefer remain hidden. All project managers make mistakes. The way most managers learn to be good managers is by learning from their mistakes or those of others. Training helps, but wisdom comes from hands-on experience. All of us have made mistakes, and the best way to deal with the difficult disclosures that arise during the implementation process is to give everyone a "get out of jail free" card. Make it clear, both at the outset and throughout the change management process that the organization is not going to persecute anyone for past transgressions. The objective of portfolio management is to increase value, which we don't accomplish by beating an organization down.

Convincing the management team that it needs to become involved in portfolio management is the first step in achieving buy-in to the change effort. It is challenging for a management team member to know how to ration limited discretionary funds to concentrate on initiatives that have the strongest probability of driving value or growth. Senior leadership should concentrate its collective attention on its own responsibility to ensure thorough and proper governance of IT, preventing the company from throwing good money after bad. In so doing, senior leadership puts pressure on middle management to systemically improve operational performance—people, processes, and technology. Senior leadership decisions may not be popular. Plenty of middle managers in IT and the business are going to complain when their pet IT projects are deferred. Savvy managers understand that difficult decisions are rarely popular, but they still support the strategy. The less savvy ones will complain, but they are likely to complain no matter what senior leadership does.

One of the challenges for senior leaders in trying to influence the behavior of middle managers is that senior leaders have limited visibility into the systemic problems and opportunities created by the weaknesses and strengths of various individual managers. For senior leaders, middle management constitutes a FOG, consisting of *fearful, overachieving,* and *gifted* employees. Fearful managers obsess about issues and problems, either unable or afraid to focus on solutions lest they be tasked with delivering results. The fearful do not want to change the status quo and risk losing their organizational power. Overachieving managers, by contrast, have grandiose plans to change the organization. Overachievers think that they could do a better job of leading than the leadership team is doing, but in reality they are oblivious to the complexity and magnitude of the issues at play. They haven't completely thought through a plan to address these issues and lack the competence to implement such a plan even if they had one. Then the truly gifted are those rare managers who have both the perspective to understand what needs to be done and the ability to execute in a comprehensive way. Gifted employees are few, and many lack sufficient voice in the organization because they spend most of their time managing instead of politicking. Hopefully, senior leaders, who cannot do everything themselves, have surrounded themselves with enough gifted employees to overcome the plethora of personal fears and ambitions within the management team as a whole.

Under these circumstances, launching a portfolio management process and making it successful requires creating a coalition. The coalition will help achieve buy-in to the change effort and will lend it credibility by assisting in the process design and implementation. The coalition must be comprised of all three types of managers. Gifted managers provide immediate support. Overachievers can provide vision. Once converted, even the most fearful managers often become the greatest champions of the effort, because they can often best communicate the value proposition to others who are equally fearful of the change. The coalition needs champions and sponsors, subject-matter experts and ordinary participants in the new process. Champions speak out in support of the change effort, but may not have money to fund it. Sponsors fund the change effort, but may wish to remain impartial in the eyes of their constituents. Subject-matter experts know how the process is executed today. Participants will be required to use the transformed process. Some in the coalition will want formal recognition, others will prefer anonymity. All members of the coalition serve a purpose. The coalition is built one person at a time, one conversation at a time. Don't expect executive mandates and large initiatives to suffice as a substitute for such a coalition. The mandate *du jour* might lend temporary credibility, but without coalition support the change effort will stall or backslide as soon as executives focus elsewhere. The coalition looks at the change effort from multiple angles, assesses the ripple effects, and determines the expected value proposition for the organization. In time, the coalition will need to recruit or override the fearful, who generate the FUD factor: fear, uncertainty, and doubt. The organization must overcome the FUD factor to be successful in the long run and not be doomed to passive and active resistance.

Portfolio management gives the organization no place to hide. It sounds great to overachievers, but it scares managers who suddenly find themselves accountable for results. Anyone who has actually experienced accountability understands that it is a burden, not a perk. Authority is a perk. Accountability is an obligation. Unfortunately, authority without accountability can create nightmares for an organization. Few managers experience true accountability in the course of their careers. Legal precedent impairs an organization's ability to hold

Improvement Implementation Curve

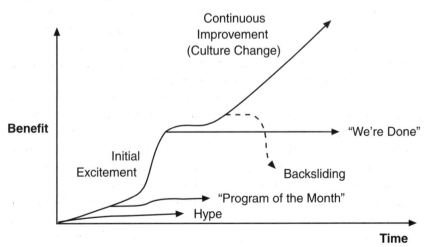

employees accountable. Some organizations attempt to use compensation as a means of instilling accountability, but personal relationships, unclear roles, ambiguous requirements, and ill-defined deliverables end up diluting any real accountability. The system is imperfect, which results in imperfect accountability for results. Navigating these murky waters when, as a member of a PMT, one is accountable for "fixing" this portfolio and generating results in the current fiscal year sounds like fun only to overachievers and the ignorant.

So why would anyone willingly strengthen accountability by improving portfolio management? Why would middle managers want to increase visibility into project results knowing that they have made suboptimal decisions in the past? Why should shareholders pay for the transformation to a state that should already exist? Who is going to explain to the shareholders why it doesn't exist? An organization will need to answer all these questions if it wants the portfolio change effort to succeed.

To make matters worse, improving a portfolio management process requires change at the most senior of management levels. Surprisingly, many senior managers are unaccustomed to following processes. In fact, many managers became managers so that they could make and break all the rules. For years, management has been an art as opposed to a science. Increasingly, universities are better understanding the behavioral science of management. Portfolio management is the result of one of these sciences—the science of governing sets of projects to achieve an intended result. Portfolio management imposes structure on traditionally undocumented or unstructured decision-making processes in which organizations have executed their workflows without formal guidelines and roles. Although this informality works for some processes, we found it to be mostly ineffective for management processes. Management processes need to be clear, lest managers use them to exploit every loophole and ambiguity. The problem is that gaining consensus from senior executives is like herding cats—you can coax and gesture, but getting them to do what you want will be a challenge. Each manager has a unique personality. We can't change personalities, so we need to understand different individuals' needs and motivations, to help them to understand how portfolio management will help them achieve their individual goals. We need to answer the question, *What's in it for me (WIIFM)?* Knowing the WIIFM for each manager provides us with insight into what the process must do to achieve management's buy-in. It also provides clues to where we may have to compromise in our process design to achieve buy-in—for example, we may not be able to do everything we intended at the outset of the change effort until we gain credibility with senior management.

It is necessary to convince and entice management to change, because no single individual, from the CEO on down, is capable of making managers change. For everyone affected by the portfolio process you need to provide an analysis supporting the business case for change as well as answer the WIIFM question. Why should the process participants change what they are doing? How will your process make them successful? You won't be able to answer this question definitively for everyone, but if you want your coalition to support the change effort, answer the WIIFM question as best as you can. Your coalition can help. If you want senior management to fund the effort, answer the WIIFM question for them. Sometimes it can be helpful to develop a written value proposition (business case) for senior management to justify improving the portfolio management process. For some leaders in some organizations, a qualitative value proposition may suffice. If you've answered the WIIFM question for all the major constituents, then all you need to do is summarize the answers in a presentation. Then add in the expected cost of implementing the change effort. Other leaders in other organizations may require a quantitative cost-benefit assessment. Such an assessment is more challenging because you will need to translate the WIIFM answers into bottom-line implications.

Changing the way that upper management behaves takes more diplomacy, time, and strength of mind than most people anticipate. Many organizations turn to professional facilitators and change agents to help with this effort. Internal staff members are career conscious and conditioned not to challenge the status quo. Those who "tell it like it is" are rarely rewarded for their good intentions; the potential career repercussions may not be worth the sacrifice. (How many managers, for example, are willing, at first, to risk their careers by telling the division head that his or her behavior needs to change?) Those managers who *are* willing to utter hard truths may not have the time, experience, or expertise to handle these issues with delicacy. In actuality, it may be impossible to facilitate the transition to effective portfolio management without stepping on toes. Yet avoiding such confrontations may result in a suboptimal process. Outside agents are immune from career repercussions—at least within your organization. Experienced executive facilitators know how to deliver difficult messages diplomatically. External agents are expected to ruffle a few feathers because it is what they get paid for. Sometimes an outside agent's opinion holds more weight because decision makers perceive the outside agent as being more experienced and objective. Think it's a double standard? Perhaps, but remember that the facilitator's engagement is short-lived. When facilitators complete their mission or outstay their welcome, external agents need to find work elsewhere. You will be around long after they leave. Most leading companies can afford outside help. Those reluctant to spend the money probably have the greatest need to do so.

Facilitation and change management are real skills. Contrary to popular belief, many managers lack them. Most managers do not have the objectivity, discipline, patience, interest, or time to nurture these skills. Most managers are conflict-adverse and are not used to hearing the unvarnished truth. Most staff are unaccustomed to, or too impatient for, spoon-feeding managers what they need to know when they need to know it. A good change agent can aid in the transition to a new portfolio management process by defining what needs to be presented and how it needs to be presented, as well as by coaching managers on what to expect and how *not* to react if they want to promote the continued sharing of the unvarnished truth. A good change agent will work outside and across organizational boundaries, reducing the time it takes for unfiltered information to flow from managers to their fellow managers and to decision makers. They are a catalyst for shared situational awareness. They are educators, mentors, and counselors to the organization.

Most professional change agents spend most of their time communicating with managers, both orally and in written form. The oral communication generates buy-in. The written communication generates common understanding. Many executives will buy in to the process conditionally, depending on how well it is designed. Remember that one of the WIIFM questions is how the process will make everyone involved successful. If poorly designed, all the portfolio management process does is shift decision authority from one power base to another. So ultimately you will need to put the process on paper to engage executives and process experts, ensuring that all have a common understanding of how the process will operate. The documentation should clearly communicate accountabilities and responsibilities to the rest of the organization. When you consider what you want to document, you don't want to create a tome that nobody will read. You don't want to create a thousand flow charts and "wiring diagrams" that mean nothing except to those who created them. We recommend documenting only that which is useful for communicating with your audience. In addition to the business case, at a minimum the documentation should include the following:

- A workflow overview depicting high-level activities and inter-dependencies with other IT management processes
- A depiction of roles (see the RACI matrix presented in *Governance Design*), describing the accountabilities and responsibilities of process participants and explaining who will be consulted and informed throughout the process
- A data flow chart depicting where information will come from and what databases or applications need be integrated
- Business rules that will determine the guidelines and delegation of authority for process participants
- Tools and templates that will be used in the near term for process efficiency (automation)
- IT requirements for any longer-term portfolio software acquisition

The documentation can be Web-enabled, stored online for easy access, or stored in static documents and presentations. Remember that every document has an audience, so your objective should be not just to document but to do so in a manner that facilitates learning, buy-in, and adoption of the process. Once you have the basics in place, you can continuously improve the efficiency and effectiveness of portfolio management. A more disciplined and institutionalized process will outperform an informal one regardless of organization size, structure, or politics. For example, can you imagine that a large, bureaucratic $20 billion company can effectively review and approve a multimillion-dollar project in less than a half-hour? Well, it can.

Finally—as should be crystal clear by now—in implementing a new portfolio management process it is also essential to understand from the outset that it will take a lot of time and attention to detail. We tell clients, in fact, that it will take a year to fully absorb and institutionalize a new process. Many doubt this statistic, perhaps because they lack the change management experience or just don't want to face reality. A typical process implementation will take one to three months to design, but plan on it taking as long as nine months of really using the process before it "sticks" in the organization. Making change stick takes a lot more care and feeding than most people expect; changing the way an organization does business is a major effort. It requires hundreds of small changes, many of them involving seemingly insignificant cultural nuances. Continuous fine-tuning makes the difference between a process that sits on a shelf and a process that is institutionalized into your culture.

Making the Process Stick

A computer storage manufacturer found that it took only a few months to design a portfolio management process around best practices that met the organization's needs. The company piloted the process through the design and implementation phases with relative ease, but it took nine months of fine-tuning and facilitation to institutionalize it. It didn't take long to establish the new governance teams, and the new structure started to return benefits from the outset. However, getting the organization to fully understand, buy in to, and begin using the new process took much longer. The CIO thought that all he had to do was tell others what to do. In reality, getting the process working required several months of continual communication and education. Although building a business case template took just one day, getting the organization (which had a strong financial discipline and a results-oriented culture) to effectively use the new template took months. The organization had difficulty quantifying (or even qualifying) and committing to the benefits of a new application. Critical IT resources were wasted calculating the total cost of projects that lacked sufficient business value. Eventually, the CIO changed the process to require business managers to articulate, document, and agree upon the value proposition before allowing IT resources to cost a project. Only when the portfolio decision makers were satisfied with the benefits statement would they allow the IT staff to develop a TCO statement.

There is nothing more difficult to carry out, or more doubtful of success, nor more dangerous to handle, than to initiate a new order of things. For the reformer has enemies in all those who profit from the old order.

—Niccolo Machiavelli, *The Prince*

Key Themes

- IT portfolio management practices can be grouped into four stages in terms of their efficiency and effectiveness: *informal, functional, collaborative,* and *enterprise-wide.* Practices in the areas of strategy, implementation, operations, governance, metrics, and organization together reveal how efficient and effective an organization's overall portfolio management process is. Step-function improvements (as opposed to continuous improvement) assume a greater magnitude as organizations move in the direction of enterprise-wide practices and cross-functional practices become more tightly integrated.

- Step-function improvements in portfolio performance comprise improvements in three particular areas: increasing throughput, optimizing resources, and expanding the efficient frontier of projects.

- Portfolio decision making impacts throughput by managing two variables: project cycle time and portfolio capacity. Portfolio decision making affects project cycle time by determining the size, charter, and deliverables of projects and by ensuring effective project governance. Portfolio decision making affects portfolio capacity as portfolio managers determine how many resources exist, what skills are required, and how fast to release (launch) new projects.

- In order to maximize portfolio capacity, it is also necessary to optimize resources. For resources to be optimized they must be both busy and productive, while the portfolio management process itself must be effective and efficient.

- Effective portfolio management expands the efficient frontier of projects. The two analyses required to expand the efficient frontier are determining what projects to pursue (*doing the right things*) and determining what will make the projects successful (*doing things right*).

- Apart from the many qualitative benefits it provides, improving the IT portfolio management process can and should improve the bottom line. An improved IT portfolio management impacts the bottom line by creating increased efficiency, increased capacity, and increased value.

- Portfolio management is different from most processes in that it is a management process that affects managers more than their staff members, which makes driving change tricky.
- When setting out to convince people to change their behavior, it is important to recognize that some type of portfolio management process already exists. The uncertainties involved in transformation projects make people wary of them, so that managers will push back when the organization attempts to implement a new process. For this reason, the change needs to be driven from the top down.
- Improving a portfolio management process requires change at the most senior management levels. In order to convince and entice any managers to change, it is necessary to give them answers to the question *What's in it for me?*
- Implementing a new portfolio management process takes a lot of time and attention to detail. It will normally take a year to fully absorb and institutionalize a new process.

Epilogue: A Method for Strategic Transformation

Now this is not the end. It is not even the beginning of the end. But it is, perhaps, the end of the beginning.

—Winston Churchill, November 1942

We know when our clients *get it*. We know when they really understand what IT portfolio management is all about. Once they begin to see the possibilities of a robust portfolio management method, they generally come to us and say, "You shouldn't call this *IT* portfolio management. It is much more than IT. It is really *enterprise transformation* portfolio management." That's when we know they get it.

We've touched several times on the fact that most big "IT projects" are not merely IT projects. They involve other kinds of work streams too. Most of these projects require changes to organizational structure, responsibilities, processes, policies, and decision rights. They are business transformation (enterprise transformation) projects. These projects have an IT work stream, but the IT work stream should not be managed independently. Because the IT work stream needs to be managed jointly with other work streams, the investment management decision making also needs to be managed jointly, preferably guided by an enterprise architecture. Organizations should not make decisions about the IT work stream that adversely affect the other, interdependent work streams. Project managers should develop and govern the IT work stream in collaboration with the business process and people changes required for successful transformation. Interdependent activities must be fused to ensure holistic and optimized business transformations. Business improvements should not be chartered and executed piecemeal with insufficient consideration for cross-departmental dependencies. Workflow should not be designed to optimize one department's efficiency rather than overall customer impact.

247

These transformation projects are often treated as "IT projects" because most organizations don't know what else to do with them. Where else can they report? Perhaps the business units could manage them, but few business units are set up to staff and manage project-based investments. The business units are typically staffed for steady-state operational activities. Few business units have the project management savvy, skills, and disciplines to manage transformation projects effectively. It makes matters even more complex when transformation projects span the *enterprise* (multiple departments, divisions, business units, etc.). Who might have the ability and capacity to manage enterprise transformation other than the IT department? Not many departments cut across the enterprise. The IT department happens to be one that does, at the same time it happens to be a nucleus of project management capabilities. The other cross-enterprise departments are administrative departments, which are typically poorly suited to managing project-based investments. It explains why many transformation projects are run out of the IT department. Because they are run out of the IT department, senior executives too often treat transformation projects as "IT projects."

In a perfect world, an enterprise transformation portfolio is managed by an enterprise transformation portfolio management team (ET-PMT). An enterprise transformation portfolio management method would be the organization's focal point for bringing about change and would govern and coordinate these projects. It would drive the strategic management agenda, the vision, enterprise architecture, and accompanying road map that determine the future state of the organization. Who drives the strategic management agenda today? The CEO or COO? The CEO and COO might create the vision statement, but they rarely have time to execute the vision. The CFO? CFOs are too busy governing the finances. The CIO? CIOs are too busy trying to address the tactical IT challenges. The answer is that in most organizations, nobody is accountable for driving the strategic management agenda. These CxOs may navigate, but most organizations lurch down the road with nobody at the strategy wheel. The only things keeping them on the road are the ruts the wheels ride in. Occasionally someone sees a sharp bend in the road and grabs hold of the wheel for a bit, but soon that person becomes distracted again and lets go. Most organizations that succeed do so in spite of themselves, not because of any strategic management capabilities.

The ET-PMT coordinates and governs enterprise transformation projects. It makes objective trade-off decisions regarding how it wants to spend investment funds and resources. Discretionary funds are pooled at the highest level, instead of trickling down to middle management coffers. Middle management coffers are really just buffers, created by middle managers to hedge against the future. When scattered around the organization, these buffers grow larger over time. Funds squirreled away by middle managers in this way can't be leveraged across the organization. It becomes difficult to rob Peter to pay Paul, even though Paul has a much better project concept than Peter. Too often, Peter's coffer is bigger because of political clout, historic spending levels, and sometimes just because senior management hasn't bothered to look. Even the wealthiest organizations, when seeking to implement a major transformation project, can find themselves impoverished because they can't get their hands on the requisite funds. It is too late to go looking for discretionary funds after the need has arisen. The time to locate them is before the need arises, so the organization has the resources when they are needed.

With the necessary funds and a portfolio management method in place, an ET-PMT made up of CxOs increases accountability for results. If it charters a project to improve a business process, the ET-PMT effectively creates a contract with the project team and project governance team. The contract provides funding in exchange for bottom-line improvements. The CFO holds the leadership team accountable for these improvements by adjusting the financial plan (budget) based on the intended result. For example, if a supply chain manager promises to reduce cost by implementing an ERP software application, the CFO reduces the supply chain manager's operating budget accordingly, commensurate with the business case assumptions for the project. This adjustment causes the supply chain manager to think a little more conservatively when estimating benefits, rather than exaggerating the benefits to sell the project internally. It also causes the supply chain manager to think twice about whether he or she really needs a new ERP application or would rather consolidate a warehouse or two. The portfolio management method helps organizations make better trade-off decisions, not just within departments but also across departments. They can more objectively compare, for example, something like the ERP project just described with a salesforce effectiveness project. They can ensure that the salesforce manager is willing to commit to a higher revenue target in return for funding. They can decide whether they want to invest in a new application, a better process, a new factory, a new warehouse, a new service, a new product, or none of these options.

A portfolio management method provides CxOs with improved awareness of the implications of decision making. A decision to change the scope, approach, or timing of a change initiative has a direct impact on financial and resource planning. Many CxOs are powerless to ensure that their directions are carried out appropriately. Middle managers promise resources but later withhold them due to conflicting priorities. In some cases, the organization simply can't handle the volume of change efforts underway at any given time, or the organization can't absorb that much change that fast. Hence, projects may begin with the best of intentions but deliver mediocre results. Issues that should be aired with senior management are buried because of poor judgment or political ineptitude. Without an apolitical, unbiased process for managing change efforts, CxOs have no way to ensure that middle managers take proper action.

The portfolio management method provides CxOs with better visibility into project status and results. CxOs too often hear too late that projects are struggling. They lack both catalysts and methods for adjusting strategic priorities in response to transformation project learnings, evolving market conditions, and unfolding business trends. Middle managers manually collect, assess, augment, and filter project information, because their incentives motivate them to make themselves look good. With no real-time information available on project status, nobody can be required to report it. A portfolio management application, on the other hand, can capture and disseminate project information to the CxO. It doesn't solve the filtering problem completely, but it increases visibility as well as the probability that information will be provided to the CxO.

The enterprise transformation portfolio management method is a focal point for change, and the transformation road map is the enterprise architecture. Yet most organizations lack an enterprise architecture, with nobody accountable for developing it. Who has accountability for developing the future-state vision of how the entire organization will operate, addressing people and processes as well as technology? The ET-PMT is accountable, but few organizations have an ET-PMT. So, lacking both the ET-PMT and an enterprise architecture, organizations continue to throw good money at half-baked improvement initiatives. Managers continue to improve their own pieces of the system with point solutions at the expense of the whole. They drive blindly onward "improving" the business without any consensus on where the organization is going, what will make it successful, or how it will get there. Without a common vision, how will managers ever obtain a common situational awareness of how the enterprise operates? Without a comprehensive perspective and the motivation to make the "right" decision, managers make the wrong decisions regardless of how well-intentioned they might be.

Right Strategy, Wrong Execution

The CIO of a multibillion-dollar company had a plan to save the corporation money. The CIO figured that they could consolidate applications. The CIO thought the idea was sound, so he convinced the CEO to invest in the project. The CEO funded the project and then disengaged. The project should have been handled as an enterprise transformation effort. The business leaders should have been involved from the beginning, because it was their business and bottom line that were affected. Instead, the project was managed as an "IT project" and the IT department was left to convince the business to change. The middle managers in the business were uncooperative and saw the initiative as something the IT department "was doing to them" rather than "doing for them." The initiative failed, not because of the IT department, but in spite of it. The project would have saved the company millions in annual operating expenses. The senior management team should have driven the project from the top.

Portfolio management is a strategic management method. It enables organizations to transform their processes generally. It is how CxOs translate strategic intent into real change efforts and ensure that those change efforts are successful. If one believes that an organization should adopt a "process approach" to management, it follows that a method is needed to manage changes to enterprise processes (meaning people, business processes, *and* technology). Portfolio management is such a method. Portfolio management is a universal management system that enables senior executives to take a process approach to managing multiple types of investments, including assets and projects. It manages investments before (strategy), during (implementation), and after (operations) the investment occurs. It is well suited to manage projects of all types including technology, business process, restructuring, mergers, services, acquisitions, research, engineering, and construction. It provides a live-and-in-person governance method that ensures that humans (executives) are aware of their accountability for results. It provides executives with a method to ensure that the project team is held responsible for execution. It provides the means to rationalize the number or size of investments based on consistent business case analysis across investment options of all types. It provides the means to allocate discretionary spending (capital and expense) to the highest-value initiatives. It provides the oversight to ensure investments address mission assurance, with proper risk and contingency planning. It enables centralized and standardized oversight and leadership while allowing for decentralized execution.

The chief *information* officer (CIO) was never intended to be the head of the information *technology* department. The CIO position was first conceptualized in response to a specific problem, which was not solely an IT problem. It was a decision-making problem—a leadership problem. Thought leaders saw a need to amalgamate enterprise information (not data) as a corporate asset, available to any knowledge worker with a need. They wanted to standardize, streamline, and organize this information according to business processes, rather than leaving it pigeonholed in organizational silos and replicated in multiple point solution software applications. The CIO was going to fix this issue and, in so doing, optimize all those workflows across the enterprise that collected, maintained, reported, and utilized the information. The CIO was going to break down the organizational silos, transforming the organization so that it revolved around a value chain focused solely on delivering customer value. Good intent. Terrible execution. Somehow it was decided that the CIO should head up the IT department. The analysis behind this decision appeared to consist of looking at the terms CIO and IT and realizing that they both had an "I" in them. Rather than create a new position, most organizations simply gave a new title to the VP of IT. And so the CIO was born, saddled with the IT dilemma, and rarely given a chance to address the transformation opportunity.

Meanwhile, most organizations continue to lack an enterprise-wide investment management method. It does not make sense to manage IT investments separately from other corporate investments because IT investments are an essential part of other corporate investments. The more one studies IT management and the business transformation process, the more evident it becomes that IT is a piece of an organization's value chain—an integrated piece of the value chain as opposed to a discrete process. Even though it may make sense, from a human resource perspective, to manage IT service provision staff as a separate department, it does not make sense to govern transformation investments discretely. Take another look at the enterprise-wide portfolio management practices depicted in the table "IT Portfolio Practices at Various Stages of Adoption" in *Articulating—and Achieving—the Benefits of IT Portfolio Management*. Note that most of the enterprise-wide work streams have fused IT with business process and people work streams. It doesn't take a huge leap of reasoning to see how the future of IT portfolio management becomes so tightly integrated with other investment management decision making as to make it virtually impossible to make large IT investment decisions discretely.

The destiny of IT portfolio management is for organizations to stop obsessing about technology and start obsessing about *transformation* (results). If CIOs are really sincere about living up to their titles and the original intent behind the creation of the job, they should seek to take portfolio management to a higher level. Before they begin, they need to get a basic handle on IT portfolio management and establish an internal market economy to govern IT investments. They need to realize that IT management is not an IT department problem; it is an enterprise problem. It is also a fixable problem. CIOs can attain the higher purpose they were meant to fulfill as they put their IT house in order. They need to prove that portfolio management has a future by first demonstrating what it can do for IT management, and then proving what it can do to enable enterprise transformation.

All the scientists hope to do is describe the universe mathematically, pre-dict it, and maybe control it. The philosopher, by contrast, seems unbe-comingly ambitious. He wants to understand the universe; to get behind phenomena and operation and solve the logically prior riddles of being, knowledge, and value. But the artist, and in particular the nov-elist, in his essence wishes neither to explain nor to control nor to under-stand the universe. He wants to make one of his own, and may even aspire to make it more orderly, meaningful, beautiful, and interesting than the one God turned out. What's more, in the opinion of many readers of literature, he sometimes succeeds.

—John Barth, *How to Make a Universe*

Appendix:
Business Case Analysis

Business case analysis is critical to effective portfolio management, yet organizations struggle with creating and reviewing business cases. A business case typically considers the following elements:

- *Business value*: How will the project directly or indirectly increase value for the organization?
  - *Quantitative value*: Explicit commitments to improve measurable performance metrics such as financial measures, cycle time, defect rate, units processed per period, etc.
  - *Qualitative value*: Explicit commitments to create value that the organization cannot easily measure such as customer experience, usability, employee satisfaction, etc.
- *Implementation impact:* How will this project affect the organization's productivity during implementation?
- *Risk:* How risky is the project? Ideally, risk should be broken down into standardized risk drivers such as[1]:
  - *Business risk*: How could the project impede bottom-line business performance?

---

[1] Risk should also be broken down into what is controllable (dependent on events that the organization can control or at least influence) and uncontrollable (dependent on events that organization can neither control nor influence).

- *Technology risk*: Has the IT service provider ever implemented the technology? Has anyone ever implemented the technology?
- *Third-party risk*: How viable are the third-party providers? Have these third parties ever served the organization in this capacity?
- *Complexity risk*: Has the service provider, vendor, or organization ever implemented a project of this complexity (number of software packages, proprietary systems or interfaces, lines of code, etc.)?
- *Scale risk*: Has the service provider, vendor, or organization ever implemented a project of this complexity on this scale (number of users, locations, modules, etc.)?
- *Uncertainty risk*: What is the project team aware that it doesn't know? What are the key assumptions that, if proven incorrect, could dramatically affect the business case?
- *High-level approach:* What approach is proposed?
  - *Tasks:* What is the end-to-end, top-level work structure of the project? Tasks should address planning, designing, building, certifying, and implementing, as well as the transition to steady-state. Tasks should include everything required from every organization including in-house IT departments, business departments, and third parties.
  - *Risk mitigation and contingency plans:* What is the organization planning to do to mitigate the risks? What alternative action does the organization plan to take should the anticipated risks materialize?
  - *Timing:* What is the rough order of magnitude (ROM) end-to-end timeline? What is the ROM duration of each phase?
  - *Resources:* What skills are required? What specific subject-matter experts are required? Consider resources required from both the IT departments and the business departments. How many full-time resources are required? How many part-time ones? What specific people are needed to participate in the project, and in what roles?
- *Cost:* What incremental cost will be incurred as a result of executing the project?
  - *One-time cost (cash flow):* One-time expenditures required to implement every aspect of the project. (Sometimes it is

easier to think in terms of what the organization theoretically would not spend or utilize if the PMT were to cancel the project.) Include all in-house and third-party resources required to execute the project in the one-time cost estimate.

- *Life cycle cost (cash flow):* Annual expenditures required to operate, administer, maintain, support, and upgrade the system for its entire life (from production to retirement). This estimate should include IT-related as well as business-related expenditures such as database administration, user support, table maintenance, document management, etc.
- *Other costs:* Other opportunity costs of executing this project using the specified approach rather than using other approaches. This estimate might also include increases in employee responsibilities that might not be incremental, such as asking an employee to administer one more system. The increment might not affect cash flow, but the organization cannot continue to pile more work on employees without eventually affecting cost or quality.
- *Net present value (NPV):* What is the net financial impact when the time value of money is accounted for? What was the rate used to calculate the NPV and why is it an appropriate risk measure for a project of this type? (Note that we recommend NPV over ROI, because NPV comparisons across projects are more meaningful.)
- *Sensitivity analysis:* Which cost or value factors have the greatest affect on the NPV calculation?

It is difficult for the PMT to evaluate a project's merits without a robust business case. However, at the outset of a project the organization may lack comprehensive information on its costs and benefits. At best, the organization has only a rough order of magnitude (ROM) understanding of the business case. At worst, the organization hasn't really given the business case much thought. So how does an organization compare across projects when the accuracy estimates are so broad? It doesn't. It first reduces the variance in the estimates. The PMT should not allow a project to pass without at least an ROM business case.

The PMT should revisit the business case at the beginning of every stage of a project's life cycle (concept, plan/design, build/integrate/ test, certify, deploy, and retire) to determine whether the project should proceed as planned. The PMT is not merely checking the status of projects when it reviews the business case. It is also considering the expected value of in-process projects in the portfolio relative to other pending opportunities. The PMT is accountable for making the decision to shelve or terminate the project in view of other opportunities.

The number of terminated projects should not be zero. If the PMT is not canceling at least a few projects, the organization is likely either avoiding risk completely or allowing low-value projects to proceed. Excess risk avoidance leads to a suboptimized portfolio with overall lower value. Allowing low-value projects to proceed has an opportunity cost that also lowers overall portfolio value. PMTs should motivate and even reward project teams for recommending projects be shut down or deferred at any time throughout the project life cycle when the business case ceases to look attractive, even after a lot of money has been sunk into the project. The PMT needs to concern itself with the decades of ongoing operating expense for inefficient or ineffective applications rather than obsessing about the initial sunk cost of the project. Sometimes the best thing for a project to do is start over with new objectives, clarified constraints, and aligned assumptions.

It is a best practice for the project team to refresh the business case at the end of every phase of the project. Business cases and plans mature as the project team learns. It may happen that a seemingly dull project turns out to be foundational, once the organization better understands why it is needed. A project with an attractive business case often becomes less attractive as the organization learns what it will really take to make it successful. Many legitimate reasons may justify shutting down a project without blaming the project team members for "failure." The foundational benefit assumptions may have proven false. The organization may not be ready to change. The managers may not have understood the change implications. The commercial off-the-shelf application may not be sufficiently mature. Other, higher priorities may have arisen. Economic conditions may have changed. Organizations should regard projects shut down early in their life cycle as successes, not failures.

Is the PMT better off reviewing the project only after the business case is complete, so that it will have a clearer picture of the costs and benefits? The answer is no. First, the business case is never truly complete until all the project life cycle learnings are incorporated, which might not be until well into the integration phase. Furthermore, if the business case is objective and well thought out, the PMT will know if the project has potential just by looking at the ROM impact, cost, and benefit analysis. The PMT can always reengage later in the life cycle if the business case changes significantly, but it cannot recover resources wasted on low-value projects.

Too often, organizations waste time on the initial business case or drag out business case development over months. Too often, critical resources work on the business case in their spare time, as a low-priority activity. Not only is this wasteful and ineffective, it impedes the organization's response time. Avoiding this waste is the reason for the *concept* phase at the beginning of a project's life cycle. The deliverables from the concept phase are limited to the project charter and ROM business case. The concept phase is predominantly a thinking exercise among a select few visionaries and subject-matter experts, and its duration is time-boxed to one staff-member-month (160 hours). The benefits of a time-boxed concept phase are that it:

- Emphasizes the value that the organization places on a well-thought-out business case
- Forces the organization to acknowledge the cost and resources required to develop a good ROM business case
- Mitigates the risk of the project becoming embroiled in technology issues too early in its life cycle
- Limits the mindshare wasted on lesser-priority project concepts

References

"Are Budget Pressures Overwhelming You," *CIO Insight Magazine,* February 2003.

"Best Practices in IT Portfolio Management," *MIT Sloan Management Review,* Spring 2004, pp. 41–49.

"Budget for Information Technology Reflects Administration Priorities, Commitment to Fiscal Restraint," Executive Office of the President Office of management and Budget, February 5, 2004.

"By the Numbers: Upward and Onward with Outsourcing," *CIO Magazine,* August 1, 2002, p. 26.

"Can Strategy Thrive When Money Is Tight?" *CIO Insight Magazine,* October 2003.

The Chaos Report, The Standish Group, 1994.

"CIO 100 Honoree Survey," *CIO Magazine,* August 15, 2003.

"CIO Research Reports: Best Practices of Resourceful CIOs," *CIO Magazine,* August 4, 2003.

Cobb, Martin, *Unfinished Voyages: A follow-up to the CHAOS Report,* Standish Group Report, 1996.

Cohen, Shoshanah, and Joseph Roussel, *Strategic Supply Chain Management* (McGraw Hill, 2004).

The Columbia World of Quotations, Columbia University Press, Bartleby.com, 2001.

Edgett, Scott, Elko Kleinschmidt, and Robert Gravlin Cooper, *Portfolio Management for New Products*, 2nd ed. (Perseus Publishing, 2001).

Frese, Robert, and Vicki Sauter, *Project Success and Failure: What Is Success, What Is Failure, and How Can You Improve Your Odds for Success* (UM-St. Louis, 2003).

Goldratt, Eliyahu, *Theory of Constraints* (North River Press Publishing Corporation, 1999).

Highlights of GAO-04–394G, an executive guide. Information Technology Investment Management A Framework for Assessing and Improving Process Maturity, United States General Accounting Office (no copyright), March 2004.

Hoffman, Thomas, "Value of Project Management Offices Questioned," *Computerworld*, July 21, 2003.

Hoffman, Thomas, "Corporate Execs Try New Ways to Align IT with Business Units," *Computerworld*, October 27, 2003.

"How Bad Is the Bite in Your Budget," *CIO Insight Magazine*, January 2003.

ICT Infrastructure Management, Office of Government Commerce Staff, Bernan Assoc., May 1, 2002.

"IT Doesn't Matter," *Harvard Business Review Online*, Harvard Business School Publishing, May 2003.

"IT Effectiveness Survey," PRTM and *CIO Magazine*, 2002.

"The IT Organization: Why Is IT Morale So Bad?" *CIO Insight Magazine*, November 2004.

Kerr, Steven, "On the Folly of Rewarding A, While Hoping for B," Academy of Management Executives, 1995.

King, Julia, "Survey shows common IT woes," *Computerworld*, June 23, 2003.

McGrath, Michael, *Next Generation Product Development: How to Increase Productivity, Cut Costs, and Reduce Cycle Times* (McGraw-Hill, 2004).

McGrath, Michael, *Product Strategy for High Technology Companies*, 2nd ed. (McGraw-Hill Trade, 2000).

McGrath, Michael, *Setting the PACE in Product Development, A Guide to Product and Cycle-time Excellence,* rev. ed. (Butterworth-Heinemann, 1996).

Merriam-Webster Online Thesaurus, available at www.Merriam-Webster.com.

Meyer, Marc, and Alvin Lehnerd, *The Power of Product Platforms* (Free Press, 1997).

Nash, Kim, and Mel Duvall, "PepsiCo Case Dissection–PepsiCo: No Deposit, No Return," available at www.baselinemag.com (May 1, 2003).

Service Delivery (It Infrastructure Library Series), Bernan Assoc., May 1, 2001.

Service Support (It Infrastructure Library Series), Renouf Pub Co Ltd., 2000.

Stack, Jack, and Bo Burlingham. *The Great Game of Business* (Currency, 1994).

"The Strategic Alignment Research Study: Strategy," *CIO Insight Magazine,* 2002.

Tabor Greene, Richard. *Global Quality: A Synthesis of the World's Best Management Methods* (McGraw-Hill Trade, April 1, 1993).

United States Information Technology Management Reform Act: Clinger-Cohen Act , 104th Congress of the United States of America, Second Session, January 3, 1996.

Weill, Peter, and Jeanne Ross, *IT Governance: How Top Performers Manage IT Decision Rights for Superior Results* (Harvard Business School Press, 2004).

Womack, James, and Daniel Jones, *Lean Thinking: Banish Waste and Create Wealth in Your Corporation* (Free Press, 2003).

Youngblood, Mark. *Eating the Chocolate Elephant: Take Charge of Change Through Total Process Management* (Micrografx, November 1994).

Index

integrated financial systems, effect of IT
spending on, 36, 47
integration
between business units and IT department, 65, 73
common taxonomy for, 67
within IT management system,
65–69, 73
of processes across organizations, 103
integration budgets, 13
interdepartmental workflow, managing,
59, 73
interdependencies, 156–173
management of, 59, 73, 184, 247
reducing, 178
internal IT market economy
cost allocation in, 172
equilibrium in, maintaining, 76,
123–124
management of, 55
inventory and calibration work stream,
133, 135–139, 184
business case analysis, 136–137, 147
decision-support data collection, 189
investments in IT
accountability and decision making
disconnect, 3–4, 17
awareness of, decision making for, 152
booking, 155
budget pressure and, 13
business strategy as driver of, 9
centralized versus decentralized, 33–34
cost crisis in, 34–38
decision costs and implications, 175
decision making for, 152–153
decision making responsibility for, 4
downward spiral of, 7–8, 29
enterprise-wide management methods for, 253
planning, 118
senior management accountability
for, 12–13, 17
waste, cutting from, 13–16
involvement
definition of, 107–108
and delegation, balancing, 107–108

IT
business issues versus technology issues, 8–9, 17
business unit demand for, 3–4, 17,
33, 55, 77
as capital asset, 13
competitive advantage from, 13,
175–177
competitive parity from, 176
cost increases in, 33
cost structure alterations, 33–34
decentralized responsibility for, 33–34
demand and supply management, 55,
76–77
enhancements in, necessity of,
228–229
evolution of, 29–38, 41
as growth enabler, 1–2, 17
mainframe era, 30–31, 47
maturity curve of, 175–177
new applications, 175–176, 208. See
also new IT
obsolescence of, 178
planning for, integration into business planning, 69–72
requirements for, documenting, 242
scheduling investment in, 180
spending cuts in, 13, 18
strategic versus critical, 228
technology introduction methodology for, 208
as value chain link, 253
value of, 17. See also value
IT customers
and IT assets, disconnect between,
30–31
portfolio information use, 191
voice of the customer, 208
IT department
and business units, 31–32
caps on head count, 44
CIO in, 252–253
consolidation of responsibilities
under, 38–39
core missions, 5–6, 17
as cost center, 43

About the Author

Jeffrey D. Kaplan is a lead partner in the Strategic IT Management Practice of global management consulting firm Pittiglio Rabin Todd & McGrath (PRTM), Inc. He is also in the firm's Government Business Group, and has experience working with the defense-related agencies. Kaplan has more than 18 years of experience, primarily in effecting process transformation via the strategic application of technology, across multiple business areas including marketing, sales, service, engineering, supply chain and information technology. His expertise comprises IT governance, strategy, performance management, customer management, and organizational change management. Kaplan also oversees intellectual property and affiliations related to the Strategic IT Management Practice. He has helped organizations in industries spanning the banking, chemical, computer equipment, government, pharmaceutical, software, and telecommunications fields dramatically improve business processes through the strategic deployment of technology investments.

Prior to joining PRTM, Kaplan worked in the IT industry, where he held IT management positions in multiple business areas including customer management, service provision, and vendor and project management. He holds an M.B.A with a focus on marketing, production and operations management from the University of Chicago, and a B.A. in computer science from the University of Iowa.

PRTM management consultants want to help organizations achieve superior value from technology investments. Please visit us at www.PRTM.com.